"Dr Susan Hetrick has produced a very timely, well-researched, and highly practical book on one of the most important topics in the field of management – organizational culture and its relationship with leadership. Her focus on 'the dark side' is refreshing in differing from many of the practitioner playbooks in this field which begin from the premise that strong culture and leadership are typically positive. Instead, she argues that you can have 'too-much-of-a-good-thing' – that so-called strong cultures and leadership can often turn toxic and we can learn more from these kind of cases than those that characterise the 'culture-excellence' literature. In my work as a researcher, consultant, and non-executive board member, this book will be high on my list of recommended reading to students, clients, and colleagues as a source of useful theory and ideas on how to analyse key organizational problems and build healthy workplaces."

Graeme Martin, ***Professor of Management, University of Dundee and Vice-Chair, NHS Tayside***

"Dr Hetrick makes a highly valuable contribution with this work by showing us how organizations can identify and address toxic work cultures. The practical interventions presented are tools any organization can utilize to prevent toxicity, ensure positive leadership, and when necessary, restore a healthy work environment."

Kathryn Wagner Hill, Ph.D., ***Center for Advanced Governmental Studies, Johns Hopkins University***

"With employee engagement waning and the Great Resignation upon us, this book is a timely exploration of how harmful workplace cultures can take hold and be facilitated, either wittingly or unwittingly, by organisations or individuals. In combining extensive research with pragmatic recommendations, this book offers both an engaging diagnosis and workable remedies to bolster cultural health in the workplace."

Richard Fulham, ***HR Director***

Toxic Organizational Cultures and Leadership

Toxic organizational cultures and leadership have led to major reputational failures, with the greatest impact felt by the people who dedicate their careers to working for these organizations. And yet organizations do not become toxic overnight. They do not consciously set out to break rules and regulations, nor do they actively seek wrongdoing. This book defines toxic culture, explains how toxic cultures emerge over time, and provides practical approaches supported by in-depth research for overcoming a toxic culture at the individual, team, and organizational level.

Pragmatic and applicable, the book provides a call to action that can be applied in any type of organization. While the role of leadership in toxic cultures is acknowledged, the book sets out four distinct stages to embedding toxic cultures and draws on examples from leading organizations and companies to illustrate each stage. The book then identifies interventions and levers that can be implemented by executives, boards, and HR practitioners to prevent toxicity and to change toxic cultures back to healthy, positive workplaces. Drawing on research and interviews with senior HR leaders and executives, the book provides:

- An understanding of the four stages of toxic cultures and the impact of performance pressures in driving toxicity
- An appreciation of the role of senior leadership and personality traits
- Practical tools and guidance on interventions for practitioners to build and sustain a healthy and positive workplace

Senior executives, HR, and organizational development practitioners in local and global organizations spanning a range of industry sectors will find this book invaluable. The book is also highly relevant to consultants working in the field of corporate culture and change.

Susan Hetrick is the founder of Zuhra, an HR consultancy. She has held senior HR leadership roles and worked with executive teams for a number of organizations, including the World Bank Group, Arab Banking Corporation, the NatWest Group, Aegon, HSBC, and Deloitte. Susan is a published author and speaker on corporate culture in global organizations and holds a Doctorate from City University Business School and a Master's degree in Industrial Relations from Warwick University.

Toxic Organizational Cultures and Leadership

How to Build and Sustain a Healthy Workplace

Susan Hetrick

Routledge
Taylor & Francis Group
LONDON AND NEW YORK

Designed cover image: © Getty Images

First published 2023
by Routledge
4 Park Square, Milton Park, Abingdon, Oxon OX14 4RN

and by Routledge
605 Third Avenue, New York, NY 10158

Routledge is an imprint of the Taylor & Francis Group, an informa business

British Library Cataloguing-in-Publication Data
A catalogue record for this book is available from the British Library

ISBN: 978-1-032-36129-1 (hbk)
ISBN: 978-1-032-36131-4 (pbk)
ISBN: 978-1-003-33038-7 (ebk)

DOI: 10.4324/9781003330387

Typeset in Goudy
by codeMantra

Being in a minority, even in a minority of one, did not make you mad. There was truth, and there was untruth, and if you clung to the truth against the whole world, you were not mad.

George Orwell, 1984

For my sons, Alexander and James

Contents

List of Illustrations xiii

Acknowledgements xv

List of Acronyms and Abbreviations xvii

Introduction 1

PART I
The Four Stages of Toxicity **11**

1 Why Culture Matters 12
1.1 Introduction 12
1.2 Culture and Leadership 14
1.3 Toxic Cultures 17
1.3.1 Toxic Origins – A Word 19
1.4 Positive Cultures: The Opposite of Toxic Cultures? 23
1.4.1 Corporate Culture and Change 26
1.4.2 Culture Levers 28
1.5 Culture and Corporateness 31
1.5.1 Toxic Organizational Norms 34

2 The First Driver of Toxic Culture – The Normalization of Deviance 40
2.1 Normalization of Deviance 41
2.2 What Is Meant by the Normalization of Deviance? 42
2.3 What Parallels Can We Draw for Business? 45
2.4 What Was the Normalization of Deviance for RBS? 47
2.5 The Reinforcement of Success Leads to the Normalization of Deviance 48
2.6 The Slippery-Slope Effect 50

3 The Second Driver of Toxic Culture – Cognitive Dissonance 54
3.1 Introduction 54
3.2 Defining Cognitive Dissonance 54
3.3 The Case of the Volkswagen Carbon Emissions Scandal 55

3.4 Linking Image, Vision, and Culture: Corporate Reputations 60
3.4.1 Culture, Image, and Identity 62
3.5 Carillion – A Case Study 67
3.5.1 Cognitive Dissonance 69
3.5.2 Normalization of Deviance 70
3.5.3 Toxicity Spreads 72
3.5.4 The Lessons of Carillion 73

4 The Four Stages of a Toxic Culture 77
4.1 Introduction 77
4.2 Performance Pressures 77
4.2.1 Performance Pressures at Boeing 78
4.3 Triggers of Toxicity 82
4.4 Stages of Toxicity 84
4.4.1 Stage 1: Performance Pressure Leading to a Bold New Vision 84
4.4.1.1 Performance Pressures 85
4.4.1.2 Toxic Behaviours by Senior Leaders Become Tolerated 86
4.4.2 Stage 1 and the Normalization of Deviance 87
4.4.3 Stage 2: Demand for Loyalty and Alignment 87
4.4.4 Stage 3: Reverence from External Stakeholders 95
4.4.5 Stage 4: Cult of Singularity 97
4.5 Summary 107

PART II
The Toxic Triangle **113**

5 Toxic Leadership 115
5.1 Introduction and Context 115
5.2 Approaches to Leadership: The Three Camps 116
5.2.1 Defining Toxic Leadership 117
5.2.2 The Impact of Toxic Leadership 120
5.3 Dysfunctional Behaviour in the Workplace 123
5.3.1 Measuring the Dark Side of Leadership 124
5.3.2 Bullying in Leadership 124
5.3.3 Bullying Tactics 127
5.4 The Dark Triad 129
5.4.1 Machiavellian Leadership 131
5.4.2 Narcissistic Leadership 132
5.4.3 Psychopathic Leadership or the Corporate Psychopath 133
5.5 Toxic Leadership in the Workplace 140
5.5.1 Abuse of Power 140
5.5.2 Unrealistic Demands 140
5.5.3 Demand for Perfection 141

5.5.4 Control, Control, Control 141
5.5.5 Them versus Us 141
5.5.6 Enticing You In 142
5.5.7 Divide and Rule 142
5.5.8 Threats 142
5.5.9 Selling a Vision 142
5.5.10 Requirement of Unquestionable Loyalty and Devotion 143
5.6 Is the Poison in the Person or in the Bottle? 145
5.7 Summary 145

6 Susceptible Followers 151
6.1 Introduction 151
6.2 Leadership and Followership 151
6.3 Expectations of Followership 153
6.4 Followership and Toxic Leadership 154
6.5 Followership in Toxic Cultures 156
6.6 Susceptible Followers 157
6.7 Positive and Negative Followers 160
6.7.1 Narcissistic Followers 162
6.7.2 Machiavellian Followers 162
6.7.3 Psychopathic Followers 163
6.8 Toxic Followers Working for Toxic Leaders 164
6.8.1 Other Types of Followers 165
6.8.1.1 The Quiet Resistance 165
6.8.1.2 The Survivor 166
6.9 Summary 167

7 Conducive Environments 171
7.1 Introduction 171
7.1.1 Instability 171
7.1.2 Perceived Threats 173
7.1.3 Favouritism 173
7.1.4 Absence of Checks and Balances 174
7.2 Cultural Values 176
7.3 Measuring a Conducive Environment 178
7.4 The Pressure of Performance on Individual Behaviour 178
7.5 Performance Management Systems 181
7.6 The Negative Consequences of Performance Management Systems 184
7.7 Bullying 185
7.8 Rewarding Toxic Behaviours 189
7.9 The Impact of Harassment and Bullying 190
7.10 The Impact of Harmful Behaviour on Corporate Reputation 191
7.11 Summary 192

PART III
How to Build and Sustain a Healthy Workplace Culture **195**

8 How to Build and Sustain a Healthy Workplace Culture 197
8.1 Introduction 197
8.1.1 Defining a Healthy Workplace Culture 197
8.1.1.1 Extreme Collectivist Cultures 198
8.1.1.2 Extreme Individualistic Cultures 199
8.2 Realign Corporate Values and Measure Engagement, Inclusion, and Respect 199
8.2.1 Values 202
8.2.2 Consensus on Values 202
8.2.3 Measure Values 205
8.2.4 Drivers of Employee Engagement 205
8.2.5 Measure Engagement . . . and Disengagement 209
8.2.6 Measuring Disengagement 209
8.3 Enable Psychological Safety and Support Employees to Speak Up 213
8.3.1 From Evaluating to Coaching 214
8.3.2 Multidirectional Feedback 215
8.3.3 Speaking Up 216
8.4 Strengthen and Enable Leadership to Act as Role Models 216
8.4.1 Train, Promote, and Develop Leadership Capability 217
8.5 Promote and Align HR Policies and Processes 220
8.5.1 Embedding Values through HR Policies and Processes 221
8.6 Elevate Well-being 224
8.6.1 Flexible Working Arrangements 225
8.6.2 Create a Sense of Community 226
8.6.3 The Business of Well-being 227
8.6.4 Elevate Well-being Questions Using the 5-Point Likert Scale 228
8.7 Call Out Toxic Behaviours 229
8.8 Transform Career Development and Learning through the Growth Mindset 231
8.8.1 Career Management at the World Bank Group 232
8.8.2 Talent Marketplace 237
8.8.3 Questions to Test Career and Talent Engagement Using the 5-Point Likert Scale 237

9 A Framework for Action 241
9.1 Introduction 241
9.2 Framework for Action 241

Conclusion 248

Index 255

Illustrations

Figures

1.1 Analysis of Organizational Culture 16
1.2 Changing Mindsets and Behaviours 28
3.1 The Relationship Between Culture, Identity, and Image 63
4.1 Triggers for the Normalization of Deviance and Cognitive Dissonance 82
4.2 The Four Stages of Toxicity 84
5.1 The Toxic Triangle 114
8.1 Conceptualization of a Healthy Emotional Culture 198
8.2 The Values Most Valued by FTSE 100 Companies 203
8.3 Principles of Career Management at the World Bank 233
8.4 Illustrative Career Paths 235

Images

4.1 The "dieselgate" Timeline 104

Tables

1.1 Organizational Culture Awareness 17
1.2 Definitions of Toxic Culture 20
1.3 Table Illustrating Intrinsic Motivation Factors and Their Key Differences in Positive and Toxic Work Cultures 24
1.4 Table Illustrating Extrinsic Motivation Factors and Their Key Differences in Positive and Toxic Work Cultures 27
2.1 Timeline of RBS Post-Acquisition of ABN Amro 47
3.1 Definitions Related to Corporateness 60
4.1 The Four Stages of a Toxic Culture 88

5.1 Toxic Leadership Terms in the Literature 117
5.2 Definitions of Toxic Leadership 118
5.3 Taxonomy of the Dark Side of Personality and Related Measures 125
5.4 Types of Bully in Organizations 126
5.5 Bullying Tactics 127
6.1 Examples of Harmful Leadership Behaviour 155
6.2 Followers' Coping Strategies 155
6.3 Definitions and Examples of Followership 158
6.4 Thody's Typology of Positive and Negative Behaviours 160
6.5 Red Flag Behaviours for each of the Dark Triad Traits 163
7.1 Financial Reporting Council: The UK Corporate Governance Code, July 2018 175
7.2 Survey Questions to Measure Toxic Work Environments 179
7.3 The Key Steps in Performance Management 182
7.4 Bullying Tactics 188
8.1 Most Frequently Cited Values Across a Wide Range of Organizations 202
8.2 Questions for Boards 204
8.3 Engagement Survey Questions to Test Culture Values 206
8.4 The FSCB Assessment Framework 36 Core Questions 210
8.5 Questions to Measure the Levels of Toxicity 213
8.6 Learning Behaviours and Beliefs in Work Teams 218
9.1 Framework for Action 242

Vignettes

1.1 The Columbia Accident at NASA 14
1.2 Toxic Culture at the World Bank 18
1.3 The Liability and Cost of a Dysfunctional Culture: The Example of AIG 18
1.4 Uber's Toxic Culture 32
3.1 VW and Toxic Culture 57
3.2 When the External Auditor Fails in Their Role 72
4.1 Boeing Case Study: Performance Pressures Leading to a Toxic Culture 79
4.2 VW CEO Fined for False Testimony and Breach of Duty of Care 105
7.1 Working in a Conducive Environment? The Case of BrewDog 177

Acknowledgements

I sincerely hope that this book will serve as a guide to improving the lives of millions in the workplace.

I started researching and writing this book just before the Covid pandemic in March 2020. It was an idea that had been bubbling for some time. My work is influenced by many academics and practitioners over the years. Yet it is only through the course of my research for this book that I have been able to fully appreciate the depths and impact of 'underlying assumptions', and how far this constrains the ability to question and challenge beliefs and perceptions.

I hope that I have done justice to everyone who has contributed to the book. Your support and belief in this work is immensely appreciated. At the end of the book, I explore the actions and levers to create and sustain a positive healthy workplace culture. One, which should never be taken for granted.

Any book is the outcome of the efforts from a number of people – from developing ideas to challenging assumptions through to providing insights and experiences. I would like to thank my friends, current and former colleagues, for their wonderful guidance and wisdom in writing this book. These include:

Professor Graeme Martin, Professor Paul Sparrow, Dr Peta Hellman, Kathy Wagner Hill Ph.D., Amanda Owen MBE, Dr Susie Tannahill, Richard Fulham, Tim Craddock, Grieg Aitken, Bernadette Bruton, Tim Chapman, John Harker, Gautam Dev, Gordon Laird, Helen Pitcher OBE, Dr Lyn Batchelor, Alexandra Frean, Catherine Muirden, Pauline Lindsay, Professor Adrian Furnham, Fatema Yusuf, John Bell, Martin Glover, Dr Consuelo Alcuaz, Sarah Schwab, Donna Marsh, Andrew Panton, Liam Sinclair, John Last, Gavin Whyte, and many more. Special thanks are due to Majd Ahsan Syed for his wonderful friendship and support over the years.

The interviews with senior executives were deliberately held on a 'not-for-attribution' basis and remain confidential. In places I have changed names and locations in order to protect the identity of the individuals involved. Some of the stories are from my own experience and interactions.

I am grateful for the research assistance and support from the diligent and excellent Dr Katie Sinclair and for her insights on followership.

Without the excellent team at Routledge, especially Rebecca Marsh and Lauren Whelan, this work would not have been possible. They have been a joy to work with and could not have done more to make the whole process smooth and effective.

A huge thank you to Hattie Hammersmith for her copious patience, proofreading, and her level-headedness, and to Carole Bonnett for her executive support.

And finally, I am indebted to my sons, Alexander and James, for their love, humour, and support while writing this book.

Acronyms and Abbreviations

ABN Amro	Algemene Bank Nederland Amro (Bank)
AQR	Audit Quality Review
ATM	Automated Teller Machine
BP	Beyond Petroleum (formerly British Petroleum)
BT	British Telecommunications
CARB	California Air Resources Board
CARE	Communications and Attitude Research for Employees
CEB	Corporate Executive Board
CEO	Chief Executive Officer
CHRO	Chief Human Resources Officer
CIPD	Chartered Institute of Personnel and Development
CO2	Carbon Dioxide
CSB	Chemical Safety and Hazard Investigation Board
DOJ	Department of Justice
Dr	Doctor
EPA	Environmental Protection Agency
EU	European Union
FRC	Financial Reporting Council
FSA	Financial Services Authority
FSCB	Financial Services Culture Board
FTSE	Financial Times Stock Exchange
GDP	Gross Domestic Product
GFC	Global Financial Crisis
GM	General Motors
HBOS	Halifax Bank of Scotland
HPMI	High Potential Motivator Indicator
HQ	Headquarters
HR	Human Resources
HRM	Human Resource Management
HSBC	Hong Kong and Shanghai Banking Corporation

IES	Institute for Employment Studies
IFC	International Finance Corporation
ILO	International Labour Organization
IT	Information Technology
J&J	Johnson & Johnson
KPMG	Klynveld Peat Marwick Goerdeler (Accountancy firm)
MIT	Massachusetts Institute of Technology
NASA	National Aeronautics and Space Administration
NLP	Natural Language Processing
NOx	Nitrogen Oxides
NHS	National Health Service
NPR	National Public Radio
OECD	Organization for Economic Co-operation and Development
P&G	Procter & Gamble
Prof.	Professor
RBS	Royal Bank of Scotland
Remco	Remuneration Committees
SHRM	Society for Human Resource Management
SME	Small and Mid-size Enterprise
TDI	Turbocharged Direct Injection
TPR	The Pensions Regulator
TTB	Alcohol and Tobacco Tax and Trade Bureau (US)
UK	United Kingdom
US	United States (of America)
USA	United States of America
VW	Volkswagen
WFH	Working From Home

Introduction

While there are reckoned to be more than 100,000 books with 'corporate culture' or 'leadership' in the title, there are few that discuss the dark side of corporate culture, toxic cultures, and leadership.

Global companies have faced billion-dollar fines for fraudulent behaviours from mis-selling and deceit to criminal negligence: companies such as Wells Fargo, Volkswagen, and BP are continuing to face charges from government agencies.[1] The Federal Reserve barred Wells Fargo from growing as a penalty for opening more than two million accounts without authorization from customers. The root cause of this fraudulent behaviour was deemed by independent investigators to be a 'culture of the division'. While corporate Annual Reports extol the alleged values of their organization and marketing campaigns reinforce these values, the reality is highlighted in these recent scandals. Government regulators, such as the Financial Conduct Authority (UK), blamed the Global Financial Crisis in 2008 as a failure of corporate culture. Business schools now talk more about 'purpose-led leadership'. Yet the cost of stress caused by bullying and harassment in the workplace in the USA is estimated at around $500bn every year.[2] Yet with the revelations from Uber, Royal Bank of Scotland (RBS), and companies such as Enron, the time to discuss the 'dark' side of organizations has never been more urgent.

Toxic cultures have been linked to higher cases of mortality, unethical behaviour, and even criminality. A Gallup study in the USA revealed that one in two people had left their job to get away from their manager to improve their overall life at some point in their career.[3] In the UK, one hospital was found to have a 'persistent toxic atmosphere' and a 'dark force' in the surgical department, which contributed to a higher death rate for patients.[4] In another NHS study using a spectrum of measures, researchers estimated that the specific impact resulting from bullying and harassment cost the UK taxpayer more than £2.2bn per annum.[5] Stock markets have seen significant financial losses and reputational damage due to whistleblowers in companies like Uber and Facebook publicly revealing a catalogue of misdemeanours.[6]

DOI: 10.4324/9781003330387-1

According to research by the Chartered Institute of Personnel Development (CIPD) in the UK, the median FTSE 100 CEO reward package was 119 times larger than a UK full-time worker on a median salary. The report concluded that this was unsustainable, arguing that Boards and Remco need to place greater emphasis on non-financial measures of CEO performance such as the impact of the organization on people.[7] With low productivity growth in the UK along with a long-standing decline in training investment in the workplace and a spate of harassment cases exposing toxic cultures in organizations, it is evident that there is a burning platform for toxic cultures to be addressed.

This book explores the dark side of organizations. It challenges conventional wisdom on engagement, leadership, and motivation. It asks important questions that are rarely addressed.

- How and why do cultures become toxic?
- What are the drivers of toxic cultures?
- Do toxic cultures emerge over time, and if so, what are the key stages?
- What roles do Boards play in identifying and preventing cultures from becoming toxic?
- What HR interventions are successful in preventing toxic cultures from thriving?
- How far do the HR policies contribute to toxic cultures?
- How do toxic leaders survive and what are the conditions for them to succeed?
- What role, if any, do 'followers' of toxic leaders perform?
- How can toxic cultures become positive workplace environments?
- What are the organizational behaviours or telltale signs of a toxic culture?
- Do corporate cultures turn leaders toxic, or is it the other way round?

This book is written from the perspective of more than 30 years in the field of human resources, with experience in a range of multinational organizations as a senior HR Practitioner and as a Management Consultant. In my career, I have worked across more than 100 countries and lived on three continents. I wrote my doctorate in the 1990s while living in Poland as it emerged from Communism. In my doctorate, I explored the corporate culture of global companies and how they did (or did not) adapt to national culture. Culture is a field that has fascinated me for as long as I can remember. In the past decade or so, I have become more fascinated by the dark side of culture.

In 2006, I published a book with my co-author, Professor Graeme Martin, titled *Corporate Reputations, Employer Branding and People Management.* Up to that point, corporate reputations were seen more as a marketing exercise. In our book, we argued that employees were vital to corporate reputations by the way they behaved and as the 'true' advocates of the organization. People, we argued, can create an excellent corporate reputation; and by their actions, they can also destroy these reputations. Uber, ING, Wells Fargo, and RBS have all featured on positive lists such as 'Best Place to Work'. Yet they have been subsequently criticized publicly for their toxic culture or toxic leadership. This book explores the relationship between culture and leadership and addresses how toxicity can become the organization's nemesis.

In the wake of scandals and corporate malpractices, the term 'toxic culture' has been coined. 'Toxic' can mean 'extremely harsh', 'malicious', or 'harmful'. The wording suggests a deviant, aberrant, or 'dark side' behaviour that is used to describe individuals as well as organizations. 'Dark side' has strong connotations of evil, dangerous, or poisonous. In researching this book, there is one constant element when defining toxicity, and that is 'harm'. Taken literally, 'toxic' is defined as 'poisonous' with its roots derived from the medieval Latin term *toxicus*, meaning poisoned or imbued with poison. The word is derived from the Greek term *toxon*, meaning 'bow'. In ancient Greece, fighters with bows would put poison on the points of their arrows. Through the lens of organizations, this evocative image suggests that toxic cultures require a continued onslaught from more than one protagonist over a prolonged period of time.

It takes time for organizations to become 'toxic' – yet most people who have worked in an organization will have experienced some degree of dysfunctional behaviours. The definition of a toxic organizational culture is based on a culture causing or sustaining harm over a period of time. Some researchers argue that organizational culture should be seen as the current reality of how the members of a cultural unit see and work with their current reality, rather than as a positive or negative experience. Cultural elements, they argue, can be dysfunctional or obsolete with respect to the environment, and cultural elements can make members feel happy or unhappy. For example, Schein argues that 'toxicity' is loaded with values that are themselves cultural from the point of view of humanism but not necessarily dysfunctional from the point of view of organizational survival.

Unfortunately, there is overwhelming evidence of toxicity in organizations. At a micro level, this toxicity may start within a team or unit. Tolerating dysfunctional behaviours causes harm and becomes absorbed by the culture as the 'way to get things done' and can spread rapidly. At a macro level, this book shows how performance pressures drive cognitive dissonance and the normalization of deviance over time, resulting in a 'toxic' organizational culture. You can work in such a culture alongside people whom you respect and trust; however, there will be a disconnect between your own values and the cultural values and focus of the organization. You may, for example, be directed to reduce costs even when you may know that it will cause potential harm say in the environment or to others. A few individuals may choose to leave but they will be replaced by others to carry out the task. A toxic organizational culture is one of apathy, hubris, and omnipotence.

This is the first book to show how toxic cultures emerge over time. While the role of leadership in toxic cultures is acknowledged, I show that there are four distinct stages that embed a toxic culture into an organization. This is a unique proposition drawn from extensive and emerging research. Corporate culture is enduring and dynamic; it is not static as defined by previous management notions of 'unfreeze and freeze'.[8] Rather, cultures need continuous management, assessment, and support. Toxic cultures, this book argues, are embedded by two drivers: (1) accepting the unacceptable or the *Normalization of Deviance*; and (2) believing rhetoric over reality or *Cognitive Dissonance*. The book draws on examples from leading organizations and companies, such as BP, VW, RBS, Wells Fargo, and others, to illustrate each of the four stages. The stages reveal how HR practices and processes can embed these drivers over time, from selecting ambitious leaders, condoning and promoting dysfunctional behaviours, implementing short-term incentives, and obsessively focusing on short-term performance measures – all under the guise of transformational change that promotes and embeds toxicity. An organization does not become toxic overnight; it does not consciously set out to break rules and regulations, nor does it actively seek wrongdoing. Yet all the organizations discussed have been described as toxic and have faced heavy fines, penalties, decline, or failure.

There are three key features of the book:

1. The four stages of toxic cultures, and the impact of performance pressures in driving toxicity
2. The Toxic Triangle: the three dimensions that enable toxic culture
3. Practical tools and guidance on developing appropriate HR policies and practices, as well as insights from non-executive directors, senior executives, and HR practitioners on managing cultures

The book provides practical examples of HR interventions and strategies that promote a better workplace environment and attempt to deal with toxicity. We explore some tools and diagnostics created to assess the level of toxicity in your organization and the HR interventions that can be used to mitigate a toxic culture. We explore the extent that your corporate values and norms are 'lived' by your leaders and managers, and we address the value of the HR function to turn toxic cultures into positive workplace environments. Finally, we explore the vital role of the Boards and governance in organizations, and why, up to now, they have failed on occasion to mitigate toxic workplaces.

In writing this book, I've seen there has been a tussle between the impact of leadership and culture and their impact on toxicity. There is little doubt that leadership and culture are two sides of the same coin, as classical cultural theorist Edgar H. Schein stated.[9] However, trying to uncover which one dominates is rather like asking which came first: the chicken or the egg. Recent research has introduced the term *Toxic Triangle* to describe three underpinning elements of destructive leadership. These elements are described as: destructive leaders, susceptible followers, and conducive environments.

This book is divided into three parts:

Part I: The Four Stages of Toxicity

This part takes a macro-level view of corporate culture. It explores two key drivers that enable toxicity and how these develop over four stages to entrench and embed a toxic culture.

Chapter 1: Why Culture Matters

We start the book by focusing on organizational culture to better understand why toxic cultures exist. We explore the definition of toxic culture before describing the differences that manifest between positive and toxic workplace environments. We explore the key levers that drive culture change on the premise that if these drive positive culture change, *ipso facto*, they could change a culture to become more toxic. These levers include the behaviours of leaders and supervisors (the role models), developing talent and skills, performance management, and people policies and processes, and we consider how these levers can reinforce a dysfunctional climate. At the level of the individual, intrinsic and extrinsic motivations are then used to detail how positive and toxic workplace environments may manifest. We conclude by exploring some of the main triggers of toxicity in organizations, and why these are typically driven by performance pressures.

Chapter 2: The First Driver of Toxic Culture – The Normalization of Deviance

In Chapter 2, we look in more detail at the first of the two main drivers for embedding a toxic culture: the *Normalization of Deviance*. This concept explores how previously unacceptable practices become acceptable over time, and even the 'norm'. Normalization of Deviance was first identified by sociologist Diane Vaughan when exploring the Challenger disaster at NASA. She identified the root cause of the Challenger disaster to be the use of the dangerously flawed O-rings at cold temperatures and how this risk had been recalibrated to become acceptable shortly before the ill-fated launch of Challenger.

Chapter 3: The Second Driver of Toxic Culture – Cognitive Dissonance

Here, we explore *Cognitive Dissonance*. As organizations come to dominate and believe their own rhetoric, there is an unrealized emergent and stark difference from the internal reality. Here, we draw on examples from BP, VW, Wells Fargo, and RBS. The chapter explores how organizations begin to create their own external narrative that is increasingly distant from the internal reality – or what is 'actually happening'. Organizations invest heavily in creating their own corporate values that are shared with Boards and in Annual Reports. Yet few organizations measure these values in terms of their own people policies and processes, leadership criteria, or managing talent decisions.

Chapter 4: The Four Stages of a Toxic Culture

In Chapter 4, we bring these two drivers together as a framework for understanding four stages of how toxicity and toxic norms are embedded over time. This framework is illustrated with examples from organizations such as NASA, VW, BP, and RBS, and we zoom in on the disastrous consequences of ignoring red flags to corporate scandals.

Part II: The Toxic Triangle

This part explores the dark side of corporate culture at the micro-level or individual level of leaders and followers. Chapter 5 explores toxic leadership, the dark triad of behaviour, and the impact on corporate culture. Chapter 6 explores the oft-neglected area of followers. Followers are regarded as either colluders or conformers, yet their role is far more complex than the current research suggests. Chapter 7 then explores the third part: a conducive environment.

Chapter 5: Toxic Leadership

In Chapter 5, we review the literature on toxic leadership. This chapter explores the three camps of literature on leadership and the growing concern around the 'dark' side of leadership. The book argues that the continued reliance on the 'superhero' theory by business schools, executive Boards, and shareholders is damaging to organizational sustainability. This populist view has placed more power in the hands of single individuals such as CEOs, and in doing so, it has perpetuated and exacerbated the tendency to idealize the leadership profile (as one similar to the psychopathic profile) in that hard-driving, results-driven, ruthless, and charismatic behaviours are all applauded as the 'right' leadership characteristics. Drawing on research from psychology and sociology, we explore a range of personality disorders present in the general population and consider how far these are reflected within organizations. We commonly see leaders who may use tactics to manipulate a 'them versus us' culture that ensures the 'psychopathic' leaders remain in command and retain loyalty among their followers. Finally, we consider the role of the 'follower' in an organization. We explore whether there are different types of followers: those who conform and those who collude. However, there is little research to draw from in this domain.

Chapter 6: Susceptible Followers

In a pragmatic sense, leaders require followers to be able to call themselves 'leaders'. In cases of toxic leadership, followers have typically been framed as innocent bystanders and passive recipients of the leader's vision, susceptible followers, colluders, or conformers. In this chapter, we explore the role of the follower to bring a more holistic understanding of their role and how these stakeholders may unwittingly play a part in promoting toxic behaviours and embedding this toxicity in the corporate culture.

Chapter 7: The Toxic Triangle – Conducive Environments

The third domain in the toxic triangle is a conducive environment, described as one without the *checks and balances* or where the organization is *tolerant of toxic behaviours* of its leader or leaders. It is asserted that toxic leaders will not survive or succeed in positive working environments. In toxic cultures, organizations justified their actions and behaviours by using rhetoric such as 'the ends justifying the means'. Loyalty to the cause becomes paramount. Non-corrupt behaviours are then punishable as deviant as the individual is 'not one of us'.[10] There are four factors that are significant in creating a conducive environment for a toxic leader and for susceptible followers: instability, perceived threats from others, favouritism, and an absence of checks and balances. In addition, this chapter illustrates how certain practices such as 'forced distribution curves' on performance ratings embed toxicity. Such forced distribution curves have all the hallmarks of toxicity: lacking empathy, pitting colleagues against each other, and encouraging the negative behaviours. We also explore certain recruitment and selection, development, talent management, and performance processes that act as complicit enablers to toxic cultures.

Part III: How to Build and Sustain a Healthy Workplace Culture

In this final part of the book, we explore how organizations can build and sustain a healthy workplace culture. There are seven key levers that need to be orchestrated to provide a remedy for toxicity, and these are called the RESPECT approach.

- Realign corporate values and measure engagement, inclusion, and respect
- Enable psychological safety and support employees to speak up
- Strengthen and enable leadership to act as role models
- Promote and align HR policies and processes
- Elevate well-being
- Call out toxic behaviours
- Transform career development and learning through the growth mindset

Chapter 8: How to Build and Sustain a Healthy Workplace Culture

Chapter 8 draws on case studies from organizations as well as the voices of a range of senior executives who have contributed to this book. We look at the use and value of surveys and other diagnostic tools, selection of senior leaders, talent management and career development, and strategies for dealing with undesirable behaviours. In addition, practical tools and techniques are proposed for practitioners to be able to measure and assess levels and/or pockets of toxicity.

Chapter 9: A Framework for Action

This chapter presents the RESPECT approach, with seven levers to build and sustain a healthy workplace culture. This framework for action can be adapted for implementation in your organization.

Conclusion

The book concludes with a call for action for organizations, senior leaders, and HR professionals, as well as Boards, to implement tools that will diagnose, identify, and measure toxic cultures. And that there must be greater accountability of Boards to monitor and address toxicity. Toxic organizational cultures and leadership are devastating for individuals, teams, organizations, and other stakeholders. The time demands action to build and continually sustain positive workplace cultures. It is time for work organizations to make a choice: to create workplaces and implement management practices that have positive impacts on physical and mental well-being, and not the reverse. Doing so will not only improve well-being but may also save lives.

Notes

1 The Financial Protection Bureau fined Wells Fargo $185m as a result of this illegal activity in 2016, when fake accounts were set up by employees to gain bonuses, with civil and criminal charges estimated around $3bn by 2020 continuing into 2021; BP paid over $60bn in criminal and civil settlements, natural resource fines, and cost of cleaning up; and VW costs continue to grow reaching £25bn in 2021 in fines and settlements.

- Chappell, B. (2016) Wells Fargo Fined $185 Million Over Creation of Fake Accounts For Bonuses. *NPR*. https://www.npr.org/sections/thetwo-way/2016/09/08/493130449/wells-fargo-to-pay-around-190-million-over-fake-accounts-that-sparked-bonuses. Accessed December 13, 2021.
- Flittler, E. (2020) The Price of Wells Fargo's Fake Account Scandal Grows by $3 Billion. *The New York Times*. https://www.nytimes.com/2020/02/21/business/wells-fargo-settlement.html. Accessed December 13, 2021.
- CNBCSon, H. (2021) Wells Fargo Hit with Another Fine, But Also Says CFPB Order from 2016 Sales Practices Has Ended. *CNBS*. https://www.cnbc.com/2021/09/09/wells-fargo-hit-with-another-fine-but-also-says-cfpb-order-from-2016-sales-practices-has-ended.html. Accessed December 13, 2021.
- Vaughan, A. (2018) BP's Deepwater Horizon Bill Tops $65bn. *The Guardian*. https://www.theguardian.com/business/2018/jan/16/bps-deepwater-horizon-bill-tops-65bn. Accessed December 13, 2021.
- Davies, R. (2021) Dieselgate: British Car Buyers' Claim against VW Reaches High Court. *The Guardian*. https://www.theguardian.com/business/2021/dec/05/dieselgate-british-car-buyers-claim-vw-reaches-high-court. Accessed December 13, 2021.

2 Harvard Business Review refers to the American Psychological Association, which estimated that the cost of stress in the workplace was $500bn annually.

Moss, J. (2019) Burnout Is about Your Workplace, Not Your People. *Harvard Business Review*. https://hbr.org/2019/12/burnout-is-about-your-workplace-not-your-people. Accessed December 13, 2021.

3 Harter, J., & Adkins, A. (2015) Employees Want a Lot More from Their Managers. *Galliup*. https://www.gallup.com/workplace/236570/employees-lot-managers.aspx. Accessed December 13, 2021.

4 BBC. (2018) Surgeons' 'Toxic' Rows Added to Mortality Rate, Says Report. *BBC News*. https://www.bbc.co.uk/news/uk-45067747. Accessed December 9, 2021.

5 Kline, R., & Lewis, D. (2018) The price of fear: Estimating the financial cost of bullying and harrassment to the NHS in England. *Public Money & Management*, 39(3): 1–10.

6

- Aiello, C. (2018) Uber's Loss Jumped 61 percent to $4.5 billion in 2017. *CNBC*. https://www.cnbc.com/2018/02/13/ubers-loss-jumped-61-percent-to-4-point-5-billion-in-2017.html. Accessed December 12, 2021.
- Kang, C. (2021) Facebook Whistle-Blower Urges Lawmakers to Regulate the Company. https://www.nytimes.com/2021/10/05/technology/facebook-whistle-blower-hearing.html. Accessed December 13, 2021.

7 CIPD in association with High Pay Centre. (2020) FTSE 100 CEO Pay in 2019 and during the Pandemic. *CIPD*. https://www.cipd.co.uk/Images/ftse-100-executive-pay-report_tcm18-82375.pdf. Accessed December 13, 2021.

8 Kurt Lewin is widely considered as the founding father of change management with his freeze-unfreeze model. Lewin has been criticized by academics as over-simplifying the change process. More recently, a team of academics found that this concept was never developed by Lewin but gained ground posthumously. Lewin is accredited with the concept of 'unfreezing', and he acknowledges that 'life was not static . . . but changing, dynamic and fluid'. See: Cummings, S., Bridgman, T., & Brown, K.G. (2016) Unfreezing change in three steps: Rethinking Kurt Lewin's legacy for change management. *Human Relations*, 69(1): 33–60.

9 Schien, E.H. (2016) *Organizational Culture and Leadership*. Hoboken, NJ: John Wiley & Sons.

10 Campbell, J.-L., & Goritz, A.S. (2014) Culture corrupts! A qualitative study of organizational culture in corrupt organizations. *Journal of Business Ethics*, 120: 291–311.

Part I
The Four Stages of Toxicity

In this Part, we explore two critical drivers that slowly change the cultural norms and embed toxicity in organizations: 'Cognitive Dissonance' and 'Normalization of Deviance'. Likened to the 'boiling frog' analogy, these drivers embed slowly and deeply over time.

Chapter 1 explores the meaning of and difference between positive and toxic workplace environments. We examine the key levers that drive culture change, such as performance pressures; the behaviours of leaders and supervisors (the role models); performance management; and people, policies, and processes, and we look at how these levers can reinforce a dysfunctional climate. Chapter 2 explores the Normalization of Deviance, which was first identified by the sociologist Diane Vaughan when exploring the Challenger disaster at NASA. Essentially, it describes how deviance from correct or proper behaviour becomes normalized in a corporate culture. This 'blindness' to the 'acceptance' of the unacceptable can be manifested in organizations such as RBS, where the belief was that failure was not possible. Chapter 3 explores Cognitive Dissonance. As organizations come to dominate their sector and believe their own rhetoric, there is an unrealized emergent and stark difference to the internal reality. Drawing on examples from BP, VW, Wells Fargo, and RBS, this chapter explores how organizations begin to create their own external narrative that is increasingly distant from the internal reality or what is actually happening. Finally in Chapter 4, we bring together the two drivers for toxic cultures as a framework to understand the four stages of toxicity and how toxic norms are embedded over time. This framework is illustrated with examples from organizations such as NASA, VW, BP, and RBS, and we focus on the disastrous consequences of ignoring red flags and corporate scandals.

DOI: 10.4324/9781003330387-2

1
Why Culture Matters

1.1 Introduction

The costs of a dysfunctional corporate culture are substantial.

Toxic cultures have been linked to higher cases of mortality, unethical behaviour, and even criminality. A Gallup study of more than 7,000 adults in the USA[1] revealed that one in two had left their job to get away from their manager in order to improve their overall life at some point in their career. BreatheHR (UK) estimated the cost of toxic workplace culture in SMEs alone is around £15.7bn per year (2020),[2] and the Society for Human Resource Management (SHRM) in the USA found that toxic workplace cultures cost an estimated $223bn over the five years prior to 2019.[3]

The Financial Conduct Authority, the UK's regulatory authority for financial services, has gone on record to say that the Global Financial Crisis in 2008 was due to 'corporate culture'. BP has paid over $60bn in criminal and civil settlements, natural resource fines, and the cost of clean-up efforts. VW's costs for its diesel cheating scandal totalled $17bn in fines and settlements.[4] Wells Fargo was ordered to pay over $1.2bn in penalties and the Federal Reserve barred the bank from growing as a penalty for opening more than two million bank accounts without authorization from customers[5]; the root cause of this fraudulent behaviour was deemed by independent investigators to be the "culture of the division" where employees opened the accounts.

The public sector is also at risk. In one UK hospital, a report found that the "persistent toxic atmosphere" and "dark force" in the surgical department contributed to a higher death rate for patients. Describing the department as "dysfunctional", the report stated that there were two camps within the department that exhibited "tribal-like activity" leading to a mortality rate that was almost twice the national average.[6] In another NHS study, using a spectrum of measures, researchers estimated that the specific impact resulting from bullying and harassment cost the UK taxpayer £2.281bn per annum.[7]

DOI: 10.4324/9781003330387-3

Some companies pride themselves on having a corporate culture with a cut-throat, high-pressure, take-no-prisoners mentality to drive their financial success. Yet a growing body of research on positive organizational psychology demonstrates that not only is a cut-throat environment harmful to productivity over time, but also a positive environment will lead to dramatic benefits for employers, employees, and the bottom line.[8] Although there is an assumption that stress and pressure push employees to perform more, better, and faster, what cut-throat organizations fail to recognize are the hidden costs incurred. In an article published in *Harvard Business Review*, authors Seppala and Cameron note that in the US, health care expenditures at high-pressure companies are nearly 50 per cent greater than at other organizations.[9]

Indeed, the American Psychological Association reckons that workplace stress costs more than $500bn annually and that 550 million workdays are lost each year due to stress on the job. Between 60 and 80 per cent of workplace accidents are attributed to stress, and it is estimated that more than 80 per cent of doctor visits are due to stress. Workplace stress has been linked to health problems ranging from metabolic syndrome to cardiovascular disease and mortality. More disturbing, the less power and influence wielded by an individual, the higher the chances of cardiovascular disease and death. One study of more than 3,000 employees by Anna Nyberg of the Karolinska Institute showed a strong link between leadership behaviour and heart disease.[10] The annual cost of poor mental health for UK employers is £56bn according to a report by Deloitte in 2022.[11]

> Toxicity is a different kind of … intensity. And sometimes you only know it when you experience it. So why did I feel that the place that I worked at was toxic? It's that feeling of awful dread when you're even walking up to the building. It's the … the smell of the place when you're in there, you can just see on the spot that there's a wariness. You can call it: meerkat syndrome - people are up there looking around, who's nearby, who's not. You can see so many side conversations going on (and) the flow of information being weaponised. So, rather than transparency with information moving around, it's 'what can we keep secret, what can we hide.' It's where you're guarded in every conversation because you feel as if it could be your last. And it's also one of those ones where, if circumstances were different, you'd want to get out.[12]

Toxic cultures harm businesses, corporations, and economies as well as individuals. In summary:

- Toxic cultures are costly in terms of sickness, absence, and health care
- Toxic cultures have been linked to higher levels of mortality
- Toxic cultures are detrimental to corporate reputations

- Toxic cultures negatively impact corporate valuations and shareholder value
- Toxic cultures can exist in any organization

Vignette 1.1 The Columbia Accident at NASA

The Columbia disaster occurred on 1 February 2003, when NASA's space shuttle Columbia broke up as it returned to Earth, killing the seven astronauts on board. It was the Board's view that NASA's organizational culture and structure had as much to do with the accident as the faulty materials. The Board's report stated:

> Cultural traits and organizational practices detrimental to safety and reliability were allowed to develop, including: reliance on past success as a substitute for sound engineering practices; organisational barriers which prevented effective communication of critical safety information and stifled professional differences of opinion; lack of integrated management across program elements; and the evolution of an informal chain of command and decision-making process that operated outside the organizations' rules.[13]

1.2 Culture and Leadership

To understand how and why cultures become toxic, we need to define corporate culture and its relationship with leadership.

In his original 1992 book, *Organizational Culture and Leadership*, Schein argues that "leadership and culture are two sides of the same coin". Culture can begin with a leader who imposes their own cause and assumptions onto the group. Leaders have the power to manipulate, manage, and change a corporate culture. Yet culture is not a static entity. It is a much more dynamic force that is constantly changing and adapting. Organizations can have different cultures even within the same industry sector. Indeed, it is also possible that different cultures or micro-cultures within teams can exist within a single organization.[14]

Culture is often cited as being the manifestation of values and attitudes, and these occur at various psychological stages from the conscious to the subconscious to the unconscious. At a conscious level, culture is defined as 'the way we do things around here' and culture is defined through the stated corporate or company values.[15] This perspective tends to see culture as a 'control mechanism' where the 'right' kind of culture can be developed and enforced via selective recruitment, promotion, and development. Schein has defined culture to be at a deeper psychological state:

> A pattern of shared basic assumptions that the group learned as it solved its problems of external adaptation and internal integration, that has worked well enough to be considered valid and, therefore, to be taught as the correct way to perceive, think, and feel in relation to those problems.[16]

The attributes of culture are defined by Schein as being shared, pervasive, implicit, and enduring. The first attribute is that culture is **shared** – it cannot exist in one person but is a group experience or phenomenon. Culture consists of shared values and assumptions and is experienced through how things get done – in other words, the unwritten rules. The second attribute is **pervasive.** Culture permeates across job levels and across geographies and boundaries. It is pervasive through the stories, physical environments, and visible symbols as well as the mindsets and unspoken assumptions. The third attribute is that it is **implicit.** It is like a language to be learned and used. Newcomers to organizations are often treated as non-natives when they are bombarded with multi-letter acronyms, for example, and must keep asking what they mean. The fourth attribute is that culture is **enduring.** As a collective experience, individuals adapt to the culture, not the other way round.

Organizational culture has been interpreted in several ways from the dominant espoused values,[17] the philosophy that guides the organization's policy,[18] the rules of the game,[19] or the feeling or climate in the organization[20] to the observation of behaviours and language in the organization. Schein's approach suggests that organizational culture exists at three levels. The first consists of what he calls **artefacts**. These are the tangible aspects of an organization's culture and consist both of the "visible and feelable structures and processes" as well as of "observed behaviour".[21] Artefacts are at the surface of an organization's culture; they are how the organization manifests its culture. They are the visible products of an organization that may include its physical environment and architecture, its technology, its creations, its style, as well as its stories and myths. Moreover, artefacts also include the published documents that cover the values, operations, rituals, and organizational charts. The second level is what Schein calls **the espoused beliefs and values** which encompass the shared ideals, goals, values, and aspirations between individuals within an organization. These can come in the form of shared ideologies and rationalizations for what the organization does. These espoused beliefs and values are deeper in the organization and cannot be directly observed but must be learned by talking to organizational members. The third and deepest level of an organizational culture is what Schein calls the **basic underlying assumptions**. These are deeply embedded within the organization and operate unconsciously through organization members. They concern taken-for-granted beliefs and values that can "determine behaviour perception, thought and feeling".[22] Beliefs are assumptions that individuals hold about themselves, their clients, their colleagues, and their organization. **Norms** are unwritten rules of behaviour that address areas such as how an employee behaves or interacts. **Norms** 'operationalize' actions which are consistent with the values and beliefs.[23]

As Figure 1.1 suggests, organization culture can be analysed at three levels: structure, values, and behaviours.

The structure relates to the rules, levels of authority, incentives, and how decisions are made. Values tend to be the explicit description of how an organization behaves with its clients as well as how employees act towards one another. These values might include statements around respect, integrity, collaboration, or excellence. Finally, the behaviours are the actions, words, and impact of the leaders and employees: how individuals and teams are treated and treat one another. An assessment of toxic corporate cultures must consider an organization's tangible and intangible manifestations and, in particular, the organizational structures (rules, governance, and power), organizational values, and organizational practices.[24] These form the core three organizational levels on which organizational culture can be evaluated. They are entry points for doing a cultural assessment but are not wholly distinct since structures can derive from and shape values and practices, values can originate in structures and

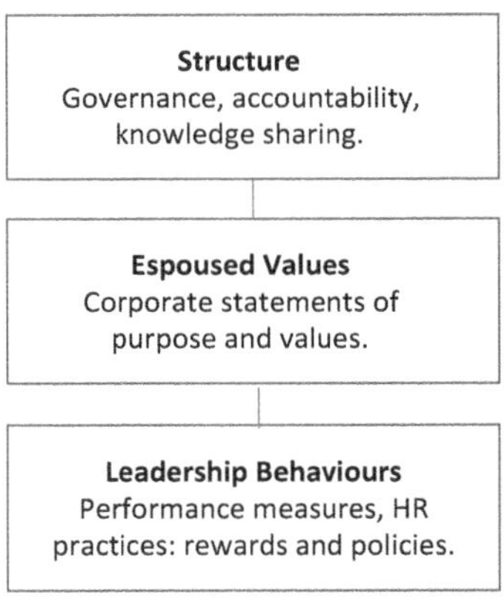

Figure 1.1 Analysis of Organizational Culture

Table 1.1 Organizational Culture Awareness

Level	*Manifested in…*	*Rooted in…*	*Awareness of…*
Structure and Governance	Rules, policies, stories	Power	Learned, manifest, and enforceable
Values	Statements, principles	Beliefs	Implicit and intangible
Behaviours	Visible behaviour	Actions	Conscious, explicit, and tangible

practices, and, of course, practices can follow the structures and values of an organization. Table 1.1 outlines the three levels of organizational culture that will be useful in identifying toxic elements in cultures.

In the next section, we explore toxic culture and examine how a toxic culture is manifested according to these three levels.

1.3 Toxic Cultures

The current challenge is that toxic cultures have not been recognized until relatively recently. There is an implicit assumption in Schein's work that all cultures tend to be positive. As such, there is a dearth of research on how toxic cultures evolve and dominate. Toxic cultures can and do exist, but in order to identify a toxic culture, a degree of understanding of what it might look like in an organization is needed.

So how should toxic cultures be defined? All corporate cultures are at risk of becoming toxic, even well-respected institutions such as global banks or supranationals. Toxic cultures within such organizations are often defined as long-term and systemic rule-breaking and damaging behaviour. Toxic culture is often associated with extremely bad or dysfunctional behaviour, but this is not the same as a criminogenic organizational culture or a criminogenic organization; organizations with toxic cultures do not necessarily have to engage in crime or break the law to be deemed 'toxic'. Toxic culture is negative and therefore different from studies that have focused on wrongdoing through a poor safety culture or compliance culture.[25] In the wake of public scandals and corporate malpractices, the term 'toxic culture' has been coined. 'Toxic' is a word used to describe workplaces, schools, cultures, relationships, and stress. 'Toxic' in this context can mean extremely harsh, malicious, or harmful. While these descriptions are accurate, they do not recognize how toxicity might develop or endure in an organization.

Vignette 1.2 Toxic Culture at the World Bank

In 2021, an investigation, by a leading law firm, into the Doing Business Reports produced by the World Bank identified elements of a 'toxic culture'.[26] The report was commissioned by the International Bank for Reconstruction and Development (part of the World Bank Group) to review the data irregularities concerning the 'improper changes to data' and the direction of and pressure from the leadership. The law firm found that there was undue pressure applied to employees from a senior level. Specifically, one leader (Djankov) was described as a 'bully who instilled fear on to the team' and managed by 'terror and intimidation'. His management style was described as 'psychological terrorism' that created a toxic environment. The law firm reported that this manager would 'dangle' promotions to ensure compliance with this team to incentivize compliance to his requests, and he retaliated against anyone who questioned his authority. This manager threatened demotions and non-renewal of contracts to ensure employees carried out his wishes. Many employees still expressed fear one year after his departure from the World Bank.

Toxic cultures have been defined in many ways from a hostile climate or hostile work environment, a negative work culture, a corrupt organizational culture, to a dysfunctional corporate culture and behaviours.

In a study by academics to explore the similarities in organizational cultures across different corrupt organizations in various industries, three levels of organizational culture were identified, closely mirroring Schein's work. These levels identify differences between manager levels and employee levels, as well as the underlying assumptions, values, norms, and behaviours. Firstly, their findings showed that the various underlying assumptions shared by managers and employees were in agreement that results were more important than the means. Secondly, both managers and employees felt that they were fighting a battle in the marketplace and held the imperative to win. Thirdly, managers valued results and performance, sometimes at a disconnect to ethical values.[27]

Vignette 1.3 The Liability and Cost of a Dysfunctional Culture: The Example of AIG[28]

AIG is an example of how a culture can become dysfunctional and lead to severe economic distress. The rapid decline of AIG was due to overexposure to the now infamous 'credit default swap'. Using its own econometric models and assuming that total economic collapse would not occur, AIG concluded that it could earn millions of dollars with virtually no risk. Yet it was not the statistical model that led to AIG's near collapse, but rather the failure to adhere to a core cultural norm. Under the previous leadership, a norm had been established where anyone could question a trade, which led to a culture that helped to avoid undue risks. Under new leadership, this norm was undermined as the leader eliminated dissenters and ensured no challenge to his direction.

1.3.1 Toxic Origins – A Word

Toxic, as a word, is defined as **poisonous** with its roots derived from the medieval Latin term **toxicus**, meaning 'poisoned' or 'imbued with poison', and this word is derived from the Greek term **toxon**, meaning 'bow'. In ancient Greece, fighters with bows would put poison on the points of their arrows before being fired over the walls or fences to attack an enemy; this probably best defines and describes how toxic cultures develop. Not that one single spear can cause devastation, but the continuous onslaught of firing the spears enables the toxic culture to take hold. Other evocative adjectives such as 'deviant', 'aberrant', or the 'dark side' have been used to describe individuals as well as cultures. 'Dark' has strong connotations to 'evil', 'dangerous', or 'malevolent'. As shown in Table 1.2, toxic culture has been described in a myriad of different ways.[29] When defining toxicity, there is one constant element and that is 'harm'; causing harm, or inflicting harm, is a consequence of the label 'dark'.

For the purpose of this book and utilizing what we already know about the topic, toxic cultures can be defined as:

> Toxic cultures are a set of **tolerated** behaviours and actions that are reinforced through the rules, policies, and actions of the leaders as a way to influence, manipulate and manage others that appear to redefine, contradict or oppose the stated values of the organization.

Now that toxic culture is defined, the question remains as to how it is created. Is it the work of a single leader or a combination of dynamic forces? Toxic cultures are far more dynamic and endemic than most observers acknowledge. Recent thinking considers toxic cultures to be a combination of toxic leaders, susceptible followers, and conducive environments.[30] This takes a perspective that the leader, or rather the toxic leader, can dominate in an organization or even a country[31] where there is a conducive environment and susceptible followers.

Table 1.2 Definitions of Toxic Culture

Source	*Definition*
van Rooij & Fine (2018)	Toxic cultures are 'organizations with long-term and systemic rule-breaking and damaging behaviour'.
	Toxic norms resist and compete with legal norms, normalize deviancy, create opportunity to violate and neutralize offending, lack support to follow rules and learn from errors, strain employees away from compliance, and delegitimize positive and social legal norms.
Khan & Rouse (2021)	Key to the dynamics of toxic organizations is power and powerlessness. Those that enact toxic behaviours have the protected space in which to do so without undue penalty; they expand their power through the regular reducing of others.
Samier & Milley (2018)	Toxic cultures dampen enthusiasm, reduce professionalism, and depress organizational effectiveness where self-interest and meaning outside of work dominate, and negativity is pervasive with organizational roles overrun by naysayers, saboteurs, rumourmongers, and antiheros.
Hartel (2008)	In an unhealthy or toxic work culture, a simple gesture of friendliness can be interpreted with scepticism and doubt due to lack of trust. Therefore, in a toxic culture where doubt and scepticism are prevalent cultural norms, the most obvious outcomes would be toxic emotions such as fear and anxiety. The authors note differences of toxicity related to the type of organizational culture: individualism or collectivism.
Lewis (2021)	A workplace culture might be described as toxic if mediocre performance is rewarded over merit-based output, employees avoid disagreement with managers for fear of reprisal, personal agendas take precedence over the long-term well-being of the company, leaders are constantly on edge and lose their tempers often, new leaders do not stay long and employee turnover is relatively high, employees are treated more like financial liabilities than assets, and bosses routinely throw temper tantrums, make unreasonable demands, or use obscenities.

Ryan (2016)	When a culture becomes toxic, so does truth. People will not speak up, at least not within the organization. Formal reporting continues but is open to being gamed.
Furnham & Taylor (2004)	The authors identify a long list of danger signals that breed malcontent: • An 'us vs. them' feel to management/employee differentiation • An assumption that loyalty and commitment is a one-way street: that employees should show unquestionable loyalty, but that management need not reciprocate this • A culture of surveillance and suspicion where nobody trusts each other and there is excessive, possibly growing, use of electronic surveillance methods • Having no, outdated, or rigged grievance procedures that people have not agreed to or have no opportunity to shape them • Hypocritical messages where the manager says one thing and does another • Where sticks are preferred to carrots to motivate and where only top managers get the 'carrot' method • Where there is no long-term view: management is reactive not proactive with a short-term view on everything, especially profit • Where people are promoted (and rewarded) by nepotism, corruption, and ingratiation rather than for their ability and effort • Where communication channels are blocked or non-existent so that people do not realize what is going on until it is too late • Where many employees feel alienated from top management • Where lots of people overtly or covertly break company rules and even legal requirements

(*continued*)

Source	*Definition*
Kusy & Holloway (2009)	Toxicity will be significantly reduced in organizations that clearly define the values in a concrete way, identify the kinds of behaviours the organization will and will not tolerate, and have a clear set of consequences when an individual does not live up to the values. The authors identify six ways in which an organization's culture promotes toxicity: 1. The organizational structure changes to accommodate the toxic personality 2. The organization tolerates the toxicity, provided the individual is productive 3. The team climate changes when the toxic person is present 4. The organization's leaders are unaware of toxic behaviour 5. Less productive team meetings are tolerated 6. The organization contributes to the toxic person getting away with counterproductive behaviours.
Roter (2019)	Dark side behaviours play a role in changing the organizational culture. Incivility and dysfunctional behaviour can permeate many different levels in the organization. As the behaviour seeps into these levels, the culture starts to morph and can quickly shift from a healthy culture to an unhealthy one.
Jain (2021)	A toxic work culture is one where workers are exposed to psychosocial hazards. They may have little or no organizational support, poor interpersonal relationships, high workload, poor rewards, and a lack of job security.
Applebaum & Roy-Girard (2007)	Toxicity in the workplace comes from multiple toxins (toxic leader, toxic manager, and toxic culture) within the organization.
de Bruijn (2021)	A toxic work environment plays an important role in affecting workplace deviance. The characteristics of leaders and how they treat their employees, as well as the characteristics of employees and how they respond to the organization, as determinants of organizational deviancy.

1.4 Positive Cultures: The Opposite of Toxic Cultures?

One way of better understanding toxicity in organizations is to distinguish between positive cultures and toxic cultures by looking at how individuals are treated in the workplace. A positive culture will quickly address toxic behaviours before they are able to be repeated or become visible to others; dysfunctional behaviours will be reprimanded quickly to prevent such episodes from becoming "the hallmark of a toxic culture".[32]

Daniel Pink, a science journalist, wrote a book titled *Drive – The surprising truth about what motivates us.*[33] Drawing on research from Deci and Ryan (2000),[34] Pink recommends a radical approach to motivation and jobs. He argues that the carrot-and-stick approach to motivation does not work anymore. It is not a sustainable approach to motivation and does not lead to excellent work or engagement. According to Pink, human beings have an innate drive to be autonomous, self-determined, and connected to one another. When that drive is achieved, people feel satisfied and fulfilled. The intrinsic motivations to learn and create new things, to direct our career path, to better ourselves, and to contribute to a better world or organization are the same the world over, irrespective of culture. Recently, the Harvard Business School published research to show that individuals were motivated by career, cause, and community; in other words, access to developing a career, working for a purpose, and a sense of belonging to a group of people.[35]

Furnham and MacRae (2017) agree that there are three components of intrinsic motivation: autonomy over work; recognition; and an affiliation to the team, business unit, or organization. In other words, individuals want to have some level of control over when they do their work, how they do it, with whom, and to receive acknowledgement for what they do. The authors go further, suggesting key work dimensions to distinguish between positive and toxic cultures. Motivating factors can be a combination of challenging work, recognition for one's achievement, being given additional responsibility, the opportunity to do something meaningful, involvement in decision making, or a sense of value to the organization. These factors correlate to positive satisfaction and are typically referred to as intrinsic motivation.[36]

Hygiene factors such as job security, salary, benefits, and working conditions are factors that are not correlated with positive satisfaction – although as classical motivation theorist Herzberg notes, dissatisfaction occurs when they are absent.[37] The term 'hygiene' is used in the sense that these are maintenance factors and have become known as extrinsic motivation. Furnham and colleagues have developed a High Potential Motivator Indicator (HPMI)[38] which is useful for helping understand why individuals hold certain types of motivation. They identified six factors differentiating intrinsic and extrinsic motivation:

For *intrinsic* motivation there are three factors:

1. **Autonomy:** This means a focus on engagement, active participation, stimulation, and personal development. Those who are motivated by autonomy want to work a job that is consistent with their own passions, career development, and self-expression. This can also be referred to as working for a cause or mission or 'having purpose'
2. **Accomplishment:** This means being motivated by achievement, advancement, and visible success. It is often related to a desire for status and recognition. This can also be referred to as 'career development'
3. **Affiliation:** This means the opportunity to work with others, and to share knowledge and experiences in a collaborative way. This can also be referred to as 'community' as a sense of belonging

Taking into account this important discussion about motivation, one would expect to see these factors appearing differently in positive versus toxic cultures.

Table 1.3 explores intrinsic motivation and the key differences between positive and toxic cultures.

Table 1.3 Table Illustrating Intrinsic Motivation Factors and Their Key Differences in Positive and Toxic Work Cultures

Intrinsic motivation	*Aspect of work*	*Positive cultures*	*Toxic cultures*
Autonomy	Time (when)	Flexible working/ Results are valued more than presenteeism.	Clock in system/ Presenteeism is valued more than results.
	Technique (how)	Coaching.	Strict procedure.
	Team (whom)	Collaboration across silos/Team working valued.	Silos/Individual contributors valued such as employee of the year.
	Task (what)	Varied, interesting, and purposeful work.	Mundane, routine, and pointless task such as rewriting a one-page board paper more than 20 times.
Accomplishment	Advance skills and knowledge	On-the-job development such as stretch assignments.	Training is perceived as remedial and targeted at poor performers.

	Mastery and Expertise	Hire and grow approach/ Recognition of thought leaders – opportunities to present at external or internal conferences or seen as a coach and mentor to more junior staff.	Hire and tire approach – hire for the skills and then after a few years with no further training the individual skills become unemployable outside of the current organization. In organizations with greater levels of toxicity, the 'hire and fire' approach is implemented to ensure that individuals are forced to agree with the leader to keep their livelihood.
Affiliation	Engagement on the purpose	Clear purpose and mission such as end poverty that drive commitment and engagement. Consistent and unambiguous direction usually achieved through a process of team meetings and clarity of the goal and purpose while enabling individuals to have the autonomy to decide on how best they can contribute to the goals. Opportunity to call out and clarify conflicting demands for the benefit of the greater good.	Unclear, confused, or absence of purpose and direction. No understanding of how an individual job supports the overall goals and purpose. Sometimes conflicting requests from senior leadership who demand different and opposing work objectives. This is usually combined with a culture of compliance and deference from the top down, making the opportunity to call out the differences career limiting.

(*continued*)

Intrinsic motivation	*Aspect of work*	*Positive cultures*	*Toxic cultures*
	Sustainability	Focus is on sustainable success – engagement is long term.	Focus is on short-term profit – engagement is short term and can lead to hiring 'mercenaries' who are only interested in their pay and bonus.
	Collaboration	Organization seen as an identity – employees talk about 'we' and 'us' as an organization.	Purpose aligned to individual leaders resulting in silos and internal competition. Leaders can perpetuate this by setting individuals against each other through side conversations or having an 'inner-circle'.

The three *extrinsic* factors are:

1. **Security**: This involves job security, personal safety, and consistency. Typically, this could mean a job with a company or profession with a consistent reputation. Valuing security is a focus on stability and reliability
2. **Compensation**: This includes material rewards such as pay, insurance, bonuses, and benefits. This could include a more flexible working schedule or the opportunity to work remotely
3. **Conditions:** This includes workplace safety and security, and personal convenience. And an environment that is conducive to the person's lifestyle

Table 1.4 explores extrinsic motivation and the key differences between positive and toxic work cultures.

1.4.1 Corporate Culture and Change

The notion that you can simply change a culture by changing the leader has dominated the corporate world (see Schein, 2010[39]; Walker and Soule, 2017[40]; Steffy, 2011[41]). Undoubtedly, the role of the leader is key. Yet as we shall explore, the role of the leader is entwined with many other factors.

Corporate cultures are complex. Executives and new recruits are often confounded by culture because much of it is anchored in unspoken behaviours,

Table 1.4 Table Illustrating Extrinsic Motivation Factors and Their Key Differences in Positive and Toxic Work Cultures

Extrinsic motivation	*Aspect of work*	*Positive cultures*	*Toxic cultures*
Security	Job Security	Job security is reassured. Individuals can feel that mistakes will be tolerated, and the organization can learn from such errors.	Threats to job security made by senior leaders. Performance management used as a 'stick' to punish individuals and threaten their livelihoods.
Compen-sation	Reward	Pay and bonuses are linked to individual as well as team/company performance. Rewards are transparent and objective.	Pay and bonuses are linked to demanding performance targets that may be regarded as unrealistic or even immoral. Rewards are opaque and subjective.
Conditions	Lifestyle	The environment is seen as equitable, just, and fair. Individuals are managed consistently irrespective of gender, ethnicity, etc. Policies apply to all irrespective of status or job role.	The environment is unfair or unjust. Individuals may be discriminated against due to gender or ethnicity. Policies are subjective and people are treated differently dependent on status and role.

mindsets, and social patterns. Culture is dynamic. It is not an end state. People create cultures, and as people change, cultures change. There is little doubt that senior leaders have far more impact on or create a greater shadow across the organization, but it is difficult to ascertain how far they can shape people's views of culture – making it both a bottom-up *and* a top-down phenomenon. Culture can be seen at the corporate level as well as at a unit level. Some of the executive HR leaders who were interviewed for this book raised the difference between micro- and macro-level cultures:

> You can have toxic groups within an organization, or you can have toxicity within most of the organization.[42]
>
> Toxicity can occur in pockets of an organization at a micro level. The HR function is well versed to deal with challenges and issues, from destructive leaders to difficult team members.[43]

1.4.2 Culture Levers

The levers that are used in changing a culture are critical to defining the concept: the importance of role models, policies and procedures, and leadership development interventions. Culture change evolves over time and becomes embedded in the mindsets and behaviours that resonate with employees, their work, and their day-to-day context. These levers may be wrapped up in insights on how to align values with behaviours, which is best illustrated from the Change Management arena. Back in 1995, John Kotter published seminal work in the field of change management in his book *Leading Change: Why Transformation Efforts Fail*. Kotter argued that less than a third of change management programmes were successful.[44]

Ten years later, McKinsey surveyed around 1500 business leaders and asked them to consider if their change programmes had been completely or mostly successful – only 30 per cent agreed.

Changing or aligning behaviours is complex and dynamic. McKinsey[45] illustrated the four dimensions that need to be addressed (Figure 1.2):

1. Role Modelling
   The role of leaders and management is critical. How managers and leaders behave and how their staff witness this behaviour defines, reinforces, and strengthens the way things 'get done'. The impact of the leader, manager, or supervisor should never be underestimated. In 2006, Graeme Martin and

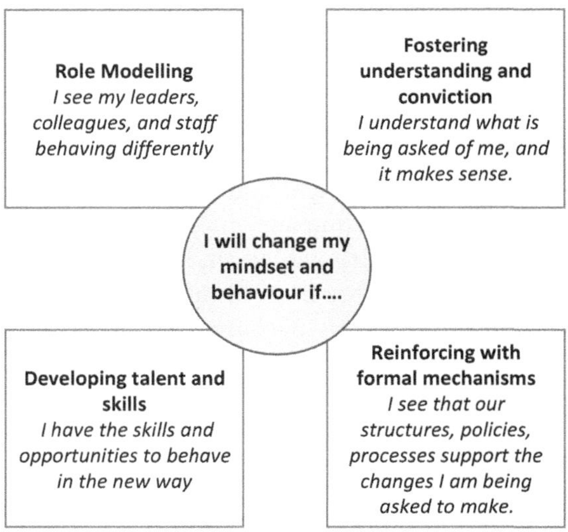

Figure 1.2 Changing Mindsets and Behaviours (Adapted from McKinsey, 2016)

I discussed in our book *Corporate Reputations, Branding and People Management* that employees are the ambassadors of the organization and critical to its corporate reputation. We showed that managers can act as a key 'control' mechanism in the corporate culture in the following ways: first, as a role model, displaying the appropriate company behaviours, values, and way of doing things; second, as a 'fixer', interpreting and adapting the corporate values and mission statements to make them readable to their teams and individuals; third, as networkers, by connecting with other units and departments across the organization; four, as agents of the corporate goals; and five, as coaches and mentors, transferring knowledge and developing skills to their teams.[46]

Some of my earlier research revealed that managers act as role models to employees.[47] They are able to demonstrate ways of behaviour that are consistent with the culture. There is little doubt that the role of managers or supervisors is far more impactful than some of the management literature acknowledges. It is not only about tone from the top – moreover, it is about how that tone is interpreted, heard, and assimilated that has the most impact. Culture is not embodied in one leader, rather it is the stories, deeds, and behaviours of any manager that has responsibility for people.

2. Fostering Understanding and Conviction
This dimension is concerned more with the communications and interpretation. People need to make sense of any change initiative, and consultants will recommend the use of 'story-telling' to define the values and behaviours of the desired culture. The idea here is that the individual will identify with the mission of the company and, by doing so, will be motivated and engaged. The idea of a sense of purpose has recently become increasingly popular as organizations compete for talent; they look to define the purpose of the organization. Corporate communication is key to culture because it signals the way the organization is to be perceived in the external world. This storytelling emerges as a key driver for embedding a culture, either positive or toxic.

For example, leading academics on RBS placed great symbolic value on the CEO's (Fred Goodwin) rigorous attention to detail, which was portrayed as reinforcing the bank's core values, thus controlling the story. Employees were reported to have had the mindset where they questioned their own decisions and asked themselves, "If Fred saw this, what would he say?"[48] The narrative that emerged at RBS was that there was one individual determining the strategy and who would not allow for dissent or alternative viewpoints.

3. Developing Talent and Skills
Being clear on the standards of behaviour expected across an organization is powerful. Many organizations have developed a 'competency framework'. These competencies might include labels such as *business acumen*,

responsible leadership, or *burning drive for results*. Done well, these competency frameworks can be a useful articulation of the corporate culture; examples of behaviours would be defined under each heading that describes 'role-model' behaviours.

For example, Aegon Asset Management, part of the Aegon Group, is one of the world's largest life insurance and pensions companies. Aegon Asset Management had historically been successful, but compared with its rivals, it was not well known in the marketplace and had not developed a corporate brand or reputation. When the CEO retired, his successor took the decision to review the company's brand and hired a new HR director to lead this work. They identified the need to consider the following: what the company stood for; what they wanted to be known for in the market, and what capabilities or competencies were required to achieve this.

The key drivers were to provide for a stronger client focus, to create a more distinct presence in the marketplace, and to develop the relevant skills and strengthen the behaviours to support this new corporate brand. The HR Director recognized the need to develop a 'capability framework' to support the brand values and to influence how people at all levels within the organization should work, interact, and make decisions. Using critical incident techniques, workshops were set up to discuss and define the key capabilities critical for success. These capabilities included having a customer focus, embracing change, acting with integrity, team working, and communication. In addition, the workshops identified the negative behaviours that were seen as 'poisoning' the culture of the company. These negative behaviours included: taking credit for someone else's work, being disrespectful to a colleague or client, procrastinating, failing to share information with other people that would enable them to do their job more effectively, continually expressing negative expectations about the team, having a one-size-fits-all approach to tasks and people, relying on status or position without explanation, unwilling to delegate, and seeing development as a cost rather than an investment. Interestingly, irrespective of the seniority or grade level of the workshop participants, the negative behaviours identified – usually given as a single statement – spanned all grade levels throughout the organization.[49]

However certain competencies may fuel toxicity. A 'burning drive for results' was considered to be the most important leadership competency at RBS according to one insider.[50] Strategy execution and the requirement to 'get things done' were the hallmarks of the RBS culture under Fred Goodwin's tenure. This focus became increasingly obsessive prior to the acquisition of ABN Amro. Two academics observed how the focus on strategy execution ultimately led to a machine-like bureaucracy that "slipped into gear to implement centrally driven strategic decisions".[51]

4. Reinforcing with Formal Mechanisms
   Human resource policies and practices are a key mechanism in shaping and moulding the corporate culture. There has been debate as to the extent that HR policies and practices can coordinate employees to achieve the same goals. In global and national companies, HRM is a mechanism of control and coordination capable of achieving integration. This control can be characterized in four areas: bureaucratic formalized control (written rules, policies, regulations), control by socialization and networks (talent and promotion, corporate culture, identification of key leadership roles), personal centralized control (influence, status of HR, structure), and output control (rewards, performance metrics). As a result, the role of human resources is a critical component in shaping and reinforcing the corporate culture. It does this in two ways: first, HR policies act as a *lingua franca* for the organization by providing the 'rules of the game'; second, the HR designs the selection criteria to identify and promote the 'role models', provides compensation structures that reward the right behaviours, and defines the learning and development programmes that teach and reinforce 'the way we do things around here'.[52]

To conclude, the four dimensions are interdependent and dynamic. If these are the dimensions that enable corporate cultures to change, according to McKinsey, then the argument follows that they are key to the sustainability of corporate cultures.[53] HRM is a key control mechanism and holds many of the solutions to mitigating and preventing toxic cultures. Tackling one or two dimensions will not sufficiently change the culture; if toxic cultures are to change, then all four dimensions must be used simultaneously – and done over a consolidated period of time.

The various HR interventions that can be used to mitigate and eliminate toxicity will be explored later in this book.

1.5 Culture and Corporateness

Culture should not be seen as only internal to the organization. In *Corporate Reputations, Branding and People Management*, Graeme Martin and I explored the impact of different actors and influences on corporate culture. We explored the idea of **corporateness** as an umbrella term for the various powerful corporate level concepts, such as reputation, identity, image, brand, vision, strategy, as well as culture, which will be discussed in more detail in Chapter 3.[54] Corporateness, we argued, implies the desire of many large and complex organizations to develop a unified approach to business and present this distinctive corporate identity to all stakeholders. This does not mean that organizations do not embrace or encourage diversity or recognize differing sub-cultures, but that the organization's common goals are embraced by employees as well as other stakeholders such as the board and shareholders.

We found that reputation and brands are one of the few sustainable strategic assets of an organization. A reputation acts as a sort of shorthand to inform shareholders and consumers. Any damage done by toxic behaviours, for example, can wipe billions of dollars from the value of an organization. Uber is reckoned to have lost around $4.5bn[55] in 2017 after a stream of harassment and bullying allegations (See Vignette 1.4).

Factors impacting corporate reputations include:

Vignette 1.4 Uber's Toxic Culture

In 2017, Uber faced a stream of revelations about the company's business practices and workplace culture, from its use of a fake version of its app to dupe municipal regulators, to a senior executive's sharing of medical records of an Uber driver's rape victim. A blog that a former employee wrote about her experience at Uber included accusations of sexual harassment and pervasive gender discrimination.[56] The central cause cited for these behaviours and actions pointed at corporate culture. The values were seen to promote bullying and boorish behaviour.

The report conducted by former Attorney General Eric Holder included major recommendations, such as curtailing the role of CEO Travis Kalanick, and more minor ones, like renaming a company conference area from the "War Room" to the "Peace Room". Uber's board agreed unanimously to adopt all 47 of the report's recommendations.[57]

Among other things, the company agreed to:

Rewrite its cultural values to remove value statements such as "always be hustlin" and "Principled Confrontation" that the report says were used as excuses for bad behaviour.

Work to change its 'party' culture, including limiting alcohol at work events and in the office. And recommended that Uber would put in place a formal ban on employee-manager relationships.

Ensure diversity is a priority at the company by doing things like blind résumé reviews and adopting a version of the "Rooney Rule", whereby it would interview at least one woman and one minority candidate for each open position.

1. *Decline in general levels of trust and consumer confidence*. Examples are VW, RBS, Enron, and Carillion. Even organizations such as the World Bank have been charged with ethical malpractice and allegations of bullying
2. *Problems associated with promoting inferior products*. Examples include Sunny Delight, which was marketed to children as healthy yet contained very high levels of sugar and led to dental decay, and VW who promoted their clean diesel cars and marketed themselves as committed to the environment and reducing carbon when the reality was entirely the opposite
3. *Concern about the global market dominance of a handful of companies that remain unregulated*. These concerns centre on companies such as Facebook (Meta) and their manipulation of algorithms to promote fake news deliberately designed to sabotage public health initiatives or undermine democracy such as in the US election in 2020. In 2021, Facebook had a market capitalization of $939bn, more than the GDP of Saudi Arabia ($793bn) or the Netherlands ($907bn)[58]; Amazon has a market capitalization of $1.7tn, compared with Australia's GDP ($1.4tn)
4. *Concerns about 'white-washing' issues as well as potential levels of toxicity within large organizations*. At the time of writing, a former Facebook employee turned whistleblower in the USA has alleged that the organization knowingly and deliberately withheld research that showed the adverse impact of social media on teenage mental health

Corporateness encapsulates corporate brands, organizational culture, and reputations. These are treated as significant intangible assets – sometimes worth two or three times the book value, as witnessed with the RBS consortium-led bid for ABN Amro. In addition, there is empirical proof of a strong and positive link between corporate reputations and financial performance.[59] The basis for both these financial outcomes arises from the ability of organizations to differentiate themselves consistently in the marketplace. The idea is that these intangible assets are difficult to copy.

It can now be illustrated how the roles of leadership, employees, and managers create and maintain these assets. This is largely achieved through unscripted and discretionary actions, attitudes, and behaviours – which lead clients and/or investors to form a favourable or unfavourable impression of the company. It is not what the company says it is or the corporate image that it promotes; reputations are also about the informal impressions created by managers and employees in the normal day-to-day conduct of their work. Over the past decade or so, organizations such as Apple have come to realize that one of the few unique and inimitable assets is their human resources in creating reputational capital.[60] Reputational capital is defined as the difference between a book and a market valuation. It encompasses and builds on the trust and confidence of stakeholders.

Corporate culture is a strategic asset. It is a source of competitive advantage and sustainable, and a strategic component of any business model.[61]

1.5.1 Toxic Organizational Norms

In organizations described as having a toxic culture, one of the key organizational norms is to not challenge, disagree with, or contradict higher level targets and demands. This social norm does not directly break legal norms or safety standards, or directly condone opening unauthorized bank accounts as was seen in the case of Wells Fargo. Once active, this norm makes it more difficult for employees to speak out and challenge or resist practices that may eventually break the law, as happened at VW with the installation of cheat devices. The focus on realizing cost savings and measuring performance based on these savings ensured that employees in these companies would find ways to achieve these targets. In these organizations, the employees and managers were under pressure to achieve these demands. Job insecurity and threats for non-compliance worked in tandem to ensure that critique and dissent were muted and minimalized.

Even when the organizations such as VW, BP, and Wells Fargo were exposed for wrongdoing, their responses were to downplay the damages and neutralize their own culpabilities.[62] This neutralization occurred by placing the blame on a few employees as 'bad apples'. However, in studying these organizations, a set of toxic norms developed over a period of time. Chapters 2 and 3 will address how these norms are underpinned by concepts: *Normalization of Deviance* and *Cognitive Dissonance*. For example, BP sought 255 budget cuts that directly impacted on safety. It had one of the worst safety records in the industry but, rather than focus on operational safety, sought to normalize deviant behaviours and instead focus on individual safety, outsourcing its engineering division so that the perception of the increasing risks was muted. Similarly, VW justified its position of fitting a cheat device to its cars by pointing out that other car manufacturers were doing the same. Interestingly, VW had been caught and fined for fitting a cheat device in 1973. It regarded being caught and fined as inevitable and a manageable risk as opposed to breaking the law.

The 'tone at the top' is a strong influence on culture – and this can positively influence organizational norms. Anglo American, the mining organization employing more than 90,000 people with operations in five continents, had a long track record of more than 200 fatalities over a five-year period due to its hazardous environment. When a new CEO was appointed, she rejected this assumption. Her approach to *zero harm* involved the unprecedented step of shutting down the world's largest platinum mine after one fatality, for seven weeks. This enabled the CEO to conduct a full-scale audit of the safety procedures. Before the mine re-opened, all 30,000 workers at the site were retrained to instil both personal and group safety. In addition, the organization invited the government and the trade unions to work together to address the industry safety records by setting up the 'Tripartite Alliance'. As a result, new safety standards based on best practices were agreed upon and implemented, resulting in far fewer fatalities. The new CEO concluded:

> I have always said that safety is a leading indicator of wider performance – if you get safety right, then other things will follow, from stronger relationships with unions and governments to greater productivity and efficiency across the board.[63]

Organizations do not become toxic by design or by any singular influence, nor is toxicity just a matter of one bad CEO, one bad set of incentives, or the 'tone at the top'.[64] Toxicity invades corporate culture in several ways, making it very difficult to see and, ultimately, to challenge right from wrong. However, toxic cultures do appear to be pressure prompted.

Chapters 2 and 3 will explore two key drivers of toxic cultures: Chapter 2, the Normalization of Deviance, and Chapter 3, Cognitive Dissonance. The Normalization of Deviance describes how previously unacceptable practices become acceptable over time. Cognitive Dissonance explores the divergence between rhetoric and reality. Chapter 4 will bring these two drivers together as a framework to understand the four stages of a toxic culture, illustrated with examples from well-known organizations.

Notes

1 https://www.gallup.com/workplace/236570/employees-lot-managers.aspx. Accessed June 5, 2022.

2 BreatheHR. (2021) *Culture Economy Report: The Impact of Company Culture on Our Wider Economy and Society*. 1–74. Accessed December 3, 2021.

3 Society for Human Resource Managmenet (2020) *The High Cost of a Toxic Workplace Culture*. https://pmq.shrm.org/wp-content/uploads/2020/07/SHRM-Culture-Report_2019-1.pdf. Accessed December 3, 2021.

4 Reuters (2017) Volkswagen Confirms $4.3bn Payment Over Diesel Emissions. *The Guardian*. https://www.theguardian.com/business/2017/jan/10/volkswagen-confirms-43-billion-us-payment-over-diesel-emissions. Accessed December 3, 2021.

5 Associated Press in New York (2018) Wells Fargo to Pay $575 Settlement for Setting up Fake Banking Accounts. *The Guardian*. https://www.theguardian.com/us-news/2018/dec/28/wells-fargo-settlement-fake-banking-accounts. Accessed December 3, 2021.
6 BBC. (2018) Surgeons' 'Toxic' Rows Added to Mortality Rate, Says Report. *BBC News*. https://www.bbc.co.uk/news/uk-45067747. Accessed December 9, 2021.
7 Kline, R., & Lewis, D. (2018) The price of fear: Estimating the financial cost of bullying and harrassment to the NHS in England. *Public Money & Management*, 39(3): 1–10.
8 Furnham, A., & MacRae, I. (2017) *Motivation and Performance: A Guide to Motivating a Diverse Workforce*. London: Kogan Page.
9 Seppala, E., & Cameron, K. (2015) Proof That Positive Work Cultures Are More Productive. *Harvard Business Review*. https://hbr.org/2015/12/proof-that-positive-work-cultures-are-more-productive. Accessed December 10, 2021.
10 Nyberg, A., Alfredsson, L., Theorell, T., Westerlund, H., Vahtera, J., & Kivimaki, M. (2008) Managerial leaderhsip and ischaemic heart disease among employees: The Swedish WOLF study. *Occupational and Environmental Medicine*, 66(1): 51–56.
11 https://www2.deloitte.com/uk/en/pages/press-releases/articles/poor-mental-health-costs-uk-employers-up-to-pound-56-billion-a-year.html. Accessed 6 June 2022.
12 Interview with Senior Executive, December 2021.
13 National Aeronautics and Space Administration and the Government Printing Office. 2003. Report of Columbia Accident Investigation Board: Volume 1. *NASA*. https://www.nasa.gov/columbia/home/CAIB_Vol1.html. Accessed December 21, 2021. Chapter 1, p.177.
14 Schein, E.H. (1992) *Organizational Culture and Leadership*. San Francisco, CA: Jossey-Bass Publishers.
15 Deal, T., & Kennedy, A. (1982) *Corporate Cultures: The Rites and Rituals of Corporate Life*. Reading, MA: Addison Wesley Publishing Company.
16 Schein, E. H. (1992) *Organizational Culture and Leadership*. San Francisco, CA: Jossey-Bass Publishers.
17 Deal, T., & Kennedy, A. (1982) *Corporate Cultures: The Rites and Rituals of Corporate Life*. Reading, MA: Addison Wesley Publishing Company.
18 Ouchi, W. (1981) *Theory Z: How American Business Can Meet the Japanese Challenge*. New York: Perseus Books.
19 Schein, E.H. (1978) *Career Dynamics: Matching Indiviudal and Organizational Needs*. Boston, MA: Addison Wesley Publishing Company.
20 Ashkanasy, N., Wilderom, C., & Paterson, M. (2000) *Handbook of Organizational Culture and Climate*. New York: Sage Publications.
21 Schein, E.H. (2010) *Organizational Culture and Leadership*. San Francisco, CA: John Wiley and Sons, p. 23.
22 *Ibid*., p. 24.
23 Flamholtz, E.G., & Randle, Y. (2012) Corporate culture, business models, competitive advantage, strategic assets and the bottom line: Theoretical and measurement issues. *Journal of Human Resource Costing and Accounting*, 16(2): 76–94.
24 *Ibid*.

25 van Rooij, B., & Fine, A. (2018) Toxic corporate culture: Assessing organizational processes of deviancy. *Administrative Sciences*, 8(23): 1–38, p. 4.

26 Machen, R.C., Jones, M.T., Varghese, G.P., & Stark, E.L. (2021) Investigation of Data Irregularities in Doing Business 2018 and Doing Business 2020. *WilmerHale LLP*. https://thedocs.worldbank.org/en/doc/84a922cc9273b7b120d49ad3b9e9d3f9-0090012021/original/DB-Investigation-Findings-and-Report-to-the-Board-of-Executive-Directors-September-15–2021.pdf. Accessed December 22, 2021.

27 Campbell, J.L., & Göritz, A.S. (2014) Culture corrupts! A qualitative study of organisational culture in corrupt organisations. *Journal of Business Ethics*, 120(3): 291–311.

28 Flamholtz, E.G., & Randle, Y. (2012) Corporate culture, business models, competitive advantage, strategic assets and the bottom line: Theoretical and measurement issues. *Journal of Human Resource Costing and Accounting*, 16(2): 76–94.

29

- Van Rooij, B., & Fine, A. (2018) Toxic corporate culture: assessing organizational processes of deviancy. *Administrative Sciences*, 8(23): 1–38.
- Kahn, W.A., & Rouse, E.D. (2021) Navigating space for personal agency: Auxiliary routines as adaptations in toxic organizations. *Academy of Management Journal*, 64(5): 1419–1444.
- Samier, E.A., & Milley, P. (2018) *Perspectives on Maladministration in Education: Theories, Research, Critiques*. New York: Routledge.
- Hartel, C.E.J. (2008) How to build a health emotional culture and avoid a toxic culture. In C. L. Cooper, & N. Ashkanasy (Eds.), *Research Companion to Emotional in Organizations*, pp. 1260–1291. Cheltenham: Edwin Elgar Publishing.
- Lewis, C. (2021) *Toxic: A Guide to Rebuilding Respect and Tolerance in a Hostile Workplace*. London: Bloomsbury Publishing.
- Ryan, L. (2016) Ten Unmistakeable Signs of a Toxic Culture. *Forbes*. https://www.forbes.com/sites/lizryan/2016/10/19/ten-unmistakable-signs-of-a-toxic-culture/?sh=2125e05f115f. Accessed December 12, 2021.
- Furnham, A., & Taylor, J. (2004) *The Dark Side of Behaviour at Work*. London: Palgrave Macmillan.
- Kusy, M., & Holloway, E. (2009) *Toxic Workplace! Managing Toxic Personalities and Their Systems of Power*. San Francisco, CA: Jossey-Bass.
- Roter, A.B. (2019) *The Dark Side of the Workplace*. Oxford: Routledge.
- Hickok, H. (2021) Why Toxic Workplace Cultures Follow You Home. *BBC: Remote Control*. https://www.bbc.com/worklife/article/20210330-why-toxic-workplace-cultures-follow-you-home. Accessed December 22, 2021.
- Hartel, C.E.J. (2008) How to build a health emotional culture and avoid a toxic culture. In C.L. Cooper, & N. Ashkanasy (Eds.), *Research Companion to Emotional in Organizations*, pp.1260–1291. Cheltenham: Edwin Elgar Publishing.
- Appelbaum, S.H., & Roy-Girard, D.R. (2007) Toxins in the workplace: Effect on organizations and employees. *Corporate Governance*, 7(1): 17–28.
- de Bruijn, A.L. (2021) Organizational factors and workplace deviance: Influences of abusive supervision, dysfunctional employees, and toxic work environments. In B. van Rooij, & D. Sokol (Eds.), *The Cambridge Handbook of Compliance*, pp. 639–661. Cambridge: Cambridge University Press.

30 Padilla, A., Hogan, R., & Kaiser, R.B. (2007) The toxic triangle: Destructive leaders, susceptible followers and conducive environments. *The Leadership Quarterly*, 18: 176–194.
31 This work takes the example of Hitler, as an example of a destructive leader, who focused on world domination. However, care should be taken here as the article implies that Hitler received an overwhelming mandate from the German people. In reality, the Nazi party received about one-third of the votes; however, due to the fragmented nature of the many political parties and the Constitution, the Nazi Party was able to secure autocratic power in 1933.
32 Ryan, L. (2016) How Important is Corporate Culture? It's Everything. *Forbes*. https://www.forbes.com/sites/lizryan/2016/09/16/how-important-is-corporate-culture-its-everything/?sh=5111650b6883. Accessed December 12, 2021.
33 Pink, D.H. (2010) *Drive: The Surprising Truth about What Motivates Us*. Edinburgh: Canongate, UK.
34 Deci, E.L., & Ryan, R.M. (2000) Intrinsic and extrinsic motivations: Classic definitions and new directions. *Contemporary Educational Psychology*, 25(1): 54–67.
35 Malnight, T., Buche, I., & Dhanaraj, C. (2019) Put Purpose at the Core of Your Strategy. *Harvard Business Review*. https://hbr.org/2019/09/put-purpose-at-the-core-of-your-strategy. Accessed December 12, 2021.
36 Furnham, A., & MacRae, I. (2017) *Motivation and Performance: A Guide to Motivating a Diverse Workforce*. London: Kogan Page.
37 Herzberg, F., Mausner, B., & Snyderman, B. (1959) *The Motivation to Work* (2nd ed.). Hoboken, NJ: John Wiley.
38 Furnham, A., & MacRae, I. (2017) *Motivation and Performance: A Guide to Motivating a Diverse Workforce*. London: Kogan Page.
39 Schein, E.H. (2010) *Organizational Culture and Leadership*. San Francisco, CA: John Wiley and Sons.
40 Walker, B., & Soule, S.A. (2017) Changing Company Culture Requires a Movement, Not a Mandate. *Harvard Business Review*. https://hbr.org/2017/06/changing-company-culture-requires-a-movement-not-a-mandate. Accessed December 21, 2021.
41 Steffy, L. (2010) *Drowning in Oil: BP & the Reckless Pursuit of Profit*. New York: McGraw-Hill Companies.
42 Senior Executive, Interview conducted on October 15, 2021 via zoom.
43 Senior Executive, Interview conducted on November 4, 2021 via zoom.
44 Kotter, J.P. (1995) Leading change: Why transformation efforts fail. *Harvard Business Review*. https://hbr.org/1995/05/leading-change-why-transformation-efforts-fail-2. Accessed December 12, 2021.
45 Basford, T., & Schaninger, B. (2016) The four building blocks of change. *McKinsey Quarterly*. https://www.mckinsey.com/business-functions/people-and-organizational-performance/our-insights/the-four-building-blocks--of-change. Accessed December 12, 2021.
46 Martin, G., & Hetrick, S. (2006) *Corporate Reputations, Branding and People Management: A Strategic Appraoch to HR*. Oxford: Butterworth-Heinemann.
47 Hetrick, S. (2002) Transferring HR ideas and practices: Globalization and convergence in Poland. *Human Resource Development International*, 5(3): 333–351.

48 Gratton, L., & Ghoshal, S. (2005) Beyond best practice. *MIT Sloan Management Review*, 46: 49–57.

49 Adapted from Hodges, J. (2021) *Managing and Leading People through Organizational Change: The Theory and Pratice of Sustaining Change through People* (2nd ed.). London: Kogan Page Limited. Note to reader: the author was the former HR Director.

50 Martin, G., & Gollan, P.J. (2012) Corporate governance and strategic human resource management in the UK finanical services sector: The case of the RBS. *International Journal of Human Resource Management*, 23(16): 3295–3314.

51 *Ibid*.

52 Hetrick, S. (2002) Transferring HR ideas and practices: Globalization and convergence in Poland. *Human Resource Development International*, 5(3): 333–351.

53 Basford et al (2016).

54 Martin & Hetrick, (2006:6).

55 Aiello, C. (2018) Uber's Loss Jumped 61 percent to $4.5 billion in 2017. *CNBC*. https://www.cnbc.com/2018/02/13/ubers-loss-jumped-61-percent-to-4-point-5-billion-in-2017.html. Accessed December 12, 2021.

56 https://www.susanjfowler.com/blog/2017/2/19/reflecting-on-one-very-strange-year-at-uber. Accessed on June 6, 2022.

57 https://www.cnbc.com/2017/06/13/eric-holder-uber-report-full-text.html. Accessed on June 6, 2022.

58 Wallach, O. (2021) The World's Tech Giants, Compared to the Size of Economies. *Visual Capitalist*. https://www.visualcapitalist.com/the-tech-giants-worth-compared-economies-countries/. Accessed December 13, 2021.

59 Martin, G., & Hetrick, S. (2006) *Corporate Reputations, Branding and People Management: A Strategic Appraoch to HR*. Oxford, UK: Butterworth-Heinemann.

60 *Ibid*, p.11.

61 Flamholtz, E.G., & Randle, Y. (2012) Corporate culture, business models, competitive advantage, strategic assets and the bottom line: Theoretical and Measurement Issues. *Journal of Human Resource Costing and Accounting*, 16(2): 76–94.

62 Van Rooij & Fine (2018).

63 Carroll, C. (2012) The CEO of Anglo American on Getting Serious about Safety. *Harvard Business Review*. https://hbr.org/2012/06/the-ceo-of-anglo-american-on-getting-serious-about-safety. Accessed December 22, 2021.

64 Van Rooij & Fine (2018:27).

2 The First Driver of Toxic Culture – The Normalization of Deviance

People are both carriers and creators of culture. Culture is enacted in everyday life. Culture reflects power and decision making through the organizational structure. Organizations can form their own norms – 'the way things are done around here'. And these norms can oppose regulations, resist and misinterpret new information, or dismiss critical evidence. White-collar crime criminologists have for a long time recognized that corporate culture matters. One strand of criminological insight is that crime originates in distress, sometimes referred to as 'strain'. This strain can result in people breaking rules or committing crimes as a way of coping with that strain. Any form of organizational deviance can come from the social norms that can obstruct compliance, such as what happened at VW, or enable rule-breaking by dismissing the evidence or new information, as at RBS.

Toxic cultures deal with errors through denial or blaming and punishing lower-level employees, the so-called 'bad apples' who failed to act when errors occurred. In failing to deal with errors, the organization will unwittingly fuel the 'dysfunctional moral climate' and hamper any positive learning from the error. All of this leads to the embedding of a toxic culture.

The first of two key drivers of toxic cultures is called Normalization of Deviance. Essentially this describes how deviance from correct or proper behaviour becomes normalized in a corporate culture. Diane Vaughan defines this as a process in which a clearly unsafe practice comes to be considered normal if it does not immediately cause a catastrophe: "a long incubation period [before a final disaster] with early warning signs that were either misinterpreted, ignored, or missed completely".[1]

This blindness to the acceptance of the unacceptable can be manifested in organizations such as RBS where the belief was that failure was not possible, yet the early warning signs of low levels of employee engagement in countries outside the UK or the lack of an international strategy in terms of people and

DOI: 10.4324/9781003330387-4

management were apparent. This process of accepting something risky becomes embedded as something normal so that it is not regarded as a risk. It becomes impossible to rally against the beliefs that there could not be failure – and we can see this in a number of so-called toxic organizations from Enron, VW, and RBS, to NASA:

> In the Board's view, NASA's organizational culture and structure had as much to do with this accident as the External Tank foam. Organizational culture refers to the values, norms, beliefs, and practices that govern how an institution functions. At the most basic level, organizational culture defines the assumptions that employees make as they carry out their work. It is a powerful force that can persist through reorganizations and the reassignment of key personnel.[2]

2.1 Normalization of Deviance

Both the Challenger and Columbia shuttles' failed space missions are described by Vaughan in terms of the Normalization of Deviance.[3]

The original example cited by Vaughan was the events leading to the Space Shuttle Challenger disaster in 1986. The Challenger exploded shortly after take-off, killing all seven astronauts on board. At first glance, the disaster is remembered as a technical failure. The 'O-rings', rubber parts, were designed to seal a tiny gap created by pressure at ignition in the joints of the Solid Rocket Boosters. In previous months, there had been concerns expressed by the engineers about the minimal temperature and the impact of cold weather on the O-rings. The design ensured that there was a secondary O-ring as a safety feature in the event of any blow-back.

The O-ring problem had been known about since 1977 – around nine years before the Challenger launch in 1986. One of the senior engineers believed that the vehicle's standing on the launch pad for several days when overnight temperatures ranged from 18 to 20 degrees Fahrenheit had impaired the O-ring resiliency – the ability of the rubber to expand to fill the gap during the launch. Reduced resiliency would slow sealing, allowing hot emissions through the gap until the joint sealed. A low temperature impaired the resilience, enabling blow-back and the ensuing disaster. Upon ignition, hot propellant gases impinged on the O-rings, creating a flame that first penetrated the joint of the Solid Rocket Booster and then the external tank carrying hydrogen and oxygen.

On the night before the launch, an emergency meeting was called with the engineers and management to discuss whether to delay the launch; the parties included NASA and the contractors. Worried engineers from the contractor, Thiokol, were concerned about the unprecedented cold temperatures in Florida and recommended that there should be a delay. There had already been several delays to the launch of Challenger, setting a NASA record for false starts. NASA managers decided to proceed.

Prior to the fateful launch, the issue with the O-rings was logged as a risk. While there was a task force set up to look into this issue, due to a lack of financial and human resources, there was little progress. To assess the extent of the problem, engineers required tests and data. Yet the results of research on the scale of the issue showed that the rings were operating as predicted.

2.2 What Is Meant by the Normalization of Deviance?

The subsequent post-Challenger analysis showed that the hot gases had reached the secondary O-ring for the first time. Another launch a few months later also revealed that the hot gases had eroded the secondary O-ring. The primary research on the degree of risk appeared to show that everything was working as predicted. Yet in hindsight, the results indicated that technical deviance had been 'normalized' (Vaughan, 2016) and had become an 'acceptable risk'. In addition, the reviews found there was scant regard paid to the effect cold weather had on the resilience of the rings. Why was this possible? The cold weather experienced in Florida, which had caused ice to form on the launch vehicle, was a once-in-a-century phenomenon.

The performance pressure to promote a 'normalized' position was significant. Even on the evening prior to the launch, the engineers were called up to present tangible evidence, aside from some photographs, or the facts needed to make a robust decision, as the O-rings were not identified as a considerable risk. Yet the pressure to perform 'blinded' senior decision makers from considering that such a tiny part might wreak such devastation.

A historical perspective shows how the structure of NASA changed. Contracting out became institutionalized. The organization grew in size in order to manage the complex administration arrangements. "As a consequence, the space agency's pure technical culture began to be compromised".[4] Many engineers were shifted to supervisory roles. Less time was spent in the lab, more time at the desk or travelling.

One of NASA's centres, Marshall, appeared to be more impacted by these changes. Marshall was responsible for the shuttle's propulsion system and was known for its strong research culture and 'can do' attitude. The director was described as a 'master bureaucrat' who "created an atmosphere of rigid, often fearful, conformity among Marshall managers"[5]:

> Saddled with a vastly more complex Marshall organizational structure and apparently lacking (his predecessor's) charisma and skill at maintaining personal contact with people at different levels in the Marshall hierarchy, Lucas relied on hierarchy and formal mechanisms to transfer information. He insisted on bureaucratic accountability for monitoring and controlling internal operations. Lucas's management style, combined with the production pressures ... resulted in competition between the other three Marshall projects. Each project manager vied with others to conform to the cultural imperatives of the original technical culture, the bureaucratic mandates, and the business ideology of production. They competed to meet deadlines, be on top of every technical detail, solve their technical problems, conform to rules and requirements, be cost-efficient, and of course, contribute to safe, successful space flight . . . it was in fact, performance pressure.[6]

In her research, Vaughan ascribes the failure of culture at NASA to be three-fold:

1. **Bureaucratic accountability**: The impact of procedural rules and a hierarchical power structure
2. **Political accountability:** The demands of cost efficiency coupled with speed of delivery
3. **Structural secrecy**: A lack of shared knowledge and information across the organization coupled with the launch decision chain that constrained and weakened a collective understanding of the entirety of the risks and issues

> Language was fundamental to structural secrecy at NASA. Talk about risk, in NASA culture, was by nature technical, impersonal, and bureaucratic – full of what to the uninitiated are meaningless acronyms, engineering terms, and NASA procedural references.[7]

In addition, the relationship between NASA and the contractors was imbalanced. There was a sense by the subcontractor, Thiokol, that NASA was considering another organization to deliver on its mandate. As such, there was a disproportionate impact on Thiokol's management to please their client. This was in evidence at the launch decision meeting.

Structural secrecy coupled with the imbalance of power meant that the information and decision-making were skewed. No rules were broken, but the dominance of the hierarchical culture meant that engineers were required to pitch their cases to senior management. The culture had been deferential to the technical decisions of the engineers; however, the change in the relationship where the engineers were now subcontracted, for the most part, meant that management took control of decisions.

Management is described as:

> Hierarchical, guided by many rules and procedures about the form, content, and structure of information exchange. Rather than the original (technical) culture's professional accountability that gave deference to those at the bottom of the organization with the greatest technical expertise, the bureaucratic accountability . . . prevailed.[8]

The night before the ill-fated launch, engineers were asked to provide reasons as to why Challenger should **not** launch as opposed to why it should. In the absence of technical engineering data, coupled with some presentational errors and reliance on observational information, the value of the information was discarded and ignored.

Culture was also blamed for the tragedy of the Columbia space flight in 2003. The Columbia Accident Investigation Board Report[9] cited that the organizational causes of the accident were rooted in the Space Shuttle Program's history and culture. Resource constraints, fluctuating priorities, schedule pressures, mischaracterizations of the shuttle as operational rather than developmental, and lack of an agreed national vision were all quoted as the organizational causes. In addition, the report alleged that cultural traits and organizational practices detrimental to safety and reliability were allowed to develop. Overall, this was regarded as the result of a reliance on past success as a substitute for sound engineering practices, organizational barriers which prevented effective communication of critical safety information and stifled professional differences of opinion, a lack of integrated management across program elements, and the evolution of an informal chain of command and decision-making processes that operated outside the organization's rules. All these were very similar to the Challenger accident only 17 years previously.

The Normalization of Deviance was evident in 'safety' as well as 'pressure for delivery'. While NASA leaders were emphasizing the importance of safety, their personnel cutbacks sent a different message. Streamlining and downsizing conveyed the importance of efficiency. Similarly, the work pressures included working evenings and weekends, coupled with the "faster, better, cheaper" NASA motto of the 1990s that dramatically decreased safety personnel, resulting in efficiency becoming a strong signal and safety a weak one.

In both incidents, Challenger and Columbia, NASA appeared to be immersed in a culture of invincibility, in stark contradiction to reality:

> The Rogers Commission found a NASA blinded by its 'Can-Do' attitude. The Board argued that this cultural artifact of the Apollo era was inappropriate in a Space Shuttle Program so strapped by schedule pressures and shortages that spare parts had to be cannibalized from one vehicle to launch another. This can-do attitude bolstered administrators' belief in an

> achievable launch rate, the belief that they had an operational system, and an unwillingness to listen to outside experts.[10]

In the 17 years between Challenger and Columbia, there had been 87 missions without major incident. NASA's Apollo-era research and development culture and its prized deference to the technical expertise of its working engineers had changed. Instead, the Space Shuttle Program was governed by 'bureaucratic accountability' – one of hierarchy, chain of command, and following the requisite procedure. In both situations, there was a difference in the definition of risk between management and the engineers. The engineers were required to demonstrate data, yet in each case, the definition of risk meant that there had not been sufficient resources dedicated to testing. As such, the data were insufficient and flawed as a basis for decision-making.

The pressure for delivery and efficiency conflicted with safety. It overrode any concerns and, in that process, 'normalized' risks. Both Challenger and Columbia engineering teams were held to the usual quantitative standard of proof, but it was a reversal of the usual circumstance: instead of having to prove it was safe to fly, they were asked to prove that it was unsafe to fly.

Management chose to ignore qualitative data and the experience of the engineers. The organizational structure and hierarchy basically blocked effective communication of technical problems.

> Signals were overlooked, people were silenced, and useful information and dissenting views on technical issues did not surface at higher levels. What was communicated to parts of the organization was that O-ring erosion and foam debris were not problems. Structure and hierarchy represent power and status. For both Challenger and Columbia, employees' positions in the organization determined the weight given to their information, by their own judgment and in the eyes of others. As a result, many signals of danger were missed. Relevant information that could have altered the course of events was available but was not presented.[11]

The many layers of bureaucracy, risk reviews, and reports served to obscure and minimize the technical risks in direct contention to their rationale. When an organization focuses on efficiency and production, these potential risks become a nuisance and are not taken seriously despite expert qualitative advice; the power in the organization shifts to production, efficiency, and delivery, rather than safety and knowledge.

2.3 What Parallels Can We Draw for Business?

RBS in 2007 launched a 'hostile bid' to acquire ABN Amro. Initiating a partnership with two other Banks, Fortis and Santander, the acquisition was the largest cash acquisition in history. The consortium announced the terms of its bid in July 2007, and 94.5 per cent of RBS shareholders voted in favour of the acquisition in August. The acquisition was completed on 17 October 2007. RBS was now the largest bank in the world by assets, totalling over $3.5tn, and the fifth largest by market capitalization. By the end of 2008, RBS imploded.

How did a successful bank, where employee engagement among its global staff stood higher than most other global organizations, fail so spectacularly?

According to the Parliamentary Report in 2012,[12] the failure was due to "poor management decisions, deficient regulation and a flawed supervisory approach". The systemic causes were applicable across the entire financial system, and in hindsight, the FSA's supervisory approach of applying a low priority to liquidity made the risk of a crisis more likely. Yet it is clear that the crux of the failure lay with RBS's management and Board. The key question that the House of Commons report asked was "whether the CEO's management style discouraged robust and effective challenge". Four answers were noted.

First, there was intense rivalry between the Barclays CEO and the RBS CEO. Barclays had already made an announcement in April 2007 of their intention to acquire ABN Amro. The intense rivalry made both organizations perceive ABN Amro as a prize; it infused the climate and atmosphere of the HQ at RBS. Second, as a hostile bid, RBS and the consortium did not have access to the same ABN Amro information and documents to inform their bid decision. There was an assumption that if Barclays was still interested in winning this prize while having access to more information, then the information (so it followed) must be positive. Third, management became more concerned when the so-called 'jewel in the crown' La Salle was sold in advance of the deal to Bank of America in the summer of 2007.[13] At that point, many senior managers suspected that the deal would be off. RBS was known for its voracious appetite for acquiring businesses. Yet the ABN Amro acquisition was known to carry some risks that were difficult to quantify. ABN Amro had been spread thinly for several years with operations across many countries; potential debts to clients in these countries had to be assumed since there was a lack of tangible evidence during the due diligence period. Fourth, RBS extolled a culture of arrogance. Its success in the marketplace, and the fact that it was the biggest tax contributor at the time to the Chancellor, made it appear invincible. When the events of October 2008 showed RBS to be close to bankruptcy, concerns were made by HR professionals as to whether the Bank could even pay the salaries of its employees.

2.4 What Was the Normalization of Deviance for RBS?

To understand this, we need to step back in time to 1999 when RBS acquired the NatWest Bank. This was an incredible acquisition as RBS was smaller in size and market capitalization than NatWest. The ultimate prize in NatWest holdings was the acquisition of Her Majesty The Queen's bank, Coutts Bank. Within a short timeframe, RBS had incorporated NatWest into its organization, leading the London Business School to publish an article on RBS declaring the organization to be 'Masters of Integration'. The integration of NatWest into its operations, coupled with the significant job losses, enabled RBS to have the lowest cost base compared with its rivals. RBS was now seen as a major bank in the UK and had operations in more than 30 countries. The upward journey continued as RBS acquired other organizations, from Angel Trains in Belgium, Greenwich Capital and Citizens Bank in the USA, to a stake in Bank of China. After being acquired, unlike NatWest, these organizations continued to operate independently while reporting at a high level to the Group CEO and completing the annual engagement survey. Prior to the ABN Amro acquisition, in 2007 RBS announced a profit of £10.3bn. It seemed RBS could do no wrong (see Table 2.1).

Table 2.1 Timeline of RBS Post-Acquisition of ABN Amro

- **October 2007:** RBS is part of a consortium that takes over the Dutch bank ABN Amro in the largest deal in financial services history
- **March 2008:** Wall Street investment bank Bear Stearns is rescued by rival JP Morgan Chase
- **April 2008:** RBS announces £12bn rights issue and puts its insurance businesses, which include Churchill and Direct Line, up for sale
- **August 2008:** RBS reports its first loss in 40 years with a half-year loss of £691m
- **September 2008:** Lehman Brothers collapses, unleashing a wave of market turmoil
- **October 2008:** The UK Government announces bailouts for RBS and other banks, including HBOS. Chief executive Fred Goodwin leaves RBS, saying he is "sad" to be going. Stephen Hester is appointed to run the bank
- **February 2009:** Goodwin gives MPs on the Treasury select committee a "profound and unqualified apology for all the distress caused" by the bank's collapse

(*continued*)

- **April 2009:** Goodwin is described as a "benefit scrounger" and a "cataclysmic failure" at the bank's annual meeting, where 90% of investors fail to back the remuneration report in protest at his £703,000 a year pension
- **June 2009:** Goodwin agrees to give up more than £200,000 a year of his pension in an attempt to appease public anger about what is seen as a reward for failure
- **December 2011:** The official report into the collapse of RBS concludes that "multiple poor decisions" were at the heart of its problems, but no action is taken against Goodwin
- **January 2012:** Goodwin is stripped of his knighthood[a]

[a] https://www.theguardian.com/business/2017/may/21/royal-bank-of-scotland-a-timeline-of-events (accessed on October 8, 2021).

In 2005, the RBS Annual Report's cover page had four statements all about profit, income, and dividend. In 2007, just before the RBS 'bankruptcy', the Annual Report records that CEO Fred Goodwin stated that the annual results "demonstrate the **resilience** of the Group in the face of testing circumstances".[14] By the time of the ABN Amro acquisition, Fred Goodwin, the then CEO, became known internally as "having the brain the size of a planet". And this assumption of genius effectively silenced internal robust debate.

2.5 The Reinforcement of Success Leads to the Normalization of Deviance

As one senior executive noted when interviewed for this book:

> Banking per se is a pretty damn arrogant sector and there is a whole 'masters of the universe' thing going on there as well. I think there was probably something in the experience, which is they (RBS) pulled off something amazing when they got NatWest, David and Goliath and all that stuff. They then did a few good European acquisitions and made something much more than it was ever going to be, and then you go 'well, this always works'. It always works until it doesn't work, but then you just force even harder and everyone else is wrong then because they can't see why this works. So that is where the arrogance comes in, the immaturity maybe.[15]

At the Parliamentary Investigation in 2009, the committee asked why RBS had reported a profit in 2007 when it should have reported a £28bn loss:

> We never imagined the parts we were holding, a large part of it was triple-A or super-senior, we never imagined, as Fred said earlier, that could end up as 10 cents in the dollar. (Tom McKillop, former Chairman)[16]

Yet during 2007, events in the USA markets, as well as Northern Rock and its liquidity crisis in the UK, should have raised questions.[17] When the Chairman was asked whether there were any internal voices expressing concerns, Sir Tom McKillop replied using the NatWest integration as the example:

> **Q801 Ms Keeble**: No internal voices inside the Bank were raised about it?
>
> **Sir Tom McKillop**: The analysis threw up the issues that would have to be managed in the integration, but this was essentially the same kind of plan that had been very successful on the integration of NatWest so, yes, there was a full analysis.[18]

The notion that the acquisition of a foreign bank with dispersed operations across 20-plus countries would be more complex was not anticipated. The Chair of the Parliamentary enquiry made the following comment:

> **Q919 Chairman:** When I look at the board of Royal Bank of Scotland, you had the brightest and the best. You had Sir Peter Sutherland, who was chairman of BP and Goldman Sachs and the director general of the World Trade Organization, you had Bob Scott, the senior independent director, the former group chief executive of Aviva and ex-chairman of the board of the Association of British Insurers, and you had Steve Robson, a former Second Permanent Secretary to the Treasury. He was there with Terry Burns when the tripartite authority was established. I could go on. The best and the brightest were there, Sir Tom.
>
> There has to be something more fundamental here. Do you not think that the vulnerability was greater than you realized because of the sheer complexity of the products or inadequate monitoring and that perhaps you did not understand the complexity? We had the auditor from KPMG here and I asked him, if he sat down for a night and looked at HSBC's books for the night, could he fully understand it, and he said no. Even the brightest and the best cannot understand that complexity. We could not have better-qualified people. There has to be systemic problems here. I put it to you that the expansion of new financial instruments increased the complexity to such an extent that people did not really understand them.[19]

The Chairman continued to ask for the reason as to why RBS had continued with the deal when the markets stated that RBS was paying three times its market value and ABN Amro had already sold LaSalle:

> Why did you and your Board allow Sir Fred to go ahead with this huge deal without an escape clause when ABN had already pre-sold LaSalle, when the credit crunch had already begun, and when everybody else said you were paying too much?[20]

The Normalization of Deviance for RBS resulted from its perceived success from the NatWest acquisition some eight years prior. It had won many industry awards and its CEO had been knighted (subsequently withdrawn) for services to the industry. At the very centre of RBS was the belief of 'resilience'.

In the RBS Annual Report, the CEO statement says: "Our proven business model delivered strong results in 2006".

In the Annual Report of 2007, the Chairman talks about the growth trajectory:

> We have a great deal to do in 2008. Markets will continue to be demanding and we have a major integration to deliver. But we also have an unparalleled set of opportunities, and their realization will allow us to continue the impressive growth trajectory that has characterised RBS over the past decade.

The Normalization of Deviance had blinded many to the risks that were there. A 'proven business model' and a 'growth trajectory' were the reasons for the acquisition, as well as what was regarded as the genius of the CEO. It was at the first meeting – during the analysis session – that Fred Goodwin came up with an idea. Could RBS buy ABN Amro as part of a consortium? That idea gained ground around the table and the Board meeting moved from analysis to implementation:

> The premise that we allowed Sir Fred to proceed implies that this was driven by Sir Fred, which is not the case. When the announcement of the ABN Amro merger with Barclays was made the Board received a presentation from our strategy group and the executive team, an analysis of the ABN Amro businesses; we looked at that in considerable detail. The Board had 18 meetings between March when we received that first analysis following the announcement by Barclays and ABN, in which ABN Amro was considered at every one of those. There was no proposition to buy ABN Amro at the first meeting; it was an analysis session. At every stage the whole Board considered this and were unanimous in the steps we took. It is wrong to characterise it as a proposition driven by Sir Fred that the Board were unable to stop.[21]

The norm of 'resilience' was so deeply entrenched that the Bank and its Board and others could only see the possibility and not the risk.

The Parliamentary Committee concluded with a sober thought:

> Anyone who doubts the need for prudence in circumstances of such vulnerability should read the story of the failure of one of the largest banks in the world – The Royal Bank of Scotland.[22]

2.6 The Slippery-Slope Effect

Enron, WorldCom, Wells Fargo, and others are all cited as examples of unethical behaviour. Indeed, as we have witnessed in Chapter 4, there is a slow journey to becoming a toxic organization. Academics and practitioners have all noted that managers in modern organizations lack strong ethical standards or are willing to abandon them in the face of economic incentives or competitive pressures. Yet questions remain as to how 'independent auditors' have been found to be complicit in their clients' activities.

Whistleblowing is regarded as the means by which an individual can raise concerns about unethical behaviour. Yet one study has revealed that where ethical standards are eroded over a period of time, then individuals are not fully aware of their ethical lapses. In the study, four laboratory tests showed that people were more likely to accept others' unethical behaviour when ethical degradation occurred over a period of time rather than in one abrupt shift. Participants served in the role of watchdogs and were charged with catching instances of cheating. The watchdogs were less likely to criticize the actions of others when their behaviour eroded gradually over time rather than in one abrupt shift. The researchers called this the 'slippery-slope effect' within the context of ethical judgement.

For an illustration of this argument:

> Imagine that an accountant employed by a well-known accounting firm is in charge of the audit of a large corporation with a strong reputation. The accounting firm and the client have an excellent relationship, and the accounting firm receives millions of dollars in fees from the client each year. For three years the accountant in charge of the audit approved the client's high quality, ethical financial statements. Suddenly in the fourth year, the corporation stretches the law, and even breaks it in certain areas … now suppose the account saw and approved the company's high quality, highly ethical financial statements for one year. The following year, the corporation begins stretching the law in a few areas, without appearing to break the law. In the third year, the firm stretches the ethicality of its returns a bit more. Some of the company's accounting decisions probably violate federal accounting standards. By the fourth year, the corporation stretches the limits of the law in more areas and occasionally breaks the law.[23]

The slippery-slope effect suggests that unethical acts may become normalized and acceptable when they become routine over time. According to researchers, "unethical acts can become an integral part of day-to-day activities to such an extent that individuals may be unable to see the inappropriateness of their behaviours".[24]

Broadly unethical behaviour can be defined as action that is "either illegal or morally unacceptable to the larger community".[25] Examples include violations of ethical norms or standards (whether they are legal standards or not), stealing, lying, cheating, or other forms of dishonesty. Unethical behaviour occurs when someone consciously exaggerates or fabricates information to achieve an outcome that benefits the organization or individual that would not have happened without such exaggeration or fabrication.

Studies show that whistleblowers tend to have higher levels of pay, seniority, and education as well as more years of service and higher levels of professional status. In addition, research shows that whistleblowing is more likely to happen when the organizational climate supports it.

Finally, there is research to show that when an environment is pressurized, people are more likely to make decisions that will be acceptable to their leaders. Research shows this 'conformity effect': when people making a decision care less about the content of that decision, that is, whether the decision is ethical, than about the potential acceptance of such a decision by those to whom they are accountable.[26]

In this chapter, we have explored how the Normalization of Deviance is one of the key drivers of any toxic culture. The acceptance of the unacceptable happens gradually over time, where the possibility of failure is ignored due to a belief that the organization is immune due to its self-aggrandizement.

Notes

1 Vaughan, D. (2016) *The Challenger Launch Decision: Risky Technology, Culture, and Deviance at NASA, Enlarged Edition*. Chicago, IL: University of Chicago Press. pp. 30–31.
2 Columbia Accident Investigation Board Report (2003) Volume 1.
3 Vaughan (2016).
4 Vaughan (2016:211).
5 Vaughan (2016:218).
6 Vaughan (2016:219).
7 Vaughan (2016: 252).
8 Vaughan (2016:357).
9 Columbia Accident Investigation Board Report (2003) Volume 1.
10 *Ibid.*
11 *Ibid.*
12 The FSA's report into the failure of RBS, House of Commons Treasury Commission, HC640, 19 October 2012.
13 https://www.reuters.com/article/abnamro-takeover-lasalle-idUSWEB8-22820071001 accessed June 6, 2022.
14 RBS Annual Report, 2007.
15 Senior Executive, interview conducted on 15 October 2021.
16 Extracts from the Parliamentary Investigation, Tuesday 10 February 2009.
17 On 14 September 2007, Northern Rock received liquidity support from the Bank of England.
18 Extracts from the Parliamentary Investigation, Tuesday 10 February 2009.
19 *Ibid.*

20 *Ibid.*
21 *Ibid.*
22 *Ibid.*
23 Gino, F., & Bazerman, M.H. (2009) When misconduct goes unnoticed: The acceptability of gradual erosion on others' unethical behaviour. *Journal of Experimental Social Psychology*, 45: 708–719.
24 Ashforth, B.E., & Anand, V. (2003) The normalization of corruption in organizations. *Research in Organizational Behavior*, 25: 1–42, p. 4.
25 Jones, T.M. (1991) Ethical decision making by individuals in organizations: An issue contingent model. *Academy of Management Review*, 16: 366–395, p. 367.
26 Brief, A.P., Dukerich, J.M., & Doran, L.I. (1991) Resolving ethical dilemmas in management: Experimental investigations of values, accountability, and choice. *Journal of Applied Social Psychology*, 17: 68–79.

3
The Second Driver of Toxic Culture – Cognitive Dissonance

3.1 Introduction

In toxic cultures, there appears to be a dissonance between the 'published values' of an organization and the actual behaviours and norms. While 'deviance' means to stray from correct or proper behaviour, 'dissonance' is defined as a lack of harmony or agreement between people and things. For organizations, 'Cognitive Dissonance' is best described as a disconnect between the external stated values of an organization and the actual practices and/or behaviours. In other words, it is the discrepancy between the rhetoric and the reality.

3.2 Defining Cognitive Dissonance

The term Cognitive Dissonance is used to describe **the mental discomfort that results from holding two conflicting beliefs, values, or attitudes**. This inconsistency between what people believe and how they behave motivates them to engage in actions that will help minimize feelings of discomfort. Cognitive Dissonance describes the discomfort people feel when two cognitions, or a cognition and a behaviour, contradict each other. *I smoke* is dissonant with the knowledge that *smoking can kill me*. To reduce that dissonance, the smoker must either quit or justify smoking ("It keeps me thin, and being overweight is a health risk too, you know").

In *When Prophecy Fails: A Social and Psychological Study of a Modern Group That Predicted the Destruction of the Word* (1956) and *A Theory of Cognitive Dissonance* (1957), Leon Festinger proposed that human beings strive for internal psychological consistency to function mentally in the real world.[1] At its core, Festinger's theory is about how people strive to make sense out of contradictory ideas and lead lives that are, at least in their own minds, consistent and meaningful. A person who experiences internal inconsistency tends to become

DOI: 10.4324/9781003330387-5

psychologically uncomfortable and is motivated to reduce the cognitive dissonance. They tend to make changes to justify the stressful behaviour, either by adding new types of information to the cognition causing the psychological dissonance (rationalization) or by avoiding circumstances and contradictory information likely to increase the magnitude of the cognitive dissonance.

3.3 The Case of the Volkswagen Carbon Emissions Scandal

At VW, executives were strategizing about how to outmanoeuvre the California regulators while at the same time portraying themselves as an organization that was leading the way in reducing the carbon footprint. When the California regulators found a discrepancy between the results of VW lab tests and actual road tests, VW sought to manipulate the narrative by lying and ordering a recall of the allegedly faulty cars: VW formally notified the regulators that the recall was required to fix the emissions problem while telling the dealers that it was to fix a safety light; instead, VW was trying to 'fix' the emissions problem by installing a more sophisticated 'defeat device' that would skew the actual emission results.

Prior to the emissions problem, the VW annual report stated, "our products combine state-of-the-art technology, comfort and safety, low fuel consumption and lower CO2 emissions with the long-term goal of zero-carbon mobility".[2] The marketing of VW's flagship brand, *Turbocharged Direct Injection* (TDI), promoted an advertising campaign about the concept of 'clean diesel'. However, VW's green branding and corporate image stood in stark contrast to its actual practices. While VW had managed to convince the EU regulators, the California regulators had begun to look at the discrepancies between the lab results and the road test results. VW responded by stating that the problems were due to the road testing by the regulators, not the lab results. As pressure mounted on VW, the company asked for a recall of its vehicles, telling dealers and customers that it was to fix a safety light. That was untrue; VW needed to 'fix' the emissions problem by upgrading the 'cheat device' so that it would produce the right results during road testing.

So, what type of corporate values did VW espouse? Prior to the knowledge of VW's emissions cheating, the corporate values for VW published in 2006 included: Responsibility, Honesty, Bravery, Diversity, Pride, Solidarity, and Reliability.[3] Yet the publication of these values does not continue after 2006. It was clear that the impression VW signalled in its marketing, to regulators and the general public, had little resemblance to their true practices.

In one account of the Volkswagen scandal, one commentator noted that "What employees and executives learned at VW was that what the company said, whether in advertisements, against regulators, and against the public, had little to no relation to what it practiced".[4] Even when VW admitted they had fitted the defeat device, they argued that they had not broken EU law, that the emissions were not so harmful, and the executives were not involved, rather that this was the work of a small group of 'bad apples' – a term used disparagingly to describe employees who were deliberately ignoring the company's policies and procedures. The pressure from external shareholders to increase profits as well as market share, coupled with neutralizing any management or employee dissent to senior leadership, enabled rule-breaking. Illegal practices were not reported.

At VW, the mission to become number one could only be achieved by becoming competitive in the number one car market, the US. When Martin Winterkorn became CEO in 2007, he wanted to increase car production from six million to ten million in the next ten years, surpassing both GM and Toyota, which would mean that VW would finally have to succeed in the difficult US car market. Despite these aspirations, employees and managers would note that what VW said publicly was not the reality within the organization. This juxtaposition between rhetoric and reality shifted employee and management perceptions. The pressure to devise a 'defeat device' to effectively alter the actual emissions to benefit VW was driven by the top leadership. Anecdotally, one executive recalled being in a senior leadership meeting where the engineers were told in no uncertain terms that "if you don't find a solution to this problem, I will find someone who can". This, in effect, ensured that there was no dissent especially as it was known at VW that CEOs Piëch and later Winterkorn often fired executives they did not like, keeping only those who would agree with them and support their positions.

Cognitive Dissonance between values and practices is a hallmark of a toxic culture. At VW, intimidation occurred at the highest levels. The CEO Winterkorn was known for his Tuesday top executive meetings that included the highest-level officials in charge of major brands like Audi or Seat. At the meetings, with all present, Winterkorn would mercilessly criticize any executive that had failed to meet set targets. Ewing explains the humiliating tactics that Winterkorn used:

> Managers who were favourites one week could suddenly fall from grace the next. Sometimes they learned they had been demoted or dismissed not from Winterkorn or a colleague but from reading about it in a German business publication, like Manager Magazine, that had somehow been tipped off.[5]

During a meeting that included 15 engineers and the head of VW engine development, they discussed how to create an economical engine that would pass stringent US emissions tests; the idea of the defeat device was presented and debated. While some pointed out the risks of breaking the law by adopting this device, others stated that this was normal across the industry and that VW had to do the same to remain competitive.[6] According to Ewing's analysis of the meeting, most of the engineers did not see this as "a grave violation of Volkswagen standards. There was plenty of precedent for using shortcuts to cope with inconvenient regulations". In all the earlier instances of cheating (see Vignette 3.1), VW as a company had turned a blind eye and condoned the behaviours that had occurred, paying the fines when they came, without creating clear boundaries that this was unacceptable behaviour. Once they had started using the cheat device in their diesel engines, there was no stopping them. As Ewing explains, "defeat devices which may have begun as a stopgap had become a habit".[7] Shockingly, on reading VW's annual report in 2014 prior to the carbon emissions scandal, the report speaks about the VW mission to significantly reduce and eliminate carbon emissions: As Prof. Dr Martin Winterkorn, previously Chairman of the Board of Management of Volkswagen, stated, "Our pursuit of innovation and perfection and our responsible approach will help to make us the world's leading automaker by 2018 – both economically and ecologically".[8]

Vignette 3.1 VW and Toxic Culture

To achieve market dominance, Winterkorn bet on clean diesel. The problem, however, was that VW was yet to produce an engine that was economical, practical, and clean. Engineers were in a bind. To achieve this target set by Winterkorn, the engineers had two main options: (1) Use a costly technology that sprayed a chemical substance to help break down the harmful emissions but required extra space, and the cars' owners would need to make frequent refills, or (2) Use the cheaper option of the 'lean NOx trap' which separated nitrogen oxide molecules and diatomic nitrogen but required an exhaust gas recirculation system that caused certain filters to wear out faster. With pressure mounting to achieve the highly ambitious targets, engineers were forced to consider an alternative solution.

They not only adopted the NOx trap but also installed a 'defeat device' that would switch on during emissions testing. This decision to install cheating devices on the EA189 engine affected more than ten million cars that VW produced and sold. In 2014, American researchers started to suspect that German carmaker Volkswagen (VW) was using a device that would lower its vehicles' emissions specifically during laboratory testing, while the nitrogen oxides (NOx) emissions under actual driving conditions would be about 40 times higher.[9]

As Eric Schneiderman, the Attorney General of New York at the time, concluded,

> Hundreds of very high-level executives and engineers knew about this. We did not find one email saying that maybe we should not be doing this, or this is against the law, or put the brakes on this system. So, this was a corporate culture permeated by fraud.

VW had first been caught using a cheating device in 1973, and it settled the case for $1,200,000 with the US Environmental Protection Agency (EPA).[10] Moreover, diesel emission violations have been widespread in the industry with 97% of cars failing emissions tests according to a 2016 report.[11] There have been major fines against other car companies for using such defeat devices as well. In 1998, major diesel truck manufacturers including Caterpillar, Renault, and Volvo came to a $1 billion settlement with the USA's Department of Justice (DOJ) and the EPA for similar violations. VW was successful in the US market with its clean diesel engine, becoming the largest car company in the world in 2015, three years ahead of the planned schedule.

When it became clear in 2014 that the regulators suspected a cheat device, VW opted to stall and deflect blame rather than coming clean with the California and US federal environmental regulators, and it even tried to argue that the harm was limited. Soon after VW learned of the tests, senior leadership discussed the costs and benefits of different response options: (1) refuse to acknowledge the problem and continue to stonewall and lie, (2) offer an update to the engine software that would decrease emissions but not to the compliant level, or (3) admit to the problem and buy back diesel cars in the US. The last option, Ewing concluded, "does not appear to have been seriously discussed at the time".[12]

VW chose the option to stonewall and lie as the California Air Resources Board (CARB) investigation sought to understand the discrepancies between lab and road emissions. The regulators regarded the VW executives' responses as evasive or dismissive – blaming CARB's testing results. Of more concern, VW decided to recall the cars, telling the regulators that they would update the software while telling the customers and dealers a different reason, that the recall was to fix a safety light.

VW used this recall to improve the effectiveness of its cheat device so that the car could detect when it was under 'test conditions'. VW continued to stonewall as CARB continued its investigations. CARB continued to request further information; when this was not forthcoming, CARB threatened that they would not approve the 2016 models onto the Californian market.

VW had managed to stall the investigation with CARB for over a year. The company provided CARB with a thick binder with the latest technical information which seemed to indicate that VW had finally solved the problem. When CARB looked deeper into the information provided, it found it was "all nonsense".[13] CARB now concluded that the only explanation was that VW had been using a defeat device all along. It was August 2015 and CARB had still not approved the 2016 VW models, which were waiting in port to enter the market. CARB was still waiting for the software information it had requested, and further, it asked VW for a 2016 model car for new testing. This proved to be the final straw as Volkswagen, eager to get its cars on the US market ready for 2016, finally confessed that its cars had had defeat devices.[14] Volkswagen later claimed that it had failed to disclose the issue earlier because executives had not known about this. According to VW, it was only a small group of technicians who knew about the device. Top executives, Volkswagen claimed, had only learned about 'conclusive proof' for the defeat device just before its confession to CARB.[15]

Volkswagen moved from stonewalling, deceit, and denial, to shifting blame downwards in the company. VW's new CEO, Müller, has maintained this discourse since then, "based on what I know today only a few employees were involved". Defending his former CEO Winterkorn, he said: "Do you really think that a chief executive had time for the inner functioning of engine software?"[16]

Volkswagen leadership maintained this line even when former CEO and grand architect of the Volkswagen growth strategy in the 1990s and early 2000s, Piëch, came forward to claim that he had learned of the emissions problems in February 2015 while still chairing the Board and that at the time Winterkorn had told them that there was nothing to worry about.[17]

In the Netflix documentary, *Dirty Money*, Oliver Schmidt, General Manager of VW America, said in a cited email to the executive leadership: "It should first be decided whether we are honest, if we are not honest, everything stays as is".[18]

3.4 Linking Image, Vision, and Culture: Corporate Reputations

Cognitive Dissonance is defined when the stated value does not mirror the actual behaviour. Are there ways that Cognitive Dissonance can be avoided? It is worth considering how the internal and external views of the organization match up. Building a corporate reputation is about an alignment with identity and external image. If we think about how corporate culture and 'the way we do things around here' is about how leaders and employees in the organization see themselves, then the external image is about what this is and how it is communicated.

'Corporate reputation' is a collective term referring to all internal and external stakeholders' views of the organization. One influential approach over the past few years has sought to measure 'corporate reputations' in terms of the 'character' of an organization. Organizational personality or character is defined by seven dimensions: Agreeableness (honest, socially responsible); Competence (reliable, ambitious); Enterprise (innovative, daring); Ruthlessness (arrogant, controlling); Chic (stylish, exclusive); Informality (easy-going); and Machismo (tough).[19] This notion of a character trait seems to provide a shorthand for the 'way we do things around here'.

In my previous book with Graeme Martin,[20] we proposed a model of the relationship between people management, reputations, brands, and performance. Over time, the importance of leadership and culture continues to dominate the impact on corporate reputations. Corporate vision, leadership, governance, and corporate strategy drive the HR strategy and influence and impact on employees and managers. These individuals – employees and managers – shape the organizational identity and culture. Therefore, how these individuals experience the HR policies and processes is important to the culture.

Table 3.1 shows a set of questions that help define the meanings behind key concepts of corporateness[21]:

Table 3.1 Definitions Related to Corporateness[22]

Key question	*Key concept*
What are our distinctive attributes in the marketplace?	Identity
To whom, what, and how should we tell our story?	Communications
What is our promise?	Brand
Who are we and how do we do things around here?	Culture
How are we perceived over time by external stakeholders?	Reputation
How are we perceived right now?	Image

The concept of how and when individuals can incorporate elements of an organization's identity into their self-perception is far more complex than most of the basic culture management literature and consultancies believe. Organizational identity (the 'who are we?' question) derives from the relationships between leadership and followers and depends on the ability of key leaders and managers to recognize the psychological contracts – the 'organizational promises' and their relative values. This psychological contract is made up of four aspects: individual identification (the 'Who am I?' question), internalization ('What do I believe in?'), psychological ownership ('Do I feel that the organization is mine?'), and commitment ('Will I stay?').[23] These questions have informed the employee engagement agenda, which is seen by many HR practitioners as more than a temperature check but as a way to validate various HR interventions. An interesting example can be seen in the case of RBS and distinguishing between their global and local organizational climates.

One Senior Executive interviewed for the book shared their insights of their time at RBS:

> It is worth thinking in terms of different segments of the organization. The day-to-day experience of branch staff, for example, wasn't the same as people working at Head Office. Whilst frankly the back of most branches was horrible, there is no doubt there was a camaraderie, there is no doubt that there was a pride in the service that was being provided, especially in the RBS branches in Scotland and as well as in the NatWest branches.
>
> Toxicity [in Head Office] wasn't played out on the ground all the time. I heard about sessions where staff had the opportunity to sit together and complete their employee opinion surveys and were helped with their answers. If you asked people who worked in that branch network in the 2000s, 'Did you like it?', a lot of them would say, 'Yes, I really did'. There is a difference between the HQ experience and the experience on the ground.[24]

Organizations are complex. To fully understand what shapes the corporate culture, as well as strategic choices, we need to explore three key areas and how they intersect:

1. **Image** – the external stakeholder's view of the organization
2. **Vision** – what leadership and senior management aspire for the organization to be
3. **Culture** – the organization's key values, behaviours, and attitudes

Using the example of the case of RBS, this section will explore these concepts. According to practitioner experts, to build an effective corporate reputation, organizations must align these three elements.[25] Not doing so causes misalignments in the following ways and, more importantly, leads to toxicity.

Vision-Culture Gap

This gap results from senior managers moving the company in a direction that employees do not understand or do not support. It may be that the vision sits uncomfortably with the values of the culture.

Image-Culture Gap

This gap results when an organization does not put into practice its brand values and, as such, there is confusion, usually from clients, about the organization's external image.

Image-Vision Gap

This gap results when there is a mismatch between the external image of the organization and senior management aspirations.

All the above contribute to Cognitive Dissonance where there is a disconnect between what is said and what is actually done and can be significant for deepening toxicity within organizations. Clarifying the connection between culture, image, and identity is important and deserves a more detailed look.

3.4.1 Culture, Image, and Identity

The challenge at times is differentiating between three dimensions that on the surface look very similar. One way of doing so is to see organizational identity – 'Who are we?' – as the link between culture and image (see Figure 3.1). The reasoning is complicated yet subtle, but it suggests a two-way recursive relationship between the three concepts of culture, organizational identity, and organizational image.

The first relationship (arrow 1) is between culture and identity. Over time, the organization may define itself in terms of 'who we are'. This is a more collective shared realization. For example, RBS collectively saw itself as strong on execution rather than innovation. The key point is that identity does not depend on people outside the organization for identification or confirmation; it is internally driven.

The second relationship (arrow 2) is the impression the organization creates on others or on external stakeholders such as investors, potential employees, and clients as well as the media and the general public.

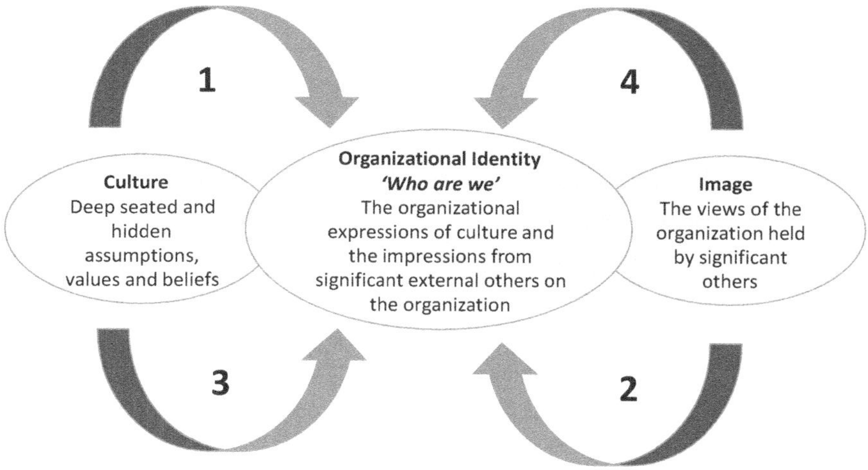

Figure 3.1 The Relationship Between Culture, Identity, and Image (based on Hatch & Schultz, 2002: 995)

These impressions reflect back (arrow 3) on the culture. The external view enforces, sustains, and confirms the organizational identity. RBS was viewed externally as an extremely successful maverick organization that went against the industry predictions and somehow achieved strategic success. Over time, this image and story fed back into the organization, leading to arrogance and a blind spot where many, both inside and externally, believed that it could not fail.

Finally, arrow 4 shows how identities can be externally driven. The need for recognized 'heroic leaders' can loop into the organizational identity. Identities are formed not only by cultural reference to internal values but also by feedback from external parties. This is seen by the dominance of the heroic leader rather than the leadership team. This helps to explain how many investors and regulators were blinded to the potential of risk and failure. The image of the RBS organization, with its campus-style HQ and state-of-the-art business school complete with Harvard faculty, reinforced the identity of success, the 'Midas touch', and potential global domination.

In this model, reinforcement of how a leader is expected to act is continually emphasized from the external image and the internal culture. The leader wears the 'organizational identity' cloak that both serves to bolster 'who we are' to the external market and stakeholders, as well as reinforces the culture for employees. The 'stories' that emerge, along with outstanding market performance, legitimize the leader's position and lead to interested academics and observers seeking to find the formula for the 'success'. When Fred Goodwin led

RBS from a small regional bank to become one of the top five global banks by market capitalization in a decade, revered business schools rushed to research this success and write a series of articles for business school publications. The external image determined and reinforced the notion of this inability to fail. The organization's identity absorbed this, and the culture of the organization increasingly reflected arrogance and superiority, as well as deference to a leader that was rumoured to have 'a brain the size of a planet'.

As one former Senior Executive commented:

> If you look at the output of business schools now and the last couple of years the whole wellbeing, empathy, and the purposeful leader agenda that they now write about is what they have always been writing about. That's just not true, they reinforced organizations that ran through the cult of the leader.[26]

Another former Senior Executive recalled:

> On the first day of our (Harvard) executive management programme in (2006) with Harvard professors, and unexpectedly, Fred appeared in the lecture room. He was clearly not expected to be there and walked into the lecture theatre. Literally, the Harvard professors bowed down in front of him. Afterwards, some of us questioned this 'worshipping' behaviour and decided that it was all very strange.[27]

RBS built much of its successful performance by having a 'lean' processing division that handled the 'paperwork' from the bank's branches. This 'manufacturing division' took out the previous end-to-end processes concerned with so-called back-end operations. The bank branch became effectively a 'shop window'. This impacted not only the individual account holder but also small and medium-sized businesses. Business decisions on loans, credit, or payments were removed from the bank's branches and centred in either large branches or regional offices. Why did this change RBS? It changed from being a regional bank where decisions were made by local branch managers to a factory of efficiency. In doing so, it reckoned that it reduced operating costs from around an average of 65 to 43 per cent[28] compared with other similar-sized retail banks.

This changed the corporate culture of the bank. The core competence was now about efficiency. This journey started with the acquisition of the London-based NatWest in 1990, a bank nearly three times the size of RBS. The relatively new CEO, Fred Goodwin, earned a 'near-heroic' reputation among the global financial community.[29] This acquisition, intended to increase revenue and profits, also contained the prize of Her Majesty the Queen's Bank, Coutts, one of the oldest banks in the world. In acquiring NatWest, the branch network and the brand were left untouched. The back-office systems such as IT, branch processing and consolidating, and decision-making moved away from branches to regional centres or offices to strip out costs and resulted in significant job losses and rationalization. This acquisition was portrayed as a success by commentators. This trajectory of 'growth through acquisition' was based on 'execution' to achieve cost efficiencies, known internally as 'make it happen'. This mantra appeared on all internal documents and presentations. It reinforced the image and identity as one of success through execution.

Up until 2007, the specific features of leadership and organization culture that were used to account for success were: (1) Goodwin's direct, acidic, and micro-leadership style, which remonstrated senior executives on a daily basis; (2) strategy execution or 'making things happen'; and (3) a focus on hard quantitative data that informed the performance management and human capital management systems.[30] Latterly, there was an investment in the top 300 executives, facilitated by Harvard Business School, to reinforce the importance of innovation in recognition that strategy execution could only achieve so much. As researchers have suggested, "There is little doubt that the financial press and the UK government were influential in shaping external and employee perceptions of Goodwin's on the organization".[31]

Goodwin was recognized as Best Bank CEO by Reuters and was knighted (subsequently rescinded) by the UK Government in 2004 – three years before the ill-fated acquisition. Goodwin and his senior executive team have been held solely accountable for the disastrous ABN Amro acquisition. This has raised the uncomfortable question about the extent to which a single leader can be attributed with the success or demise of an organization. The transformational leadership literature, as we will see in Chapter 5, exposes the over-attribution of a single leader to organizational success.

Taken from data from a research article written about the company, one Senior Executive commented:

> He (Goodwin) was probably given too much credit on the way up and came in for too much criticism on the way down . . . he came to symbolize all that was wrong with banking.[32]

When interviewing a Senior Executive for this book, they described the focus on a certain style of leadership:

> RBS Fred's predecessor, Matthewson, was sort of a warmup act for the way Fred was. Matthewson was a big macho character steeped in Scotland and Scottishness, chippy and ambitious, smart, and Fred was his protégé, so they were a double act for Fred to step up. If you look at the history, you could probably place it back to **in the making** rather than put it all on Fred's shoulders.[33]

In other words, the previous leadership style had already carved a path towards a more macho and aggressive leadership style to realize the Board's global growth ambitions. Gratton and Ghoshal reported on the meticulousness the leadership imbued across the organization's culture, citing a senior leader as saying: "He (Fred Goodwin) is very rigorous about apparently small things, and this pervades the company. People say, 'if Fred sees this, what would he say'".[34] This deepening obsession of 'what would Fred say' became endemic in the last few years before the ABN Amro acquisition. It served to direct resources, drive deference, and demand obedience. It was played out in the strategy execution.

This focus on individual contribution and accountability neglects the extent to which a corporate culture can direct and subsume an individual. Many senior leaders speak about the ability RBS had to create a "machine-like bureaucracy that slipped into gear to implement centrally driven decisions"[35]. This obsessive focus on 'strategy execution' and efficiency led to a change in the corporate culture. Success was measured on 'getting things done', measured internally as a leadership competency: a burning drive for results. The core competence of the organization had shifted away from qualitative to quantitative measures. The annual employee engagement survey, coupled with monthly pulse surveys, evolved into a Leadership Index that measured people management, sales, customer service, and financial performance and was acclaimed by Harvard academics as one of the most impressive online tools anywhere.[36] As one employee in a research study exclaimed:

> I've never known an organization like it. There was an obsession with execution … where a logo – 'make it happen' – actually reflected how an organization operated.[37]

Another explained how people were controlled by 'the machine':

> The vast majority of people were just pushed into execution, the machine just cut in. And because RBS had such great processes, we could focus on execution … The role of senior manager, and indeed my role, was on execution rather than the extent to which you were able to shape or influence strategy.[38]

Indeed, the machinery of RBS as one of execution and getting things done was seen initially as a positive trait. It attracted the brightest and the best to work at RBS.

Yet as one former Senior Executive[39] noted:

> Within a toxic culture, the individual often doesn't feel that they can be their true self. There is a prevailing orthodoxy which frankly is almost impossible to challenge, and on a more practical level, toxic organizations

> tend to reinforce themselves by retaining those who play within the rules and rejecting those who tend not to play within the rules as well.
>
> You can have toxic groups within an organization or toxicity within most of the organization … my reflection is that I worked with some of the brightest and most lovely people when I was at RBS, some tremendous people that I have contact with, people that I respect deeply, and yet everything indicates that there was a pretty high level of toxicity within that organization.

Employees who perceived that they were 'doing their best' contrast with the reflection that they were unwittingly part of a toxic organization. The concept of 'followers' is explored later in the book. Corporate cultures are more than a reflection of individual values and attitudes; the structures and processes indemnify and entrench the culture, so that individuals seek to respond rather than challenge. External stakeholders reinforce the organizational identity and may at times fan the flames for inducing or embedding toxicity through pressures for performance.

3.5 Carillion – A Case Study

> "The mystery is not that it collapsed, but that it lasted so long".[40]
>
> House Of Commons, Parliamentary Committee, 2017

In 2018, the construction giant, Carillion, went into compulsory liquidation, costing the UK taxpayers an estimated £148m. Carillion's 2016 accounts were published in March 2017 and showed the company as profitable and solvent. On the back of those results, it paid a record dividend of £79m and awarded large performance bonuses to senior executives. On 10 July 2017, just four months after the accounts were published, the company announced a reduction of £845m in the value of its contracts in a profit warning. This was increased to £1,045m in September 2017, the same amount as the company's previous seven years' profits combined. Carillion went into liquidation in January 2018 with liabilities of nearly £7bn and just £29m in cash. Carillion's collapse was sudden and from a publicly stated position of strength.

Construction firm Carillion was a major construction company and supplier to the UK Government; it was known for several high-profile, public-sector projects, including key accounts such as the £745m Aberdeen bypass, the £1.4b HS2 joint venture, and the £335m Royal Liverpool Hospital.[41] It was forced into liquidation in 2018 a few months after its annual report had published a clean bill of health.[42] At that point, it had been the largest construction company in the UK, with 43,000 employees and more than 30,000 subcontractors.

Carillion did not get off to a smooth start. Carillion demerged from Tarmac in 1999. Highly ambitious, it grew quickly and expanded beyond its roots in the construction sector into facilities management. Red flags over corporate governance practices were raised concerning the dual roles of chairman and chief executive, a lack of structure in the boardroom, and no dedicated director of finance appointed.[43]

Growth was fast, and there were several large acquisitions, including the purchase of three main rivals totalling over £1.2bn, resulting in the removal of market competitors Mowlem, Alfred McAlpine, and Eaga.[44] Balfour Beatty, the last remaining rival to Carillion, was also sought for acquisition. Carillion's offer was declined as the Balfour Beatty board did not believe Carillion's claim that the merger would bring an estimated £175m of cost savings per year.[45] Balfour Beatty was right to be sceptical. For example, in 2011, Carillion purchased Eaga, a supplier of heating and renewable energy services. Prior to the purchase, Eaga had made accumulated profits of £31m. Five consecutive years of losses followed, totalling £260m by the end of 2016. The disastrous purchase cost Carillion £298m. This came at a time when Carillion was refusing to commit further funds to addressing a pension deficit of £605m. That problem itself was largely attributable to acquisitions: when Carillion bought Mowlem for £350m in 2006 and Alfred McAlpine for £565m in 2008, it also bought responsibility for their pension scheme deficits. It was storing up problems for the future. Carillion's spending spree also enabled one of the more questionable accounting practices, which featured in its eventual demise. Carillion purchased Mowlem, Alfred McAlpine, and Eaga for substantially more than their tangible net assets. The difference between the net assets and the amount paid is accounted as 'goodwill'.[46]

The Parliamentary Report tells of hubris and greed:

> The perception of Carillion as a healthy and successful company was in no small part due to its directors' determination to increase the dividend paid each year, come what may. Amid a jutting mountain range of volatile financial performance charts, dividend payments stand out as a generous, reliable and steady incline. In the company's final years, directors rewarded themselves and other shareholders by choosing to pay out more in dividends than the company generated in cash, despite increased borrowing, low levels of investment and a growing pension deficit. Active investors have expressed surprise and disappointment that Carillion's directors chose short-term gains over the long-term sustainability of the company. We too can find no justification for this reckless approach.[47]

In July 2017, the company issued a profit warning and later announced that the value of existing contracts had losses of £845m, which increased to £1045m a few months later. This loss amounted to the total of the previous seven years' profits.[48]

3.5.1 Cognitive Dissonance

Carillion presented accounts that misrepresented the reality of the business and increased its dividend every year. Carillion's accounts were systematically manipulated to make optimistic assessments of revenue in defiance of internal controls. Long-term obligations, such as adequately funding its pension schemes, were treated with contempt.

Carillion's final annual report, *Making Tomorrow A Better Place* published in March 2017, noted proudly, "the board has increased the dividend in each of the 16 years since the formation of the Company in 1999". Despite financial discrepancies, Carillion continued to paint a positive picture in its final annual report accounts and stressed the importance of company values:

> More than any policy document, our values define the way we behave, with each other, with our customers and partners, and how we approach our challenges and opportunities on a daily basis.
>
> Our vision: to be the trusted partner for providing services, delivering infrastructure and creating places that bring lasting benefits to our customers and the communities in which we live and work. Our values: We Care, We Achieve Together, We Improve, We Deliver.[49]

Carillion relied on an extensive network of suppliers to deliver materials, services, and support across its business. At the point of the company's collapse, Carillion's supply chain spanned 30,000 companies. Despite being signatories of the Prompt Payment Code, Carillion treated suppliers with contempt and gained a reputation as a notorious late payer. Suppliers could be paid within 45 days but had to take a cut for the privilege. This enabled Carillion to borrow more money under so-called supply chain financing. When it collapsed, it owed around £2bn to its 30,000 suppliers, sub-contractors, and other short-term creditors. Carillion's use of supply chain finance was unusual in both the harshness of the alternative standard payment terms and the extent to which the company relied on it. Shortly after the launch of the Supply Chain Finance Scheme, Carillion changed its standard payment terms to 120 days. Suppliers could sell their invoices at a discount to Carillion's bank to receive their payment after 45 days. Carillion, however, would not be expected to reimburse the bank until the standard payment terms had expired, providing them with a generous repayment period. This was a deliberate strategy. Carillion explicitly used this to avoid 'damaging working capital' and served to highlight the fragility of Carillion's business model.

The UK Government monitored Carillion as part of its risk management system for strategic suppliers. Carillion dominated the market for government services, with the Cabinet Office monitoring Carillion as a strategic supplier. Carillion reported £1,719 of UK public sector revenue in 2016. However, it was increasingly criticized by sub-contractors for late payments. Yet in April 2015, Carillion told the Cabinet Office that it was paying sub-contractors on government contracts within 30 days.[50]

Cognitive Dissonance was evident in Carillion's demise. The UK Parliamentary report stated:

> Carillion's directors, both executive and non-executive, were optimistic until the very end of the company. They had built a culture of ever-growing reward behind the façade of an ever-growing company, focused on their personal profit and success. Even after the company became insolvent, directors seemed surprised the business had not survived.[51]

3.5.2 Normalization of Deviance

As shown in the previous chapter, the Normalization of Deviance is often present in toxic organizations. At Carillion, three distinct types of deviance became normalized over time:

1. Late payments to suppliers
2. Aggressive accounting
3. Payment of high dividends to shareholders despite the troubled financial status of the firm

Considerations of the factors that determine Normalization of Deviance are:

1. To become deviant, an action must be contrary to norms maintained by actors external to the subject organization
2. The action must find support in the norms of a given level or division in the organization
3. The action must be known to and supported by the dominant administrative coalition in the organization
4. New members must be socialized to participate in it

At the time of collapse, Emma Mercer was the financial director in post and the only director who spoke openly about Carillion and their 'aggressive accounting'. Mercer was previously employed for three years in the Canadian part of the business. On returning to the UK in 2017, she became concerned about the increasingly aggressive trading of contracts and raised a formal concern with the Board of Directors in May 2017. Her concerns were expressed as 'sloppy accounting'.

The Board agreed to an investigation but declined a full independent review. Instead, the company auditor, KPMG, was asked to review previous audits. KPMG concluded that Carillion had made errors in the reporting of their assets but had not misstated revenue. Mercer's speaking up about these issues acted as the turning point for a review of all contracts and led to the documentation of the £845m loss in July 2017.

The Board subsequently made a number of recommendations: (1) to run a culture audit; (2) to ensure senior management gave encouragement to staff to speak up on matters "which could lead to any embarrassment to the business"; and (3) to conduct a review of the company values to ensure "staff understand fully that behaving with transparency, honesty and integrity is as important as achieving, improving and delivering".[52] In the end, this attempt to manage a toxic culture was thwarted by the collapse of Carillion.

Normalization of Deviance occurred in a number of ways. First, payments of high dividends were made to shareholders despite the poor financial performance of the firm and while pension deficits increased. In the years preceding the collapse, Carillion's profits did not grow at a steady rate, yet the Board decided to not only continue to pay dividends but also to increase them – even without the cash flow to cover them. Later, it was discovered that Carillion paid a total of £376m in dividends to shareholders despite only making £159m cash and increasing debts. Second, transferring the consequences of its weak financial position to suppliers; Carillion was notorious as a 'late payer'. Third, ensuring that its accounting practices made the financial position look better than it actually was by hiding the increasing financial liabilities. Payment of high dividends became the 'new normal' in the company following negligence of the early warning signs of poor financial performance.

Carillion's rise and spectacular fall are described as a "story of recklessness, hubris and greed". The House of Commons report described Carillion's business model as a relentless 'dash for cash' that was driven by acquisitions, rising debt, and expansions into new overseas markets, as well as the exploitation of its suppliers. Yet it did not achieve this on its own or through corruption or blackmail. Instead, highly regarded audit and consultancy firms, such as KPMG and Deloitte, were engaging with Carillion by acting as Carillion's auditors for 19 years. Deloitte was paid £10m by the company to act as its internal auditor. The House of Commons report is scathing:

> It did not once qualify its audit opinion, complacently signing off the director's increasingly fantastical figures. In failing to exercise professional scepticism towards Carillion's accounting judgements over the course of its tenure as Carillion's auditor, KPMG was complicit in them.

In the case of Carillion, the UK's House of Commons, in a cross-party select committee, named three senior figures as culpable in the downfall of Carillion; not one single toxic leader but a 'rotten corporate culture' was blamed. The House of Commons report described the collapse of the company as:

> The rise and spectacular story of recklessness, hubris and greed. (Carillion's) business model was a relentless dash for cash, driven by acquisitions, rising debt expansion into new markets and the exploitation of suppliers. It presented accounts that misrepresented the reality of the business, and increased dividends every year, come what may. Long-term obligations, such as adequately funding its pension schemes, were treated with contempt. Even as the company very publicly began to unravel, the board was concerned with increasing and protecting generous executive bonuses. Carillion was unsustainable. The mystery is not that it collapsed, but that it lasted for so long.[53]

The Parliamentary reports concluded that Carillion's board was both responsible and culpable for the company's failure. The Board presented itself as "self-pitying victims of a maelstrom of coincidental and unforeseeable mishaps" and pointed to difficulties in a few key contracts in the Middle East. But the report concluded that the problems that caused the collapse of Carillion were long in the making, as was the "rotten corporate culture" that allowed those problems to occur.[54]

> Corporate culture does not emerge overnight. The chronic lack of accountability and professionalism now evident in Carillion's governance were failures years in the making. The board was either negligently ignorant of the rotten culture at Carillion or complicit in it.[55]

3.5.3 Toxicity Spreads

Vignette 3.2 illustrates how the 'rotten culture' had spread to lead to collusion from external auditors. KPMG gave Carillion a clean bill of health only months before its collapse in 2018. In a court case in 2022, former partners and staff of KPMG were accused of forging documents and have faced fines and sanctions. KPMG faced a £250m negligence claim over the Carillion audit.

Vignette 3.2 When the External Auditor Fails in Their Role

Carillion collapsed with £7bn of debts in January 2018, resulting in 3,000 job losses and causing chaos across hundreds of its projects – including two big hospitals, schools, roads, and even Liverpool FC's stadium, Anfield.

A tribunal investigating claims made by the Financial Reporting Council (FRC), which regulates accountants, found that KPMG and its staff had misled FRC inspectors by forging documents in relation to its work on the accounts of Carillion and a software company, Regenersis.

The FRC published a settlement with KPMG and its former employee over the 2014 Regenersis audit. One of the former partners has agreed to pay a fine of £150,000 and is barred from accountancy for three years. Much of the evidence focused on KPMG's 'misleading' disclosures to the FRC over its audit of Carillion.

KPMG has admitted misleading the FRC during routine checks on the quality of its audit, but former staff members accused of misconduct by the FRC disagree over who was to blame. They include one of its most senior staff members, known as partners. The partner was suspended by the company in 2019 and left in 2021. A senior staff member repeatedly denied being involved in the alleged falsification of documents. He told the tribunal that he was "shocked and devastated and angry" to find that members of his team had allegedly duped the regulator.

KPMG will now pay one of the largest fines in UK audit history after former staff forged documents and misled the regulator over audits for companies, including the collapsed outsourcer Carillion.

The FRC confirmed the £14.4m settlement at a London tribunal hearing and said KPMG would also face a "severe reprimand" over the "extremely serious" misconduct related to employees' false representations to the watchdog.

The fine relates to misleading information provided to the FRC as part of audit quality reviews (AQR), meant to confirm the integrity of audits conducted for both Carillion and the software firm Regenersis between 2014 and 2016. The tribunal upheld allegations by the FRC that KPMG and former staff created false meeting minutes and retroactively edited spreadsheets, before sharing those documents with the FRC.

(https://www.theguardian.com/business/2022/may/12/kpmg-fined-frc-audit-carillion accessed 27 June 2022)

3.5.4 The Lessons of Carillion

The Board and senior executives were culpable in the demise of Carillion. However, key regulators, the FRC and The Pensions Regulator (TPR), were regarded as feeble and timid. The FRC identified concerns in the Carillion accounts in 2015 but failed to follow them up. TPR threatened on seven occasions to use a power to enforce pension contributions that it never used. The Government's Crown Representative system provided little warning of risks in a key strategic supplier. Carillion's senior executive and the Board performed with "reckless short-termism . . . Carillion became a giant and unsustainable corporate time bomb in a regulatory and legal environment still in existence today". The UK's Parliamentary investigation is critical of the senior executives and the Board in the running of Carillion, as well as being critical of the auditors, advisers, and regulators in challenging, advising, or regulating it, who they note were "often acting entirely in line with their personal incentives".[56]

In this chapter, we have explored the second driver of toxic cultures: Cognitive Dissonance. This driver is defined as the growing divergence between the image, vision, and culture of the organization. Yet the case of Carillion illustrates the impact of both of the two key drivers: Normalization of Deviance and Cognitive Dissonance. As the UK Parliamentary Committee noted, toxic cultures do not emerge overnight, rather they develop and are embedded over time. In the next chapter, we will explore how both drivers, the Normalization of Deviance and Cognitive Dissonance, serve to enable and embed a toxic culture.

Notes

1 Festinger, L., Riecken, H., & Schachter, S. (1964) *When Prophecy Fails: A Social and Psychological Study of a Modern Group that Predicted the Destruction of the World.* New York: Harper Torchbooks. (Reprint 2009). Festinger, L. (1957). *A Theory of Cognitive Dissonance*. Stanford, CA: Stanford University Press.
2 Volkswagen. (2014) Volkswagen Annual Report 2013 https://annualreport2013.volkswagenag.com/servicepages/filelibrary/files/collection.php. Accessed December 21, 2021. p. 174.
3 Volkswagen. (2007) Volkswagen Annual Report 2006. https://www.volkswagenag.com/presence/konzern/images/teaser/history/chronik/annual-report/2006-Annual-Report.pdf. Accessed 21 December 2021.
4 Ewing, J. (2017) *Faster, Higher, Farther: The Volkswagen Scandal.* New York: Norton. p. 157.
5 *Ibid.*
6 *Ibid.*, p. 122.
7 *Ibid.*, p. 178.
8 Volkswagen. (2015) Volkswagen Annual Report 2014. https://annualreport2014.volkswagenag.com. Accessed 21 December 2021.
9 Volkswagen. (2015) Volkswagen Annual Report 2014. https://annualreport2014.volkswagenag.com. Accessed 21 December 2021.

10 *Ibid.*
11 Carrington, D. (2016) The Truth about London's Air Pollution. *The Guardian*. https://www.theguardian.com/environment/2016/feb/05/the-truth-about-londons-air-pollution. Accessed 28 December 2021.
12 Ewing (2017), p. 179.
13 *Ibid.*
14 *Ibid.*, pp. 197–198.
15 *Ibid.*, p. 200.
16 *Ibid.*, p. 216.
17 *Ibid.*, p. 271.
18 "Hard Nox". (2020) *Dirty Money*. Season 1, Episode 1, Netflix. https://www.netflix.com/title/80118100. Accessed 28 December 2021.
19 Davies, G., Chun, R., Vinhas da Silva, R., & Roper, S. (2004) A corporate character scale to assess employee and customer views of organization reputation. *Corporate Reputation Review*, 7(2): 125–146.
20 Martin, G., & Hetrick, S. (2006) *Corporate Reputations, Branding and People Management: A Strategic Appraoch to HR*. Oxford: Butterworth-Heinemann.
21 Balmer, J., & Greyser, S. (2003) *Perspectives on Identity, Image, Reputation, Corporate Banking and Corporate Level Marketng*. London: Routledge.
22 *Ibid*.
23 *Ibid.*
24 Senior Executive, Interviewed in October 2021.
25 Hatch, M.J., & Schultz, M. (2001) Are the strategic stars aligned for your corporate brand? *Harvard Business Review*. Accessed 21 December 2021.
26 Senior Executive, 1, interviewed in October 2021.
27 Personal experience.
28 Royal Bank of Scotland: Annual Report and Accounts 2005. https://investors.natwestgroup.com/~/media/Files/R/RBS-IR-V2/annual-reports/rbs-group-accounts-2005.pdf. Accessed 14 December 2021.
29 Kennedy, G., Boddy, D., & Paton, R.A. (2006) Managing the aftermath: Lessons from The Royal Bank of Scotland's Acquisition of NatWest. *European Management Journal*, 25(4): 368–379.
30 Martin, G., & Gollan, P.J. (2012) Corporate governance and strategic human resource management in the UK financial services sector: The case of the RBS. *International Journal of Human Resource Management*, 23(16): 3295–3314.
31 *Ibid.*, p. 3302.
32 Martin & Gollan (2012).
33 Senior Executive, Interviewed in October 2021.
34 Gratton, L., & Ghoshal, S. (2005) Beyond best practice. *MIT Sloan Management Review*, 46: 49–57.
35 Martin & Gollan (2012), p. 3303.
36 Groysberg & Sherman (2008).
37 Martin & Gollan (2012), p. 3303.
38 *Ibid.*
39 Senior executive, interviewed in November 2021.

40 https://publications.parliament.uk/pa/cm201719/cmselect/cmworpen/769/76903.htm#:~:text=Carillion%20was%20unsustainable.,that%20it%20lasted%20so%20long. Accessed 5 January 2022.
41 https://www.bbc.co.uk/news/uk-42731762. Accessed 5 January 2022.
42 Carillion's final annual report (2016) was published in March 2017, certified by auditor KPMG, who were paid a staggering £29m as Carillion's auditor over a period spanning 19 years. In June 2017, the Carillion board declared a year-end dividend of £55m, along with large performance bonuses to senior executives – including Richard Adam, who was the retiring Finance Director.
43 https://www.theguardian.com/business/1999/jul/02/12. Accessed 5 January 2022.
44 (1) February 2006: acquisition Mowlem £350m; (2) February 2008: acquisition Alfred McAlpine £565m; (3) April 2011: acquisition Eaga £298m.
45 Carillion Joint Report (2006), p. 13.
46 *Ibid.*, p. 14 citing annual reports 2006 and 2008.
47 https://publications.parliament.uk/pa/cm201719/cmselect/cmworpen/769/769.pdf
48 Carillion Joint Report. p. 7.
49 *Ibid.*, p. 52.
50 House of Commons Business, Energy and Industrial Strategy and Work and Pensions Committees Carillion Second Joint Report HC 769. Published on 16 May 2018. p. 24. https://publications.parliament.uk/pa/cm201719/cmselect/cmworpen/769/769.pdf. Accessed 5 January 2022.
51 *Ibid.*, p. 47.
52 "Key Lessons Learnt" cited in Cabinet Office. p. 11.
53 House of Commons Business, Energy and Industrial Strategy and Work and Pensions Committees Carillion Second Joint Report HC 769. Published on 16 May 2018.
54 *Ibid.*
55 *Ibid.*, p. 27.
56 *Ibid.*, p. 86.

4 The Four Stages of a Toxic Culture

4.1 Introduction

Pressure for increased performance, overly ambitious goals, and 'toxic' leadership can provoke a toxic culture. The actions of the leader, such as berating and mocking individuals in front of their peers (VW, RBS), holding almost omnipotent power vested by the Board and other external stakeholders (BP), and driving internal resources or directing orders through phrases such as "the (CEO) wants this to happen", are key to the journey of organizations becoming toxic.

This chapter sets out to explore the four stages of the journey to becoming a toxic organization. Some organizations may not reach all four stages, but each stage should enable diagnosis.

4.2 Performance Pressures

One of the significant triggers for a toxic culture is pressure for performance. Many of the organizations that we have explored started as underdogs with high ambitions. These high ambitions were often ascribed by a new CEO to become the biggest and dominate their industry sector. For BP, the trigger was the highly ambitious target to become one of the industry giants, coupled with the desire for superior financial returns to shareholders. When John Browne, then CEO, sought to capitalize on BP by raising revenues, he did so by cutting budgets by 25 per cent, which enabled BP to raise its profit margins and increase shareholder value. Within a decade, under John Browne's leadership, BP became one of the world's leading oil companies, and its structure and governance were driven by high risk and high growth. The pressure on BP managers to reduce costs directly impacted the health and safety of their operations,

DOI: 10.4324/9781003330387-6

resulting in the Deepwater Horizon spill some years later. It was not a case of 'if' but rather 'when'.

One senior executive interviewed for this book explained how performance pressures and management behaviour could mix and produce toxic results:

> When an organization starts focusing more on financial results and only financial results, that organization embarks on a journey to become very toxic because the focus is on what you have delivered (and) how much money you have made for the company; it is not how you made that money. People are driven to be recognized as 'great achievers', but in reality, they are achieving the short-term financial gains for themselves (yet) they are destroying the long-term impact on the organization.
>
> Secondly when managers start getting appreciated for being tough, [it] can really manoeuvre the team when we start appreciating toughness. That will start giving birth to a very toxic environment because people will start to look at that as an example of 'how I should behave' and, 'if I want to be on the top then that is how I should be'.
>
> Another element is when people speak up, i.e., whistleblowing, and a complaint is parked. That complaint is not acted upon. I had a lot of anonymous emails. Whilst the organization didn't have a formal whistleblowing policy, the general reaction of the top management was, 'Well, he is stirring up the team, trying to get more performance out of the team, so people have moved out of their comfort zones, and they have complained about it' … The manager against whom the complaints have been made will become more aggressive. These are the elements of primarily how organizations start their journey on a toxic culture.[1]

4.2.1 Performance Pressures at Boeing

In 2018 and 2019, two crashes of the Boeing 737 MAX 8 killed 346 people. The crashes exposed a toxic corporate culture. Throughout the last 20 years of Boeing's corporate history, the organization and its senior executives had "skimped on testing and pressured employees to meet unrealistic deadlines and convinced the regulators to put planes in service without properly equipping them or their pilots for flight".[2]

Boeing, once an industry innovator and previously featured in bestsellers such as *Built to Last* and *In Search of Excellence*, had become fixated on the bottom line and a drive to beat the competition. Its focus on cost at the expense of safety, as well as its obsession to reward senior executives and its shareholders, came at a very high price with two tragic crashes within a matter of months.

The Boeing Case Study (Vignette 4.1) shows how performance pressures sustained over a period of time led to a toxic culture.

Vignette 4.1 Boeing Case Study: Performance Pressures Leading to a Toxic Culture

Pressure to outperform rivals, coupled with its acquisition of the military airplane producer McDonnell Douglas in 1997, changed the Boeing corporate culture. One year after the acquisition, the company was at war with itself.

McDonnell Douglas's culture was described as 'cut-throat' and 'win at all costs', while Boeing just wanted to design the world's best airplanes. At the time of the acquisition, two senior executives from McDonnell Douglas became Boeing's two largest shareholders and both joined the Board. McDonnell Douglas executives became known as 'hunter killer assassins'.

Over the next few years, the culture began to change in the way people communicated, how people were held to account, and how their performance and careers were managed.

A new 5–15 rule was introduced: memos should take no more than five minutes to read and 15 minutes to write. This was anathema to the engineers who wrote carefully worded emails.

Senior executives began to lecture managers that Boeing needed to be a team and not a family. At an AGM meeting with several hundred attendees, a senior executive asked two Boeing managers to stand up and apologize for falling behind on their commitments and causing the entire company to miss its goals. This senior executive announced to all that the threat to Boeing came from inside due to a *failure to execute*. Senior leaders were fired.

Fraud and Wrongdoing

In 2004, a former senior executive and an employee in the USA Air Force were fired and both pleaded guilty to conflict-of-interest charges and served time in prison. According to reports, Boeing's former chief financial officer pleaded guilty to a criminal charge of acting improperly over a scandal-hit deal to provide the US Air Force with refuelling tankers.

Financial Incentives Aligned to Delivery Rather Than Safety

Performance bonuses were linked to delivery at the expense of safety. In 2012 for example, because of the financial incentives managers overrode their own specialists' concerns at the last minute to approve the Sikorsky S-76D helicopter.

Employees Ranked by Individual Performance

GE's 'rank and yank' performance system was introduced at Boeing around 2004, where each year ten per cent of management was eliminated. In 2014, Boeing introduced an employee ranking system that made it more likely that older and more experienced workers were made redundant – similar to the approach at 3M, where the latest CEO had come from.

Broken Promises to Employees

In 2008, Boeing faced the largest white-collar strike in US history, encompassing 27,000 workers from six states, due in the main to concerns about the declining quality of the Boeing planes, outsourcing, job security, pay, and benefits. As a compromise to end the strike, senior executives promised no change to employee benefits but behind the scenes, they did lower benefits.

In late October 2008, a tentative deal was reached between Boeing and the SPEEA Professional Aerospace Union, in which Boeing made a number of concessions. Boeing told the union engineers that the company planned less outsourcing on future airplanes, including the next 787 Dreamliner model.

Safety is not mentioned from 2010 to 2014 in any of the company's annual reports.

Compromises on Safety and Outsourcing

After a series of serious incidents, the US aviation authority, the FAA, decided in 2013 to ground all Dreamliners worldwide. Prior to this, Boeing had outsourced key components of the Dreamliner 787, which finally had to be brought in-house at a cost of $50bn to complete the job. The high degree of outsourcing in terms of aircraft safety drastically increased the complexity of the production process and therefore posed a challenge to testing the integration of key components. Some parts simply did not fit together. Boeing was able to borrow money on calculating future upfront expenses. Finance staff complained to others that 'we're all going to jail'.[3] The SEC launched an investigation based on a whistleblower's complaint, but no action was taken.

Performance Pressure to Meet Deadlines

After the Dreamliner, the focus was on the upgraded 737 MAX 8, and a new phrase became dominant in the company: 'more for less'. Performance pressures included a 'countdown clock' in conference rooms where the programme was taking place, with the clock marking the remaining time for a new plane's first flight.

Whistleblowing Concerns Ignored

In 2014, Al Jazeera sent a hidden camera into the plant and caught some employees on tape saying they'd never fly on the planes because of shoddy workmanship. In 2017, senior managers filed a complaint with the ethics department, saying managers were "more concerned with cost and schedule than safety and quality".

Safety and Training Seen as Optional Extra

Boeing had known one year before the crash in 2018 that the warning signal alerting crews of a bad angle of attack vane wouldn't work for most airlines. Boeing sold its planes on a core offering, with additional equipment adding to the overall price. Many airlines that acquired the new 737 MAX 8 did not have this indicator as it was seen as an optional extra.

When there is a launch of a new plane, all pilots are required to undergo training. Boeing lobbied and argued that the 737 MAX 8 was just an upgrade and, as such, required only a minimal amount of training. In doing so, Boeing could ensure costs were kept low; in addition, airlines did not have to bear the costs of their pilots attending a formal course. The training for the 737 MAX 8 was delivered as an online course via an iPad.

Post-Crash: Blaming Others

In the 2018 crash, an internal flight in Indonesia, the two pilots wrestled with the controls. Boeing initially blamed the inexperience and lack of expertise of the two pilots. Lion Air, the airline, also had a poor safety record. For 11 years until June 2018, the airline was banned, along with other Indonesian carriers, from the European Union because of concerns about maintenance and training practices in the country.

Outcomes

The US Department of Justice levied a $2.5bn fine on Boeing based on their two test pilots' inaccurate representations to the Regulator about how the software worked. The bulk of this fine was for compensation to the victims' families. The amount of the criminal penalty of just under

$250m was what the cost would have been for the training in a simulator for the MAX pilots.

According to one study on corrupt organizations,[4] managers put pressure on employees through goal setting, rewards, and punishment. In doing so, they punished employees who did not facilitate the corruptions and rewarded those who did. Employees started to separate themselves from non-corrupt co-workers and established an 'inner-group' where secrets of corruption would be shared. Outside of that group and across the organization, a veil of secrecy reinforced a 'them versus us' culture.

Based on the research for this book, this chapter will explore how performance pressures cause strain in an organization. This strain will restrict management and employee input and dissent; obstruct successful critique of such high-risk targets; normalize risky, immoral, and/or illegal behaviour; reward behaviours that deliver these ambitions; and promote individuals who comply with these orders.

4.3 Triggers of Toxicity

The premise of this book is that two dimensions embed and deepen toxicity: (1) the Normalization of Deviance, and (2) Cognitive Dissonance. Figure 4.1 shows how performance pressures, demanding and aggressive goals, and

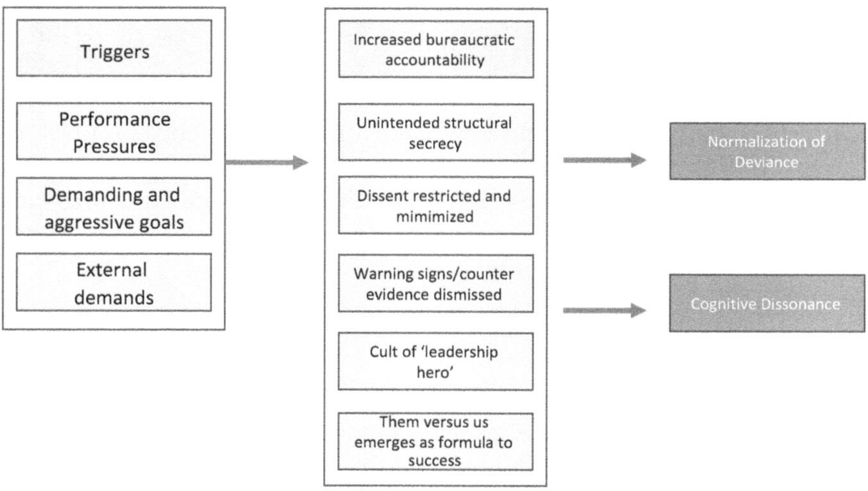

Figure 4.1 Triggers for the Normalization of Deviance and Cognitive Dissonance

external demands trigger a number of areas that lead to the Normalization of Deviance and Cognitive Dissonance over time.

Organizational toxicity exists not only when corporate norms are directly opposed to legal norms, but also when an organization: (a) condones, neutralizes, or enables rule-breaking; (b) disables and/or obstructs compliance; and (c) actual practices contrast to the expressed values.

The most important trigger that leads to toxicity is 'performance pressure'. In the examples discussed, VW, BP, and RBS were under strain from the shareholders' expectations for growth and revenue. New leaders responded to these pressures by setting highly ambitious goals. Due to their high risk and low feasibility nature, such goals brought external strain into the company's operations, ultimately trickling down to the employees. Crucially, there were instances which forced employees to make or go along with decisions that were damaging, and in the worst cases, illegal. Through the lens of culture, these responses to strain and the resultant negative outcomes came at the cultural level of structures, laid down in targets and incentives, but soon moved deeper into explicit 'shared values' and visible 'common behaviour'.

A strong norm developed in these 'toxic culture' companies that employees should not resist or disagree or raise concerns in response to higher-level commands. Many researchers and practitioners acknowledge that all organizations will have some degree of toxicity in their corporate culture.[5] As one senior executive noted:

> You have to discriminate between where a corporate culture is toxic and where there are behaviours that lead to toxicity in micro cultures. The former first, there will be an amalgam of this, it is where there are very aggressive targets/business objectives potentially infused and skirting at the very least ethical behaviour and ethical outcomes. Where those actual business objectives are tied to the line of what one might regard as really good ethical behaviour. Often where there are really directive and senior leaders, you know the German expression 'der Fisch stinkt aus dem Kopf', the fish stinks from the head. Leadership magnifies. Leaders and particularly the CEO, Exec Team, what behaviours they show, the way they are as individuals and the way they run that company or organization really helps drive and create that culture.
>
> There is that amalgam where you have particularly aggressive, particularly thoughtless, particularly challenging, particularly uncaring, particularly focused, particularly selfish individuals running companies. Fundamentally their view is that (people) are dispensable resources to achieve a business end and they put the pressure on to deliver on whatever capacity that is to deliver that amplifies through the organization. That then creates pressure, stress, division and a lack of collaborative working, and all of that creates an atmosphere where people become inhibited, frightened and intimidated and under particular stress and then that can generate toxic behaviours.[6]

Let us now explore how toxicity becomes embedded and entrenched over time.

4.4 Stages of Toxicity

So, how might toxicity become embedded? Drawing on organizational examples, there are four stages that take effect over time. The first stage typically begins with performance pressures – internal or external – often fuelled by ambitions for growth and dominance (Figure 4.2).

4.4.1 Stage 1: Performance Pressure Leading to a Bold New Vision

In the first stage of toxic culture, we see a pattern emerging. A new leader, focused on responding to the 'strain', such as a significant performance pressure, may promise the ultimate vision to the Board. Many of the organizational examples given started as underdogs with high ambitions and had new CEOs with a vision of complete dominance in the marketplace that would enable high returns for shareholders. This manifested as 'arrogance', resulting in an obsession with high performance and over-competitiveness, and an acceptance of any type of behaviour which is deemed to add value or relieve the performance pressure.

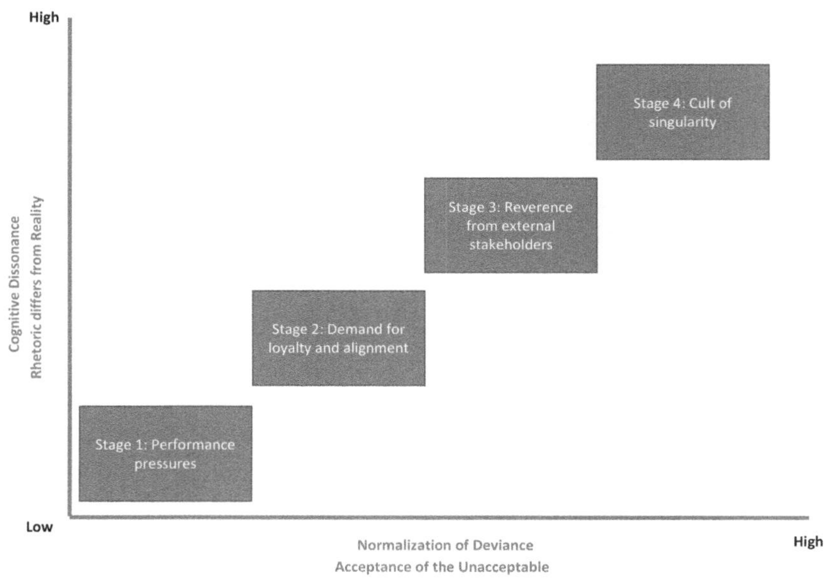

Figure 4.2 The Four Stages of Toxicity

4.4.1.1 *Performance Pressures*

Typically, the new CEO is appointed or joins the organization with a bold vision for the future. This vision is portrayed as becoming the 'biggest', 'strongest', or 'greatest'. The strain created by very aggressive targets or business objectives puts pressure on individuals to deliver. Performance management and targets can typically drive individualistic ways of working. For Goodwin at RBS, the drive for growth and market dominance was noted at a Smith Institute Seminar in 1999: "Certainly in our organization growth is key. Large numbers of our people, the vast majority of our people, are incentivized around targets of customer acquisition, growth, provision of products to customers".[7] This led to pressure within the organization to continually grow market share. In order to do this, it sought acquisitions that started with NatWest and included Angel Trains in Belgium and Citizens Bank in the USA, as well as a joint venture with Tesco to create Tesco Bank.

The RBS Group may be viewed as an example of the obsession with dominance and power. In one decade, the company went from a retail bank in Scotland to one of the biggest global banks by market capitalization. Fred Goodwin's ambition was to become a global bank, *the* global bank. It began with the desire for UK domination, which was achieved by the acquisition of NatWest Bank in 1999. The strategy was two-fold: cut costs and build new business areas. Cost-cutting was achieved by making job redundancies and streamlining back-office operations by moving them to central processing units.

At BP, to achieve profit and market share, budgets were slashed. In the early 1990s, BP was struggling as oil prices had declined, many oil reserves in the Middle East had been nationalized by local countries, and the production costs of onshore drilling had hampered profits.[8] When John Browne became CEO of BP in 1995, he saw that BP could close the gap between it and the largest petroleum giants by rigorously focusing on divesting on-shore operations with low profits, cutting costs, and doing new oil exploration for major off-shore fields (so-called 'elephants') in areas with higher risk but also higher profits.[9] The risk came as the new strategy required two opposing interventions: cutting costs and laying off a large part of the engineering expertise, while at the same time developing new oil exploration in high-risk areas that required extra engineering resources.[10] After John Browne took the helm, he started to cut costs aggressively with across-the-board cuts of 25 per cent, first in 1999 and then again in 2004. This affected not just material costs but also personnel, resulting in forced layoffs, thus shrinking BP's pool of engineering talent.[11]

Take the example of VW in 2007, the CEO Martin Winterkorn set the goal that, by 2018, VW would be the largest carmaker in the world. Volkswagen had major difficulties in the US market where it had been unable to find a successor to the counterculture successes of the Beetle and the Transporter Van in the 1960s. Further, it struggled with the image of being unreliable and requiring frequent repair, had high labour and production costs, and barely broke even financially in 1992.[12] Yet the seeds for dominance were set in 1993 when Ferdinand Piëch (the grandson of Ferdinand Porsche who had designed the original Beetle for Hitler) took over as CEO of VW; he soon declared that within a decade the German carmaker should become the largest in the world.[13] The mission to become 'Number One' could only be achieved by dominating the US market. To do so meant increasing car production from six to ten million within a decade, surpassing both General Motors and Toyota.

Another example of this obsession with dominance is Wells Fargo, a local bank operating largely in California that had been acquired by Minneapolis-based Norwest in 1998. It opted to drop its old name (Norwest) when Richard Kovacevich became CEO and adopt the name of Wells Fargo.[14] Seeking to guide the bank to the top nationally and globally by outselling competitors, Kovacevich adopted the "Go for Gr-Eight" motto. This strategic direction promoted the selling of eight products per customer – four times the average rate for banks in the industry.[15]

4.4.1.2 Toxic Behaviours by Senior Leaders Become Tolerated

During Stage 1, toxic behaviours by the CEO are increasingly tolerated. In the previous examples, a bullying leadership style was invoked at meetings with senior executives: RBS's and VW's CEOs held meetings which would regularly involve berating one executive in front of their peers. At RBS, the morning meetings were nicknamed the 'daily beatings'. At VW, the pressure to become the largest carmaker in the world invoked toxic leadership. According to Zinkin, leadership at VW was described as 'autocratic and fear-based'. Winterkorn and his predecessor, Piëch, created a culture of tight control, involving themselves in minor decisions:

> The Company's leadership set aggressive goals and senior executives involved themselves in minor decisions. Former employees described a workplace in which subordinates were afraid to admit failure or contradict superiors. Company leaders bullied employees. Piëch bragged that he forced superior performance by 'terrifying his engineers' and at times fired engineers or executives who displeased him.[16]

Within days of arriving at RBS in 1995, Fred Goodwin (Deputy CEO) alienated almost the entire management team. He was regarded as a control freak obsessed with minutiae, who delighted in tearing a strip off his colleagues. While at the Clydesdale Bank, Goodwin had launched a verbal onslaught at his associate and former best man in front of his colleagues.

One former ex-RBS colleague recalled:

> In his first few weeks, Fred's tactic was to unsettle people by being deliberately confrontational. For example, he had my personal assistant in tears. I remember having to calm her down afterwards and just thinking "What an arse". It was by no means an isolated incident. It was part of a deliberate pattern of behaviour which bordered on the psychotic. My experience of Fred at a personal level was that he was utterly charming, very good company, good fun. But he had this weird capacity to switch between business and pleasure in the blink of an eye. For example, you might have had an excellent evening with Fred and then the next morning he would be demolishing you in front of colleagues for some minor transgression without so much as a flicker.[17]

Goodwin seemed to derive pleasure from humiliating people and used this as a way of exerting authority, eliminating dissent, and suppressing rivals. One senior ex-colleague stated: "Fred was both evil and mad. He would punish, pulverize, and beat people up".[18] After a verbal battle at one of the HR leadership meetings where Goodwin had shown up, another ex-colleague recounted that "usually when you wave the white flag, the attacker stops. He just kept attacking".[19]

In the same way that the CEOs had exercised tight control at VW, one former senior executive recalled a similar approach at RBS[20]:

> Someone from the reward team sent a paper up to the executive group, it came back covered in old school red ink, including a comment in the margin saying, "Who wrote this pish?" Why was the CEO at the time of a major company bothering with this and writing that sort of bullying language?

4.4.2 Stage 1 and the Normalization of Deviance

During Stage 1, previous corporate misdemeanours become accepted. Volkswagen was first caught using defeat devices in 1973; it was fined $120,000. As far back as 1999, the company had installed a device within the software that controlled the highly polluting noise control system in its Audi engines which would switch off this system and reduce pollution when it recognized the car was being tested.[21] So when engineers frantically sought to find a solution to making the new VW diesel not only clean but also economical and practical, they had models to turn to (see Table 4.1).

4.4.3 Stage 2: Demand for Loyalty and Alignment

As discussed earlier, at VW, CEOs Piëch and later Winterkorn often fired executives they did not like, keeping only those who would agree with them and support their positions.[22] This intimidation occurred at the highest levels.

Table 4.1 The Four Stages of a Toxic Culture

Level	*Stage 1* *Performance pressures*	*Stage 2* *Demand for loyalty and alignment*	*Stage 3* *Reverence from external stakeholders*	*Stage 4* *Cult of Singularity*
Structure and Governance				
Governance and Structure	Leadership dominates decision-making as empowerment is reduced.	Leadership demands delivery of metrics to deliver high-risk returns (i.e., budget cuts).	Inner circle determines who is in and who is out.	Inner circle dominates and controls resources and decisions.
Measures of success	Focus on quantitative metrics increases in importance.	Quantitative metrics dominate.	Rewards and promotions determined by performance numbers.	Leadership rewards compliance and execution.
Values				
Perception of external world	Image begins to promote an 'us versus them' narrative, typically to become the best, biggest, to achieve 'domination' in the market or industry sector.	Image extolls 'us versus them' – the narrative depicts the organization as taking on 'battles' or reinforcing 'David and Goliath' imagery such as RBS acquiring NatWest.	Belief that the organization may need to circumvent external rules/regulations to achieve its goals. The narrative continues to criticize any organization or regulations that are perceived as 'blockers' to achieving the 'vision'.	Prevalence of Groupthink at senior levels believing that the organization is omnipotent and as such may need to break rules that impact on its overall mission.

Internal perceptions of reality	Naysayers 'tolerated' or required to collude.	Naysayers 'isolated' or required to conform.	Naysayers leave.	Deference to leader.
Behaviours				
Role of CEO	Leader criticizes the past and sets out 'new vision'. Leader berates senior leaders on previous performance or capability, resulting in (In)voluntary exits.	Leader dominates all decisions through daily meetings and continues to berate senior leaders.	Leader is coveted and applauded by external stakeholders such as business academics and media, and receives accolades from governments, industry, and academia.	The role of the CEO or leader becomes 'omnipotent' in that work is guided at all levels by what would the (CEO) think and do…
Leadership behaviours	Individual toxic behaviour tolerated at senior level.	Individual toxic behaviour promoted subject to delivery – focus on the 'what' and not the 'how'.	Individual toxic behaviour extolled as virtue, with leadership competencies (i.e., labelled as 'driven by results').	Deeply held assumptions are that there is only one way to do things and how to behave, that are engrained as way of doing things in the organization.

Other examples can be seen in relatively small and meaningless issues which are perceived as lack of loyalty. One senior RBS executive was berated for paying for a coffee with a Bank of Scotland banknote – the rival of RBS. When the individual replied that the money had come from an RBS ATM, an extreme new rule was implemented that all of RBS's ATMs in Scotland must only contain RBS printed notes. In another example, after the initial opening, all the luxury toiletries that were to be provided to delegates at the RBS Business School were destroyed for not being the right colour.

At this stage, the organization has an increasingly low tolerance for errors. How an organization responds to and deals with errors is crucial to the conduct and ethical behaviour at all levels. Organizations that promote ethical behaviour and psychological safety recognize that errors are part of normal work and foster employees to acknowledge errors and learn from them. Organizations that foster unethical behaviour deny that errors can and do occur, fail to act when they do occur, and fail to assess the cause and make necessary changes to prevent future errors. Instead, employees are blamed and punished. Cited from Ian Fraser's 2014 book on the demise of RBS, one senior HR executive recounted events at RBS:

> There was a rollout of something in HR that didn't go all that well … a very RBS phrase that was used all the time was: "Who is on the hook . . . like a fish".[23]

> Goodwin's arrival at RBS changed the corporate culture from one of being open and collegiate that promoted entrepreneurialism to one that stifled it. Goodwin's rottweiler-ish approach to managing people meant that people kept their heads down and launched initiatives without telling him for fear of being knocked back.[24]

As toxicity becomes more embedded, it appears that organizations reduce tolerance for anyone raising concerns or challenging the overall strategy. In 1999, a group of 77 BP workers at the Alaskan operations – where later a major oil spill would occur – wrote a letter to BP CEO John Browne trying to dissuade him from implementing intended cuts as they feared this would further undermine the already appalling safety conditions. The letter points out the difficulty in communicating critical information upwards,

> Anything we say either stays at this level or gets filtered on the way up to a version of 'yes can do, sir' . . . Our feedback is ignored because it doesn't support the preordained agenda … Your frontline management will continue to cut as long as you direct and sanction it, right up to the precipice of disaster.

John Browne did not reply and one month later announced another $4bn budget cut.[25]

Five years later in 2004, the new Plant Manager at the BP Texas City Refinery conducted a detailed report on the operations and sent his report to Head Office. His report shared the appalling safety record at the plant where over three decades 23 workers had died – one of the worst records in the industry. The new manager used the report to ask for a budget increase to upgrade the safety at the plant. The Head Office denied his request and asked him to focus on the 25 per cent budget cuts required for that year – despite the fact that the refinery was making $100m per month for BP.[26] Employees were impotent in their ability to raise concerns. This norm cemented the view among employees that even if they did raise concerns, they would be ignored or silenced; it created a norm in these organizations that it was detrimental to their careers and livelihoods to raise concerns with management and leadership. A strong norm developed in all these companies not to resist or disagree with higher-level targets and commands.

Wells Fargo was found to have fraudulently opened 3.5 million accounts without customer authorization between 2009 and 2016. Independent investigations suggested that these fraudulent practices had been occurring for about 15 years, but had been dealt with internally as individual misdemeanours, resulting in the individual being fired. However, these sales practices resulted from corporate incentives that pushed employees to achieve unrealistic targets and sell as many products as possible. This was described by the Independent Directors of the Board of Wells Fargo investigation report in 2017:

> The root cause of sales practice failures was the distortion of the Community Bank's sales culture and performance management system, which when combined with aggressive sales management, created pressure on employees to sell unwanted or unneeded products to customers and, in some cases, to open unauthorized accounts.[27]

Employees would be under constant scrutiny with daily and monthly 'motivator' reports tracking their sales volumes.[28] If they failed to meet targets, employees would undergo 'coaching sessions'. These coaching sessions were, in reality, a 'dressing down' with the threat of firing. One employee explained later to National Public Radio (NPR) journalists that these sessions were not there to support the workers but just to pressure them to sell more.[29] During special sales campaigns, such as the "Jump into January" campaign, employees were instructed to reach even higher targets than usual, sometimes even up to 20 per customer. In one local branch office, employees were forced to 'run the gauntlet' by running past costumed district managers to write their sales numbers on a whiteboard.[30] It became increasingly clear that employees had started resorting to creating unauthorized or fake accounts in response to these extreme pressures, communicated in the format of 'games', to boost their sales targets and achieve the overall goals set in the company. Yet, for a long time, no change was made to the targets themselves or the pressures through which they were implemented. As one report found, Wells Fargo "was hesitant to end the program because (Carrie) Tolstedt (the head of community banking at the time) was 'scared to death' that it could hurt sales figures for the entire year".[31]

At RBS, the performance management system generated a sales-orientated culture in the branches, emphasizing the prioritization of sales over anything else. The system ranked employees using a bell-shaped curve, with the vast majority of employees ranked as 3 or 3+. The ratings determined the bonus pot at the end of each year as well as the potential for promotion. This bell-shaped curve caused stress, as it had to be manipulated to ensure that the ratings of a team fitted into the curve. There was a relentless focus on market share and numbers at RBS. The Human Capital Toolkit introduced in 2005 collated data on individual employees and brought together the data from the engagement surveys with customer service and financial performance. It was able to compare high-performing retail branches against low-performing ones. The increased focus on measurement meant that data and numbers dominated the culture and created competitiveness between branches.

In a similar way at BP, cost-cutting and profits were rewarded. Safety was not. CEO John Browne was described as giving "the impression that he was transforming BP, but his management skills were very traditional – chop, chop, chop".[32] The rotation of managers also had an impact on safety; managers might be in their supervisory role for six or ten months before moving on to another job. Their bonus payments were tied to meeting specific goals, typically cutting costs. One observer said: "There was always this attitude that the manager would come in and cut, cut, cut, then get out and leave the consequences to their successors".[33]

At BP, there was a growing dissonance between the rhetoric and reality. BP continued to claim that it cared about safety – especially at times following major incidents. There was a growing emphasis on individual and personal safety rather than operational safety; this placed responsibility on the individual rather than on the operations and the company. Yet with substantial budget cuts, operational safety was at risk. In 2000, for instance, BP's Grangemouth refinery in Scotland had three separate accidents all in one week. As a result, BP received a criminal fine of £750,000. The investigation found that BP's goal of cost reductions had created the safety hazards, and that its fractured management structure had undermined a safety prevention strategy.[34] BP's response was to state that it had got the message and that it had "shared the lessons it learned with its 11 other refineries in the world".[35] However, in fact, BP did not change its practices of cost-cutting, ignored safety concerns, and deflected blame even onto those who themselves had been hurt in accidents BP had caused. With each new incident, BP claimed improvement and change, yet real change did not happen. Instead, BP's internal communications on safety focused on minor, low-cost matters. As one former exploration engineer recalls, the company and its executives

> focused so heavily on the easy part of safety, holding the handrails, spending hours discussing the merits of reverse parking and the dangers of not having a lid on a coffee cup, but were less enthusiastic about the hard stuff, investing in and maintaining their complex facilities.[36]

Yet BP officials continued to talk about BP's outstanding safety record; in reality, they were looking at individual injury statistics. Safety was viewed as an overhead. The rhetoric and communications said that safety was important to the organization, but this did not translate to reality.

Around this narrative, BP was changing within, with greater focus on sustainability and climate change. In BP's Annual Report 2004, Browne states:

> To deliver sustainable performance, we require a combination of factors. Our investments must be for the long term. We have to attract and retain the best people. We must work with others towards a sustainable environment. And we must build trust through relationships based on 'mutual advantage' – relationships that bring benefits to everyone concerned. Along with standards such as those set out in our new code of conduct, the consideration of mutual advantage keeps our ambition within legitimate bounds and marks out the path we take towards creating value. To achieve our purpose, we follow a strategy that is itself founded on the principles of sustainability.[37]

Yet the disconnect between cost-cutting and sustainability was visible and evident. The cognitive dissonance of engaging shareholders and employees with the green agenda and rebranding BP as *Beyond Petroleum* enabled the organization to communicate laudable goals. Safety was not specifically mentioned in BP's group values at this time, rather a vague statement on "no accidents, no harm to people, and no harm to the environment". BP's brand values were being performance driven, innovative, progressive, and green. An investigative panel in 2005 studied not just Texas City, but also all five of BP's US refineries. It found a disturbing pattern. Inspections were long overdue, and near-catastrophes were never investigated; known issues such as pipes thinning were left in disrepair for more than a decade; and tests of alarms and other emergency shutdown systems were either not completed or not completed properly. The Panel concluded that the 'entrepreneurial culture' that Browne had implemented was at the core of the problem. Managers were not sufficiently accountable for process safety. Safety was mentioned in BPs code of conduct, but the panel concluded that this message was diluted. The panel found that Browne was generally noted for his leadership in various areas, including reducing carbon dioxide emissions and developing the use of alternative fuels, but the panel believed that if Browne had demonstrated comparable leadership and commitment to safety, the result would have been a high level of process safety performance in BP's US refineries.[38]

Demands for unquestionable loyalty and alignment can also be seen at VW. It had a highly centralized structure with strong power vested in the CEO at the top. There was a centralized authority in decision-making that forced decisions to go up the chain of command. As one former management trainee described it: "VW was like North Korea without the labour camps. You have to obey everyone".[39] VW's CEOs played a central and direct role in day-to-day decisions, first with Piëch and then his successor Winterkorn, micromanaging engineering decisions all the way down to the interior colour of cars promoted at auto shows. VW's highly centralized hierarchy meant lower-level employees had trouble getting their information heard at higher levels. Thus, at VW, it was hard for lower-level employees to correct faulty central-level decision-making and targets. Unquestionable loyalty became entrenched as both Piech and Winterkorn became known for firing executives who disagreed with them and did not support their agenda.[40]

In comparison to VW's centralized authority, BP's decentralized structure also did not allow for information flow. At BP, CEO Browne's management structure was driven by shareholder returns as it regarded engineering and design work as overheads rather than as key components of the business. Browne built a management structure that reinforced this view and replaced experienced managers, who might have challenged his view, with a group of young executives. This group of young executives were known as 'the turtles' after the *Teenage Mutant Ninja Turtles* cartoon characters; they were on the leadership fast track with a promise that they would succeed Browne as CEO. The turtles were shifted around frequently, often staying in a division for only a year or two. This constant shuffling ensured that they were not able to accumulate power in any one division and potentially challenge Browne. However, this shuffling reduced accountability and ensured that there remained an internal competition between the 'turtles' to succeed Browne. This lack of accountability was noted by contractors hired by BP, who often found it difficult to determine who was ultimately in charge of a project.

The top-down demands for cost-cutting "created a stifling environment of intimidation".[41] Browne set up business units to run as separate companies within BP, and each had its own profit-and-loss reports. The idea was that this would create a more entrepreneurial culture where each unit could act autonomously. As Steffy discussed, after the Amoco and Arco mergers in 1999, the number of business units exceeded more than 300 and the structure became unwieldy.[42] Structural secrecy was reinforced because each unit leader was more concerned about meeting their own targets rather than being concerned about the bigger picture.

At RBS in 2001, there was growing concern from senior leaders about an emerging culture of fear. After the NatWest acquisition, there was an executive conference where the executives were asked to identify the biggest problems facing the bank. According to observers, there was near unanimity that the biggest problem was a culture of fear. One group said that it was not possible to be open and honest at RBS as there was a lot of paranoia. When Goodwin took the stage to hear the results, he commented,

> We should lock the doors because the people who make the decisions in this bank are all in this room. That is you, not me. So, what are you going to do about it ... don't tell me, you're frightened of little old me?[43]

4.4.4 Stage 3: Reverence from External Stakeholders

At this stage, the image of the organization becomes a subject of interest for business schools and academics who are keen to find out the 'secret' of the organization's success. Due to our excessive focus on leadership, the deductive logic is that the success must be due to the leader or leadership. Reverence can be seen in the articles published by business schools and in business journals.

John Stumpf, the then CEO of Wells Fargo, appeared majestically on the cover of Forbes magazine in 2012 with an article titled "The Bank That Works". The article applauded the 'cross selling' results of Wells Fargo and said, "Well Fargo which averages 5.9 products per customer in its retail banking business, does it better than anyone".[44] Eight years later, Stumpf was fined $17.5m for the improper sales practices and fake accounts and received a lifetime ban from the banking industry.

In 1999, after cutting costs and taking over several competitors, BP quadrupled in value and finally caught up with the top oil companies. Its stocks soared and its CEO, Browne, was dubbed "Sun King" in British newspapers. Yet the overall targets of cost reduction played a crucial role in BP safety issues, as the Chemical Safety and Hazard Investigation Board (CSB) concluded in its 341-page report in response to the Texas explosion that killed 15.[45] As a supervisor told lower-level managers who had questioned the 2004 budget cuts and their implications for ensuring operations: "Which bit of 25 per cent do you not understand?"[46] Another manager explained how this forced them towards risky and illegal practices:

> The focus on controlling costs was acute at BP, to the point it became a distraction. They just go after it with a ferocity that's mind-numbing and terrifying. No one's ever asked to cut corners or take a risk, but often it ends up like that.[47]

As discussed in previous chapters, RBS was the subject of two prestigious business school articles from Harvard Business School and London Business School titled "The Masters of Integration"[48] and "The Strategy of Not Having a Strategy".[49] Howard Davies, currently the Chairman of RBS Group and former Chairman of the Financial Conduct Authority, noted in a speech in 2018 that academics were persuaded that RBS had found a "secret sauce recipe".[50] In *The Masters of Integration*, a leading academic proclaimed that "RBS has undoubtedly developed a word-class acquisition integration capability . . . and had also demonstrated an ability to flawlessly execute exceedingly technical and change programs in very short periods of time".[51] Soon after, London Business School wrote a positive account of RBS which lauded the NatWest integration, noting that "All of NatWest's systems, for example, were moved onto RBS's platform". Yet as Chairman Davies noted, RBS and NatWest were still on different systems in 2018, so he found this a "surprising conclusion".[52]

According to critics and insiders, RBS's acquisition of NatWest for £21bn in 1999 was a 'botched job'. The banks ran on different operating systems and the technology side was not well integrated. According to one author,[53] it was not possible to pay an RBS cheque into the NatWest branches, illustrating the fragmented architecture of the two financial systems. RBS noted that the success of the deal was based on the share price comparison – it used 800p as the starting share price, when the price should have been 2100p – the value of the shares before the Bank announced its intention to bid for NatWest. As one former executive remarked: "Having been sucked into a bidding war with Bank of Scotland, Goodwin overpaid for his prey. This meant that irrespective of the success of the integration, the numbers were never going to work".[54]

Yet the adoration from industry experts and academics reinforced the norm that RBS had found the 'secret sauce recipe' for success. Prior to ABN Amro, RBS had made a number of acquisitions such as First Active in Ireland and Citizens Bank in the USA. Jonny Cameron, the director of Corporate Banking, was quoted in the FSA report as saying:

> One of the things that went wrong for RBS was that . . . we bought NatWest as a hostile acquisition. We did no due diligence. We couldn't because it was hostile. After we bought NatWest, we had lots of surprises, but almost all of them were pleasant. And I think that lulled us into a sense of complacency around that. The fact is that the acquisition was also hostile. We got bits and pieces of information but fundamentally it was hostile.[55]

Despite many commentators expressing concerns regarding the ABN Amro acquisition, the organization was determined to follow through. When the LaSalle portion of the business was acquired by Barclays, staff thought that this was the opportunity to step away from the deal. However, Goodwin was determined to win. ABN Amro covered 53 countries and the consortium was designed to split the business in three ways. Yet RBS's success was due to its business in the UK. While it operated in 30 countries, the engagement survey clearly showed high levels of disengagement from staff outside the UK.

It was also apparent that RBS did not have an operating platform for this complex acquisition. In countries such as Germany, the respective businesses of retail, insurance, and corporate would all operate individually. As such, there was no common operating framework, with each business offering differing employment policies. The acquisition of an international bank that was spread thinly in 53 countries was regarded as highly ambitious, and there was little in the way of planning for the integration of ABN Amro once it had been acquired. The sheer complexity of the ABN acquisition was downplayed by RBS executives. The mantra of RBS directors was that there was nothing to fear as they were experts at large-scale bank integration and would be able to reduce the cost-to-income ratio at ABN's investment banking business.

The norm that had been established was that RBS could buck the market trends and ignore the negative commentators, as its history of acquisitions had been deemed 'successful' by external stakeholders. As such a norm emerged where naysayers were perceived as 'negative' within the organization. One Human Resources Manager said:

> I will never forget the positive feeling running right through RBS. You could almost touch it. We all had implicit faith in the executives and Fred Goodwin in particular. Despite adverse commentary in the press, we utterly believed that Sir Fred would land the deal of the decade and create a global platform for RBS to continue its unbelievable expansions in size, income, and reputation.[56]

According to one commentator, RBS had a preponderance of Scottish nationals on its Board and this lack of diversity served as an impediment to good corporate governance. As such the Board was:

> Dominated by Scots and almost a patriotic pride in the Royal Bank of Scotland and this national pride. It meant that the Scottish directors were not disposed to challenge the management because they shared this national pride. It got in the way of good governance. The board was too big, and it was not diverse enough and this Scottish thing went to the selection of senior executives.[57]

4.4.5 Stage 4: Cult of Singularity

At this stage, the organization is dominated by a singular mantra, typically with an unhealthy reliance on a single leader. There is a fear of 'getting it wrong'. At RBS, employees would try to second guess Fred's reaction to any issue: "What would Fred think?" or use the phrase "Fred says" to bulldoze any objections to a particular initiative. The 'untouchable leader' can do no wrong.

One former senior executive[58] has recounted an incident when he had been called to a meeting with Goodwin at the London office shortly after the bid for ABN Amro had been announced, and it aptly highlights the nature of such power when vested in one person and the impact this can have on the atmosphere and culture:

> (We were) in his upstairs deluxe executive suite and we were all gathered around, and someone had the temerity to ask a question about whether … I think the markets were just changing a little bit … whether the material change (contract) clause should be invoked. And I remembered there was almost this hush, Christ, someone is challenging, and Goodwin basically just shot him down. I paraphrase, it was like 'shut up, what do you know, you idiot'.
>
> Now would I have asked a question like that? Not on your nelly in an open format, because it killed the whole atmosphere. Where I think we ended up with RBS, whilst it was a toxic culture it didn't mean it was always unpleasant, although there was unpleasantness in it. But it was toxic because there was an immensely powerful leader who had become inviolable in terms of his position, who in my view absolutely believed his own hype and became grandiose in his visions for RBS. But then of course because it had a track record for share price growth and dividends, he was feted by the city, so nobody was criticizing him or pointing out, 'hang on a minute, are you sure', challenging him, as everyone was frightened of him because frankly if you argued against him, you wouldn't last long at RBS.

'Groupthink' becomes more prevalent at senior levels, with specialist advice ignored. Cited from an account of the meeting the night before the fateful crash of the Challenger space shuttle, specialist engineers were told: "'Take off your engineering hat and put on your management hat' to the Engineering Manager". Similarly at BP, employees were not able to voice their concerns about safety as they feared they would be punished or because their concerns would be simply ignored.[59]

At Wells Fargo, the high strain of the job resulted in massive staff turnover, reaching up to 41 per cent in one year.[60] This left the bank with highly inexperienced employees, less likely to feel secure enough to successfully raise concerns over the targets they had to meet. As discussed previously, daily intimidation practices were used to cajole and publicly shame employees to keep them focused on their targets and the overall growth of the bank. Employees at all levels worked under the pressure of constant, sometimes hourly, ranking of their sales rates in comparison with peers; when found to be lagging, they risked demotion or dismissal. As one employee recalled: "We were constantly told we would end up working for McDonald's if we did not make the sales quotas . . . We had to stay for what felt like after-school detention, or report to a call session on Saturdays".[61] This clearly did not produce an atmosphere conducive to voicing critical opinions.

Similarly at Wells Fargo, the head of community banking Carrie Tolstedt was found by an internal board review to be "insular and defensive and did not like to be challenged or hear negative information. Even senior leaders within the Community Bank were frequently afraid of or discouraged from airing contrary views".[62]

On 20 April 2010, an explosion and fire at the Deepwater Horizon drilling rig resulted in a massive crude oil leak in the Gulf of Mexico. On that day, BP, the British petroleum company that operated the rig, became responsible for the largest oil spill in US history.[63] In addition to causing tremendous economic and ecological turmoil, and negative health effects around the Gulf's coast, 11 employees died. This was not the first time BP operations had caused a major disaster in the US. On 23 March 2005, an explosion at a BP refinery in Texas City killed 15 people and injured 170 more. And in March 2006, BP caused the largest spill on Alaska's North Slope, leaking 267,000 gallons of crude oil onto the freezing tundra. That particular spill went undetected for five days.[64]

In all three disasters, the accidents occurred because BP had failed to perform sufficient maintenance, alongside constantly cutting costs, reducing its engineering capacity, and not responding to employee complaints about safety hazards. These incidents demonstrate that, well before the massive Deepwater Horizon spill in 2010, BP had continuously suffered from safety issues and had repeatedly received information about hazards. Yet incident after incident, complaint after complaint, report after report, and promise after promise, BP continued to seek ways to cut costs instead of prioritizing safety and compliance. The issues at BP were not just the product of individual decisions, but rather of broader patterns within the company. As such, these problems were endemic to the culture at BP. Indeed, William Reilly, the co-chair of the Presidential Investigation Commission on the Gulf of Mexico oil disaster, concluded that BP had been operating under a 'culture of complacency'.

Wells Fargo was found guilty of opening false accounts in 2015. John G. Stumpf, former chairman and CEO of Wells Fargo, can no longer work in the financial services industry as a result. His vision of 'Going for G-Eight' was for bank employees to sell eight products to a single customer even though the industry norm was just under two products per customer. Elizabeth Warren noted in the US Senate Banking Committee investigation in 2016,

> Okay, so you haven't resigned, you haven't returned a single nickel of your personal earnings, you haven't fired a single senior executive . . . Instead, evidently, your definition of 'accountable' is to push the blame to your low-level employees who don't have the money for a fancy P.R. firm to defend themselves.

Warren estimated that Stumpf's stock holdings had increased by $200m in value during the time that "this scam", as Warren put it, occurred, in which 5,300 employees opened unauthorized customer bank accounts in order to meet sales targets. "You should resign", she finally said. "You should be criminally investigated by both the Department of Justice and the Securities and Exchange Commission".[65]

As previously noted, in 2014, American researchers started to suspect that German carmaker Volkswagen (VW) was using a device that would lower its vehicles' emissions specifically during laboratory testing.[66] Investigations uncovered that VW had actually installed this cheat device in over 11 million vehicles. After a West Virginia University research report first discovered the discrepancy between laboratory and real driving emissions, and California regulators later confirmed this, VW stalled the investigations for more than a year, questioned the investigative methods, and even modified the cheat device to make it even more effective. Under pressure from the California Air Resource Board (CARB), which threatened to block VW from selling cars in California in 2016, the company admitted its cheating. The corporate wrongdoing in the VW case was not just the work of a single – or even a few – 'bad apples'. Rather, it appears to have been embedded within the company for quite some time. As Eric Schneiderman, the Attorney General of New York at the time, concluded,

> Hundreds of very high-level executives and engineers knew about this. We did not find one email saying that maybe we should not be doing this, or this is against the law or put the brakes on this system. So, this was a corporate culture permeated by fraud.

In BP, an independent US report[67] found that Browne's mandate to cut budgets by 25 per cent across the board in 1999 and again in 2004 had directly contributed to the Texas City accident, and the cuts were made even as BP's own internal surveys were revealing increasing safety concerns at the refinery. In addition, BP had cut its annual training budget by half and reduced its training staff from 28 to 8, switching to computer-based training to minimize costs. Carolyn Merritt, Head of CSB said: "Something was very wrong, not just at Texas City but in the corporation itself. It goes back to the culture of the corporation that was driving for maximum profits over everything else".[68]

At this stage, a cult of singularity dominates. Even when employees follow the mantra set by the leaders, they can find themselves blamed for their actions when evidence of fraudulent practices is revealed.

After the revelation of over a decade of fraudulent practices, Wells Fargo's response was to blame employees and the unrealistic sales targets that stimulated such practices. Wells Fargo blamed and fired more than 5,300 employees as so-called 'bad apples' in 2016 soon after the scandal of fraudulent practices came to light, even though there was evidence that this was not about the actions of individual employees. Wells Fargo eventually admitted that the root cause was organizational and not an individual issue. Corporate incentives had pushed employees to continually increase sales and sell customers as many products as possible. The daily sales targets were set up in a way, that if an employee missed selling their target on one day, the remaining target would be added onto the next day's target. Wells Fargo admitted in the investigation by the Independent Directors from the Wells Fargo Board (2017):

> The root cause of sales practice failures was the distortion of the Community Bank's sales culture and performance management system, which when combined with aggressive sales management, created pressure on employees to sell unwanted or unneeded products to customers and, in some cases, to open unauthorized accounts.[69]

Volkswagen ended up suspending several dozens of its mid-level engineers and executives, including the head of quality control and a member of the Audi management board.[70] Yet VW did not seriously explore the possibility the scandal involved a larger plot involving the highest-level executives. Volkswagen employees ended up paying the brunt of the costs as in November 2016 the company announced it would cut 14,000 jobs.[71]

BP's first response to major incidents was to deflect blame. One tactic was to blame individual workers – even those who had been directly hurt in the accidents. These were the same workers who had been concerned about safety operations, as years of budget cuts had led to hazardous working conditions. One employee who was hurt in the deadly Texas City refinery incident was interviewed: "Yes, I have been hurt and had management punish me and made a fool out of me".[72] In 2005, the investigation into the Texas City refinery disaster concluded that it was the result of delayed maintenance, poor safety protocols, and deferred upgrades. As a result, BP now led the USA in accounting for more than a quarter of all deaths industrywide, more than ten times the number at Exxon Mobil. BP, however, sought to blame employees for the incident. And again, for the subsequent disaster at Deepwater Horizon in 2010, contractors and employees were blamed for the event.

Within this stage of the 'cult of singularity', toxicity deepens within an organization, and we see a constant theme of stonewalling, deceit, and denial, shifting blame downwards in the company.[73]

After the 2005 explosion at the Texas refinery facility, BP followed a strategy of stonewalling and blame shifting. Firstly, it put the refinery on lockdown for eight days, not letting anybody in, claiming that it was too hazardous. Then two months later, it issued its internal investigation report and placed blame squarely on the low-level employees who were alleged to have overfilled and overheated the raffinate splitter. That ensured that blame was placed on a few inefficient or casual workers and not on the strategy of cost-cutting.[74] Steffy summarized BP's response: "Human error or workers not following rules meant that BP itself wasn't to blame". Ironically enough, a BP executive had chaired the development of safety guidelines by the Centre for Chemical Process Safety that concluded that "errant employees aren't the root cause of an accident but rather its symptom". Five years later, following the Deepwater Horizon spill, BP also sought to deflect blame. Its first tactic was to try to shield itself behind Transocean who owned the Deepwater Horizon rig, and nine of the eleven people who died in the blowout were its employees. BP issued press statements saying it 'offered its full support' to the drilling contractor. However, as the majority lease owner, BP was responsible for any pollution.

In one of the early statements, BP CEO Hayward stated: "We are responsible, not for the accident, but we are responsible for the oil". He said this despite Transocean's reliance on BP for most of its business and BP's major influence over day-to-day operational decisions – decisions that enhanced risks and neglected industry standards all to expedite the drilling and save costs.[75] At first, BP tried to use its decentralized structure with sub-contractors to deflect blame. It had done so earlier; in the 1990s for instance, BP had blamed a subcontractor, Doyon, when it was found that BP Alaska had been illegally injecting its toxic waste into the ground, even though BP was again directly in charge and Doyon relied on BP for 80 per cent of its income.[76]

BP leadership tried to downplay their role. This was most apparent in CEO Hayward's testimony during the US congressional hearings. He kept on deflecting critical questions about how BP had managed risk. Hayward instead focused on how much money the company had spent on safety.[77] Whenever he was pressed about problems, Hayward would insist that the investigation was ongoing and no firm conclusions could be made yet about the role BP had played in all this. When Hayward was asked about BP's decisions regarding particular aspects of the operation that had caused the risk, he would explain that he was not involved in the decision making. When pressed on details, he would claim ignorance. The more the panel asked, the more Hayward's responses underscored the lack of accountability in BP's management structure. He dismissed responsibility by saying he was not a cement or a drilling engineer.

BP did not stop there. It even tried to downplay the damage of the oil spill in the Gulf of Mexico. At first, BP had stated that oil was leaking at 1,000 barrels a day, a relatively modest spill. That would indicate the spill would only reach Exxon Valdez levels after one year. A little later, BP raised that figure from 1,000 to 5,000 barrels a day.[78] In fact, oceanographers from Florida had used satellite imaging data and found that the size of the leak was much larger at 30,000 barrels a day, meaning the leak could surpass the Valdez spill in only two weeks. The CEO Hayward dismissed these findings, saying that their own information was the most accurate: "A guestimate is a guestimate and the guestimate remains at 5000 barrels a day".[79] When BP was forced to release its live video feed from the wellhead or face a congressional subpoena, experts found that the leak was even larger – about 60,000–70,000 barrels per day.[80] Hayward later even went as far as to deny that such a massive spill would cause much damage. In an interview with The Guardian, he stated: "The Gulf of Mexico is a very big ocean . . . the amount of oil and dispersant we are putting into [it] is tiny in relation to the total water volume".[81]

Volkswagen also tried to downplay that it had broken the law; VW CEO Müller tried to deflect the assertion. In an interview, he stated: "It was a technical problem . . . an ethical problem? I cannot understand why you [the reporter] say that". As he explained, they did not have "the right interpretation of the American law . . . We didn't lie. We didn't understand the question first. And then we worked since 2014 to solve the problem".[82] Meanwhile in Europe, Volkswagen also took a directly confrontational legal approach, claiming that what had happened was not against the law. A Volkswagen representative who was called on to share the company's response to the scandal to the UK House of Commons Transport Select Committee described the software as a "drive trace" and said that it "was not defined as a defeat device in Europe". When committee members pressed that this was incorrect, the company's representative simply replied that "in the understanding of the Volkswagen Group it is not a defeat device" (Image 4.1).[83]

In its final attempts, Volkswagen tried to deny that it had damaged public health and refuted that NOx was harmful. In 2016, VW said: "A reliable determination of morbidity or even fatalities for certain demographic groups based on our level of knowledge is not possible from a scientific point of view".[84] In 2018, a German newspaper reported that Volkswagen had tried to back up these claims by exposing monkeys for hours to exhaust from the 'clean diesel'

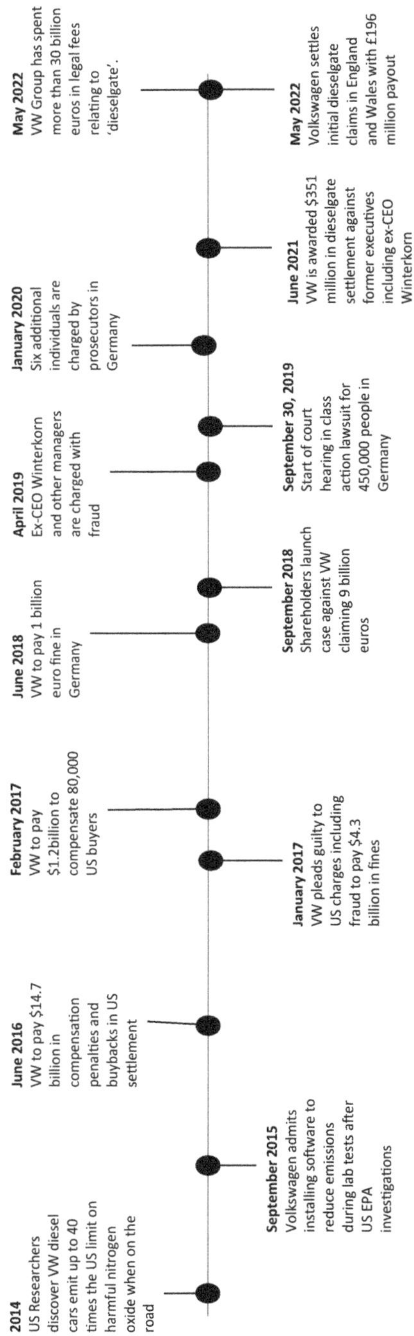

Image 4.1 The "dieselgate" Timeline

engine of a 2016 Beetle and comparing them with monkeys exposed to the fumes from a 1997 heavy-duty gasoline Ford F250 pick-up truck. Volkswagen had kept the study quiet, not in the least because the results had shown that the old Ford was less damaging to the monkeys than the state-of-the-art Beetle. Several studies have now proven that the harmful health effects are real. One of the most recent studies by MIT scientists, published in Environmental Research Letters, estimates that the extra NOx emissions emitted because of VW's cheating will cost 1200 premature deaths in Europe, each dying a decade early.[85] A Netflix documentary called *Dirty Money* was made in 2019 revealing the extent of the deception.

VW's supervisory board did not take any disciplinary action against the company's top-level executives who served on the management board.[86] And the carmaker still paid out $33.9m in top executive bonuses, even when it reported a record $1.6bn loss. This meant that even Winterkorn, who had been CEO during most of the saga, received a total compensation package of $8m in 2015, and that was for ten months only, as he had retired in October.[87] However, public outcry changed that; the company subsequently sued the former senior executives for false testimony and breach of duty of care in 2021.

Vignette 4.2: VW CEO Fined for False Testimony and Breach of Duty of Care

In 2021, Volkswagen agreed to settle claims against four former executives, including long-time CEO Martin Winterkorn, that will see the carmaker receive 288m euros ($351m) in compensation related to its emissions scandal.

Berlin prosecutors had previously charged former CEO Winterkorn with giving false testimony to the German parliament when he said he was unaware of the carmaker rigging diesel engine tests before it became public.

This settlement marks a major milestone in Volkswagen's efforts to turn a page on its biggest ever corporate scandal, which cost more than 32bn euros in vehicle refits, fines, and legal costs.

The scandal was initially blamed on a small number of rogue engineers.

Volkswagen and top shareholder Porsche SE are still subject to 4.1bn euros worth of shareholder claims in relation to the scandal, but it could take years before any agreement is reached.

Winterkorn stepped down as VW CEO in September 2015, a week after the scandal – in which the group admitted using illegal software to rig US diesel engine tests – broke.

A spokesman for Winterkorn, who served as Volkswagen CEO for nearly nine years, declined to comment on the charges brought against him by Berlin prosecutors.

Volkswagen concluded that Winterkorn had breached his duty of care by failing to fully and swiftly clarify circumstances behind the use of unlawful software functions in some diesel engines sold in North America between 2009 and 2015.[88]

At BP, the collusion of the Board – which should be an independent voice and a critical friend – was readily apparent. In the 2003 BP Annual Report, the Chairman stated:

> Innovative transactions in newer markets – and the development of our existing operations – present significant challenges for John Browne and his executive colleagues. Individually and collectively, they are an excellent team and enjoy our full confidence and support.

In 2004:

> During the year, the executive management team, so ably led by John Browne, has sustained its formidable track record. They have our full confidence and support. I would like to thank John and his team for their exemplary efforts on your behalf in 2004.

In 2005, after the Texas City Refinery explosion:

> The group suffered the explosion at the Texas City refinery in the US … 2005 was therefore, a year of contrasts, which has been testing for your board and immensely challenging for our executive management team, led by John Browne. BP's ability to meet these challenges . . . depends on the exemplary leadership provided by John Browne and the tremendously able team he heads. Their determination, experience and creativity are needed to rise to the challenges our business faces.

Culminating in 2006 with:

> John Browne is one of the great businessmen of his generation and has led the transformation of BP into one of the biggest energy groups in the world. His performance over the past 12 years has been extraordinary. He has consistently been identified by his fellow chief executives as the most impressive businessman in Britain.

At RBS as well, the Board allowed the CEO Fred Goodwin to spend £18m on a private jet, £350m on the new Head Office at Gogarburn, as well as having fresh fruit delivered daily from Paris and a permanent suite at the Savoy hotel. He also conducted an extra-marital affair with a colleague and failed to report this conflict of interest to the Board or to the Chairman.

4.5 Summary

We have defined toxic cultures as a set of **tolerated** behaviours and actions that are reinforced through the rules, policies, and actions of the leaders as a way to influence, manipulate, and manage others that appear to redefine, contradict, or oppose the stated values of the organization.

Toxicity happens over time as norms become entrenched. The organizations reviewed each held a belief of being better than any other organization, reinforcing the 'them versus us' norm, coupled with a readiness to blame others, which meant that they could not simply reverse their corporate cultures overnight. These norms become so strong that they can resist a new leader. At BP, when Hayward took over as CEO, he promised a new BP that would make safety a priority. He also promised a less complex organization with more transparency and accountability. Hayward sought to convince the Board that safety should become the priority, but many saw it as an American problem. Hayward sought to hire 1,000 engineers and improve safety despite all of BP's cost-cutting. Yet under his tenure, BP did not change its core safety problems. Hayward quickly succumbed to cutting £4bn in 2009 after a year of falling oil prices. The Deepwater Horizon spill one year later is considered to be the largest marine oil spill in history, resulting in the deaths of 11 workers, as well as an enormous environmental impact. In November 2012, BP and the United States Department of Justice settled federal criminal charges, with BP pleading guilty to 11 counts of manslaughter, two misdemeanours, and a felony count of lying to Congress. BP also agreed to four years of government monitoring of its safety practices and ethics, and the Environmental Protection Agency announced that BP would be temporarily banned from new contracts with the US Government. BP and the Department of Justice agreed to a record-setting $4.525bn in fines and other payments. In September 2014, a US District Court judge ruled that BP was primarily responsible for the oil spill because of its gross negligence and reckless conduct. In April 2016, BP agreed to pay $20.8bn in fines, the largest corporate settlement in US history. By 2018, the clean-up costs, charges, and penalties had cost the company more than $65bn.[89]

Similarly, after the global financial crisis in 2008, Fred Goodwin and others blamed the media or the US markets or the Regulators. This norm of blame shifting had become entrenched in these organizations.

The four stages illustrate how across the three levels of corporate culture toxicity becomes embedded and entrenched in organizations. From the visible processes and structures such as governance and decision-making on resources and budgets, as well as performance targets and management processes, to the deeply held assumptions and values that become embedded within the organization, they all determine 'behaviour, perception, thought, and feeling'.[90]

Part 1 has explored the concept of toxic cultures at a macro level. In Part II, we will explore the toxic triangle introduced in Chapter 1. Part II begins by exploring the role of leadership and the impact of personality disorders which become manifest under pressure, before examining the role of so-called susceptible followers and conducive environments.

Notes

1 Senior Executive interviewed for this book on 4 November 2021.
2 Robson, P. (2021) *Flying Blind*. London: Penguin Random House UK.
3 *Ibid.*
4 Campbell & Göritz (2014) Culture Corrupts! A qualitative study of organizational culture in corrupt organizations. *Journal of Business Ethics*, 120(3): 291–311.
5 van Rooij, B., & Fine, A. (2018). Toxic corporate culture: Assessing organizational processes of deviancy. *Administrative Sciences*, 8(23): 1–38. p. 4.
6 Senior Executive, Interviewed for this book by zoom in October 2021.
7 Fred Goodwin, Lecture to the Smith Institute Seminar (Wednesday 20 October 1999). 11 Downing Street, London.
8

- Lustgarden, A. (2012) *Run to Failure: BP and the Making of the Deepwater Horizon Disaster*: W.W. Norton & Co.
- Steffy, L. (2010) *Drowning in Oil: BP & the Reckless Pursuit of Profit*. New York: McGraw-Hill Companies.

9 Lustgarden (2012).
10 Steffy (2010).
11 *Ibid.*
12 Ewing, J. (2017) *Faster, Higher, Farther: The Volkswagen Scandal*. New York: W.W. Norton & Company.
13 *Ibid.*
14 Colvin, G. (2017) Inside Wells Fargo's Plan to Fix Its Culture Post-Scandal. *Fortune*. https://fortune.com/2017/06/11/wells-fargo-scandal-culture/. Accessed 28 December 2021.
15 *Ibid.*
16 Zinkin, J. (2019) *Better governance across the board: Creating value through reputation, people, and processes*. Boston, MA/Berlin: DeGruyter Press.

17 Fraser, I. (2014) *Shredded: Inside RBS, the Bank that Broke Britain*. Edinburgh: Birlinn Ltd. p. 71.
18 *Ibid.*, p.73.
19 Personal account with former senior HR executive.
20 Senior Executive interviewed for this book in October 2021.
21 Ewing (2017).
22 *Ibid.*
23 Interview with Senior Executive, October 2022.
24 Fraser (2014), p. 74.
25 Steffy (2010).
26 Steffy (2010), p. 67.
27 Wells Fargo. Independent Directors of the Board of Wells Fargo & Company: Sales Practices Investigation Report. https://www08.wellsfargomedia.com/assets/pdf/about/investor-relations/presentations/2017/board-report.pdf. Accessed 1 January 2022.
28 Frost, W. (2017) Wells Fargo Report Gives Inside Look at the Culture that Crushed the Bank's Reputation. *CNBC*. https://www.cnbc.com/2017/04/10/wells-fargo-report-shows-culture-that-crushed-banks-reputation.html. Accessed 1 January 2022.
29 Arnold, C. (2016) Former Wells Fargo Employees Describe Toxic Sales Culture, Even at HQ. *NPR*. https://www.npr.org/2016/10/04/496508361/former-wells-fargo-employees-describe-toxic-sales-culture-even-at-hq. Accessed 1 January 2022.
30 Frost (2017).
31 *Ibid.*
32 Steffy (2010), p. 145.
33 Observer cited in Steffy (2010), p. 108.
34 *Ibid.*, p. 62.
35 *Ibid.*
36 Cited in Steffy (2010), p. 57.
37 BP. (2005). BP Annual Report and Accounts 2004. https://bib.kuleuven.be/files/ebib/jaarverslagen/BPAmoco_2004.pdf. Accessed 1 January 2022. p. 3.
38 Steffy (2010), p. 114.
39 Ewing (2017), p. 93.
40 *Ibid.*
41 Steffy (2010), p. 59.
42 *Ibid.*
43 Fraser (2014), p. 125.
44 https://www.forbes.com/forbes/2012/0213/feature-john-stumpf-wells-fargo-bank-that-works.html. Accessed on 18 June 2022.
45 U.S. Chemical Safety and Hazard Investiagion Board. Investigation Report: Refinery Explosion and Fire, BP, Texas City, March 23, 2005. https://www.csb.gov/bp-america-refinery-explosion/. Accessed 1 January 2022.
46 Steffy (2010), p. 117.
47 *Ibid.*, p. 58.
48 Nohria, N., & Weber, J. (2003) The Royal Bank of Scotland: Masters of Integration, Harvard Business School, 18 August 2003.
49 Royal Bank of Scotland: The Strategy of Not Having a Strategy, London Business School, 2 June 2004.

50 Davies, H. (2018) "Royal Bank of Scotland & The Financial Crisis: Ten Years On", Speech at Kings College London, 12 September 2018.
51 Nohria & Weber (2003).
52 Davies, H. (2018) "Royal Bank of Scotland & The Financial Crisis: Ten Years On", Speech at Kings College London, 12 September 2018 https://www.rbs.com/rbs/news/2018/09/chairman_howard_davies_looks_back_at_the_financial_crisis.html Accessed 4 January 2022.
53 Fraser (2014).
54 *Ibid.*, p. 110.
55 *Ibid.*, p. 246.
56 *Ibid.*, p. 243.
57 Cited in Fraser (2014). p.416.
58 Interview with former senior HR executive, November 2021 (Interviewee 2).
59 Steffy (2010). p. 118.
60 Colvin, G. (2017) Inside Wells Fargo's Plan to Fix Its Culture Post-Scandal. *Fortune*. https://fortune.com/2017/06/11/wells-fargo-scandal-culture/. Accessed 28 December 2021.
61 Reckard, S.E. (2013) Wells Fargo's Pressure-Cooker Sales Culture Comes at a Cost. *Los Angeles Times*. https://www.latimes.com/business/la-fi-wells-fargo-sale-pressure-20131222-story.html. Accessed 2 January 2022.
62 Colvin (2017).
63 EPA. (2022) Deepwater Horizon – BP Gulf of Mexico Oil Spill. United States Environmental Protection Agency. https://www.epa.gov/enforcement/deepwater-horizon-bp-gulf-mexico-oil-spill. Accessed 2 January 2022.
64 Barringer, F. (2006) Large Oil Spill in Alaska Went Undetected for Days. *The New York Times*. https://www.nytimes.com/2006/03/15/us/large-oil-spill-in-alaska-went-undetected-for-days.html. Accessed 2 January 2022.
65 Kolhatkar, S. (2016) Elizabeth Warren and the Wells Fargo Scandal. *The New Yorker*. https://www.newyorker.com/business/currency/elizabeth-warren-and-the-wells-fargo-scam. Accessed 2 January 2022.
66 Ewing (2017).
67 See Steffy (2010).
68 Cited in Steffy (2010). p. 118.
69 Wells Fargo. Independent Directors of the Board of Wells Fargo & Company: Sales Practices Investigation Report. https://www08.wellsfargomedia.com/assets/pdf/about/investor-relations/presentations/2017/board-report.pdf. Accessed 1 January 2022.
70 Ewing (2017). pp. 223, 256.
71 *Ibid.*, p. 258.
72 Cited in Steffy (2010).
73 van Rooij, B., & Fine, A. (2018) Toxic corporate culture: Assessing organizational processes of deviancy. *Administrative Sciences*, 8(23): 1–38.
74 Excerpts in paragraph cited from Steffy (2010), pp. 89–90.
75 Cited in Smithson, J., & Venette, S. (2013) Stonewalling as an image-defense strategy: A critical examination of BP's response to the deepwater horizon explosion. *Communication Studies*, 64(4): 395–410. p. 402.

76 Lustgarden, A. (2012) *Run to Failure: BP and the Making of the Deepwater Horizon Disaster*. New York: W.W. Norton & Co. p. 61.
77 Smithson & Venette (2013), p. 402.
78 Steffy (2010), p. 184.
79 Cited in *Ibid.*
80 *Ibid*, p. 185.
81 Kollewe, J. (2010) BP chief executive Tony Hayward in his own words. *The Guardian*. https://www.theguardian.com/environment/2010/may/14/tony-hayward-bp. Accessed 2 January 2022.
82 Ewing (2017).
83 *Ibid.*, pp. 232–233.
84 Reuters. (2016) VW Says Defeat Device in Conformity with European Law. *Reuters*. November 3. Available online: https://www.reuters.com/article/us-volkswagen-emissions-lawsuit/vw-says-defeat-device-in-conformity-with-european-law-idUSKBN12Y2VJ.
85 Chossiere, G., Malina, R., Akshay, A., Dedoussi, I., Eastham, S., Speth, R., & Barrett, S. (2017) Public Health Impacts of Excess NO[subscript x] Emissions from Volkswagen Diesel Passenger Vehicles in Germany. *Environmental Research Letters*, 12(3), 1-14
86 Ewing (2017), p. 256.
87 *Ibid.*, pp. 242–243.
88 Adapted from a news article published by Reuters 9 June 2021. https://www.reuters.com/business/volkswagen-reaches-351-mln-dieselgate-settlement-with-former-execs-2021–06–09/
89 Bousso, Ron (16 January 2018). "BP Deepwater Horizon costs balloon to $65 billion". Reuters. https://www.reuters.com/article/us-bp-deepwaterhorizon-idUSKBN1F50NL. Accessed on 20 June 2022.
90 Schein (2010), p. 10.

Part II
The Toxic Triangle

Part I looked at the two drivers that slowly change cultural norms and embed toxicity in organizations. Likened to the 'boiling frog' analogy, these dimensions burn slowly over time. Unlike the boiling frog analogy that argues when the water begins to get too hot, the frog will simply jump out of the saucepan; the reality for individuals working in such environments finds that there is a lid to that pot which makes it impossible to jump out. That lid represents the harsh realities of the cost of living and the often-limited ability to change organizations.

This part will look at toxic cultures from a different perspective: The Toxic Triangle (see Figure 5.1).

The Toxic Triangle, first proposed by an academic, a psychologist, and a leadership consultant,[1] focuses on the impact of 'destructive leadership'. The premise is that toxic leadership can only exist where there is a conducive environment and susceptible followers.

According to these leading academics,[2] contextual factors support destructive leadership:

> It is hard for destructive leaders to succeed in stable systems with strong institutions and adequate checks and balances on power and control . . . effective institutions, system stability, and proper checks and balances, along with strong followers, will tend to trump the system.[3]

The Toxic Triangle has gained momentum in understanding the dynamics of a toxic culture.

As seen in Part I, organizations such as RBS, VW, BP, and others would have all ticked the boxes of being effective institutions. It is only with the benefit of hindsight that questions are raised as to why and how these organizations experienced such negative outcomes.

DOI: 10.4324/9781003330387-7

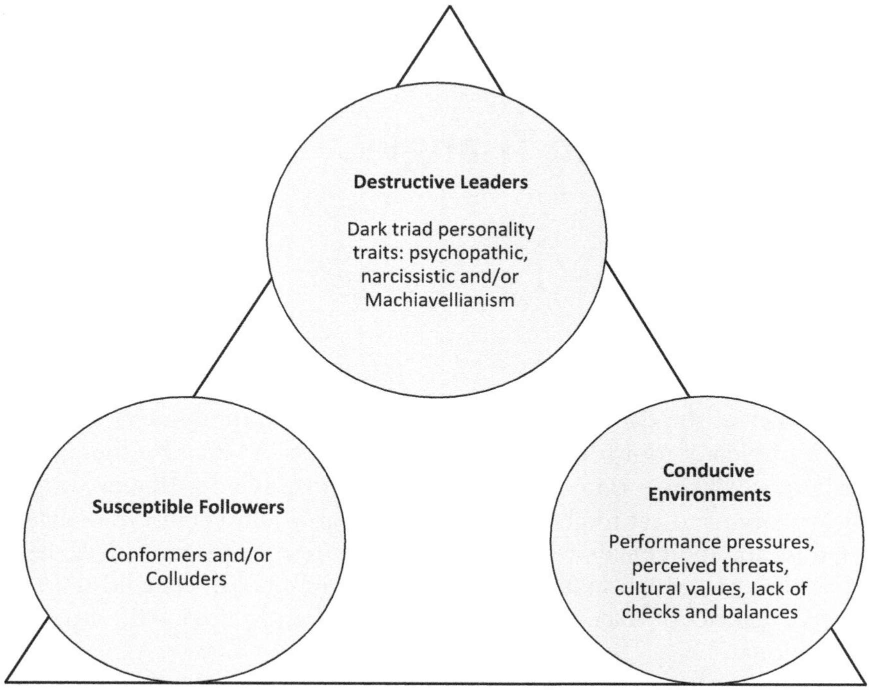

Figure 5.1 The Toxic Triangle[4]

This part will look at the three elements of a toxic culture. It is worth noting that the limitation of the toxic triangle is that each of the three dimensions appears to have an equivalence of power to each other. In addition, it appears as time-static, in that it is assumed that these dimensions occur at a single point in time. Chapter 5 will begin by exploring the dark side of leadership: how leadership impacts and shapes the culture of an organization.

Notes

1 Adapted from Padilla, A., Hogan, R., & Kaiser, R.B. (2007) The toxic triangle: Destructive leaders, susceptible followers, and conducive environments. *The Leadership Quarterly*, 18: 176–194.
2 *Ibid.*
3 *Ibid.*, p. 186.
4 Adapted from Padilla, A., Hogan, R., & Kaiser, R.B. (2007) The toxic triangle: Destructive leaders, susceptible followers, and conducive environments. The Leadership Quarterly, 18: 176–194.

5
Toxic Leadership

5.1 Introduction and Context

The culture of the organization plays a crucial role in determining what and whether dysfunctional behaviours are tolerated or not. Leadership[1] – and the position of power – is influential in demonstrating the way to get things done, and how people are treated and motivated. Leaders act as 'role models' in defining the way to behave towards others. Individuals will look up to the leader and mirror their actions and behaviours as the way to be promoted. Leaders set the expectations of how to behave in an organization.

When an organization wants to change or transform its business to become, for example, 'innovative', then it will typically hire a new CEO. Too often the new CEO only lasts for a few years before being replaced by another. Either the CEO is unable to make the changes required (the 'sad' leader), takes a ruthless approach that fundamentally impacts the business negatively (the 'bad' leader), or destroys the trust and engagement of staff leading to resignations (the 'mad' leader). Given this 'open secret' of sad, mad, and bad leaders, the costs of a failed executive are reckoned to be around \$1m to \$3m.[2]

"When dramatic organizational change is added to the normal levels of job insecurity, personality clashes, and political battling, the resulting chaotic milieu provides both the necessary stimulation and sufficient 'cover' for psychopathic behaviour".[3]

Since the Global Financial Crisis (GFC) in 2008, leadership academics have begun to question leadership, or more bluntly, the morality of leadership. A prominent business and academic scholar argues that the "worst economic downturn since the 1930s wasn't a banking crisis, a credit crisis, or a mortgage crisis – it was a moral crisis, willful negligence in extremis"[4]. This has led some observers to argue that the leadership theory needs to change due to the over-emphasis on leadership, which "in some cases, has legitimized the actions of

DOI: 10.4324/9781003330387-8

megalomaniac leaders, who have become convinced that powerful, visionary leadership is helpful, healthy and wise – and of course, that this means more power should be ceded to leaders".[5]

This chapter will explore the evolution of leadership studies, define and discuss toxic leadership, and explore the links between personality disorders and leadership.

5.2 Approaches to Leadership: The Three Camps

Books on leadership tend to fall into three broad camps. The first camp describes leaders as the 'great heroes' who are powerful and visionary. This camp dominates the field. Typically, they describe business leaders, political military leaders, or explorers who have faced adversity and 'won'. Some of these are biographies, historical accounts, or autobiographies. The vast majority are about white men. Yet as observers point out, such 'greatness' is time- and culture-specific.[6]

The second camp tends to look at leadership as a 'theory' to be learned. Situational, Servant, Participative, Action, or Transformative Leadership are just a few of these 'theories' that appear as little more than "old wine in new bottles". More recently, the trend toward 'agile' leadership theory has swept across organizations as the new way of operating. Typically, authors and researchers refer to 'best practices' that can be applied to organizations and individuals in a 'one size fits all' solution. Yet many organizations have faced disastrous consequences by uniformly applying such theories, spending millions of dollars to change organizational structures to reflect the new 'theory of leadership'. For example, ING Bank removed several managerial levels as they implemented their 'agile leadership' theory. The bank was encouraged to work through self-managed teams, and out went the checks and balances so key to banking; many middle managers resigned or were terminated. The resulting outcome led to the organization receiving one of the largest fines in banking history; the presiding judge described the organization as having a "gangster culture": the lack of managerial controls had led to significant money laundering. The lesson to be learnt is that what works in one business sector or organization does not necessarily work for another. Leadership is about context and culture. There are many leaders who have been hired to change a company, but the culture has meant they have failed.

Over the past decade or so, the third camp of leadership has focused on the 'dark side' of leadership. This is variously described as 'snakes in suits', 'sad, bad, mad', 'derailed', 'toxic', or 'manipulative' among other terms. In one study, researchers[7] asked the question, "How many bosses that you have worked for, would you be willing to work for again?" The results claimed that "two-thirds of managers are insufferable, and half will eventually fail". The idea of toxic leadership or the 'dark side' of leadership is beginning to emerge.

5.2.1 Defining Toxic Leadership

Toxic leadership is described in several ways, from despotic, restrictive, and nasty, to narcissistic, manipulative, and evil. In *Snakes in Suits*, Hare, an expert on the scientific study of psychopathy, and Babiak, a leading authority on the corporate psychopath, examined the role of psychopaths in modern corporations, and concluded that "not all psychopaths are in prison. Some are in the Boardroom" (Table 5.1).[8]

So, what is toxic leadership? Toxic leadership requires dominance, control, and coercion rather than influence, commitment, and persuasion. Ensuring close supervision of resources and expenses, implementing controls, and the removal of critics are actions designed to dominate and limit or eliminate alternative ways of doing things. For example, BP's focus on cost savings made anyone attempting to voice concerns the 'naysayer' or critic in the organization and not 'one of us'.

Toxic leadership is selfish. The desire to become the biggest and best is typically toxic. It is often cited as the vision of the leader, yet it does not account for the needs of stakeholders. To achieve industry dominance, the

Table 5.1 Toxic Leadership Terms in the Literature

Term	*Authors*[9]
Leadership derailment	McCall and Lombardo (1983); Furnham (2010)
Toxic leadership	Hogan and Hogan (2001);
Negative leadership	Kellerman (2004)
Evil leadership	Hogan and Hogan (2001); Conger (1990)
Dark side of leadership	Conger (1990); Tepper (2000)
Abusive leadership	Maccoby (2000, 2004);
Destructive leadership	Kets de Vries (1993); Hogan & Hogan (2001)

toxic leader must eliminate challengers, surround themselves with those who will believe this singular vision, and consistently 'rage' against those who do not agree. Toxic leadership compromises the quality of life and negatively impacts the well-being of the organization. Higher than average rates of turnover and absenteeism, and low levels of engagement are outcomes of toxic leadership.

As one senior HR Leader[10] reflected on the role of leadership:

> Leadership magnifies, so when you have leaders and particularly the CEO, Exec Team, what behaviours they show, the way they are as individuals, and the way they run that company or organization, it really helps drive and create that culture. So I think there is that amalgam where you have that particularly aggressive, particularly thoughtless, particularly challenging, particularly uncaring, particularly focused, particularly selfish individuals running companies where fundamentally their view is that HR are dispensable resources to achieve a business end, and they put the pressure on to deliver on whatever capacity that is to deliver that amplifies through the organization, and that then creates as I said pressure, stress, division, and a lack of collaborative working, and all of that creates an atmosphere where people become inhibited, frightened and intimidated and under particular stress, and then that can generate toxic behaviours.

Toxic leadership has been defined in several ways (see Table 5.2).

Table 5.2 Definitions of Toxic Leadership[11]

Concept	*Author*	*Definition (cited directly from source)*
Toxic leadership	Whicker, M.L. (1996)	A toxic leader is "maladjusted, malcontent, and often malevolent, even malicious". Marcia Whicker was the first to use the term 'toxic leader'. She analyzed three types of leaders: 'trustworthy', 'transitional', and 'toxic'. Such characters have a deep-seated but well-disguised sense of personal inadequacy, selfish values, and cleverness at concealing deceit. They can by virtue of their destructive behaviours and dysfunctional personal qualities inflict serious and enduring harm on the individuals, organizations, and even nations that they lead.

Lipman-Blumen, J. (2005)	Leaders who engage in numerous destructive behaviours and who exhibit certain dysfunctional personal characteristics. To count as toxic, these behaviours and qualities of character must inflict some reasonably serious and enduring harm on their followers and organizations. The intent to harm others or to enhance the self at the expense of others distinguishes seriously toxic leaders from the categories of unintentional toxic leaders, who also cause negative effects.
Walton, M. (2007)	Toxic leadership is a behaviour which is exploitive, abusive, destructive, and psychologically – and perhaps legalistically – corrupt and poisonous.
Schmidt, A.A. (2008)	Narcissistic self-promoters who engage in an unpredictable pattern of abusive and authoritarian supervision.
Watt, S.R., Javidi, M. & Normore, A. (2017)	Toxic leadership is when leaders "infringe [upon] the leader-follower relationship, abusing their powers as leaders to the detriment of the people they are leading; and when these . . . leaders move on, they leave the people who were within their sphere of influence worse off than when they originally started leading them".
Singh, N., Sengupta, S. & Dev, S. (2018)	Toxic leaders as "those narcissist, self-promoting leaders who by their divisive supervision, managerial incompetency and erratic behaviours intentionally tend to erode their self-esteem, burn out their employees, breed counterproductive performing subordinates and future overbearing bosses".
Morris, J.A. (2019)	A form of leadership that harasses, belittles, and frightens employed people, mainly followers, which causes undue stress or pressure leading to decreased performance and other undesired behaviours.

(*continued*)

Concept	*Author*	*Definition (cited directly from source)*
	Milosevic, I., Maric, S. & Loncar, D. (2020)	Toxic leadership is leadership focused on maintaining position of control via toxic influence attempts, whose harmfulness, although relatively unintentional, causes serious harm by reckless behaviour as well as their incompetence.
Destructive Leadership	Einarsen, S., Aasland, M. & Skogstad, A. (2007)	Systematic and repeated behaviour by a leader, supervisor, or manager that violates the legitimate interest of the organization by undermining and/or sabotaging the organization's goals, tasks, resources, and effectiveness and/or the motivation, well-being, or job satisfaction of subordinates.
	Thoroughgood, C.N., Sawyer, K.B., Padilla, A. & Lunsford, L. (2018)	Destructive leadership as a complex process of influence between (i) flawed, toxic and ineffective leaders, susceptible followers, and conducive environments, which (ii) unfolds over time and, (iii) on balance, culminates in destructive group or organizational outcomes that compromise the quality of life for internal and external constituents and detract from their group-focused goals or purposes.
Pseudo-Transformational Leadership	Christie, A., Barling, J. & Turner, N. (2011)	Pseudo-transformational leadership: "self-serving, yet highly inspirational leadership behaviours, unwillingness to encourage independent thought in subordinates, and little caring for one's subordinates generally".

5.2.2 The Impact of Toxic Leadership

There is little doubt that the people at the top of the organization "have a disproportionate level of influence over those they lead" and include leaders who preside over an entire company, a function, a region, or a business unit.[12] From leaders described as 'doctors' (healing a broken organization), 'visionaries' (having a dream or mission), 'commanders' (taking back control), or 'architects' (rebuilding an organization), there are too many studies that still herald leaders as the answer to everything. This preoccupation with leadership, bordering on obsession, can have detrimental effects on organizations.

Too much of the practitioner literature on leadership identifies leaders as *superheroes* who swoop into an organization and give their vision, then everyone blindly follows their lead. What is wrong with this scenario is that it assumes that one person can know everything and be correct. The transformational leadership theorists argue that to do so, the leader must understand the needs and goals of the followers and shape their attitudes towards a common unitary interest. The process is driven to align individual and organizational goals. This view of leadership borders on the messianic. It assumes that the followers are passive, waiting for guidance and inspiration. This is epitomized as:

> [Transformational leaders] are those who stimulate and inspire followers to both achieve extraordinary outcomes and, in the process, develop their own leadership capacity. Transformational leaders help followers grow and develop into leaders by responding to individual followers' needs by empowering them and by aligning the objectives and goals of the individual followers, the leader, the group and the larger organization ... transformational leadership can move followers to exceed expected performance, as well as lead to high levels of follower satisfaction and commitment to the group and the organization.[13]

Part of the reason we give leaders too much power has been the tendency to commit what has been described as the 'halo error'[14] – the over-attribution of success to those who hold top positions. This has been particularly pronounced in the management literature, notably in the work of Jim Collins who writes about top CEOs. His works, such as *Built to Last* (Collins and Porras, 1994), *Good to Great* (Collins, 2001), *How the Mighty Fall* (2009), and *Great by Choice: Uncertainty, Chaos, and Luck – Why Some Thrive Despite Them All* (Collins and Hanson, 2011), all focus on the actions of the CEO.[15] For anyone reading these books, one would be hard pushed to explain what anyone else was doing in the specific organization, as the books read as though the success of the organizations was entirely due to one man.

> Before Royal Bank of Scotland (RBS) acquired ABN Amro in its ill-fated deal, CEO Fred Goodwin was known among his staff as having a 'brain the size of a planet'. Revered by his followers, Fred Goodwin's leadership was at times vicious. In meetings, he would attack individuals who disagreed. As one former colleague said after one such encounter, "Normally when you raise the white flag (figuratively speaking), the attack stops. He continued to keep attacking".

So why was this behaviour tolerated for so long? For the most part, it was due to the success of the Bank and its profitability over the previous six to seven years. Fred Goodwin looked at strategy as winning prizes. The previous acquisition of NatWest in the late 1990s by the much smaller RBS was viewed with wonder. Fred Goodwin's prize was securing Coutts Bank, Her Majesty The Queen's bank, which was one of the NatWest businesses. Subsequent acquisitions consolidated RBS as one of the top global banks by 2007.

In 2005, RBS built a brand-new, campus-style headquarters just outside Edinburgh, complete with fountains, gym, restaurant, tennis courts, a conference centre, an executive suite, and a state-of-the-art executive learning centre, as well as a children's nursery. The opening was conducted by HM The Queen followed by live music and a ceremonial lap of the building by a famous F1 racing driver. To access the building, a new road bridge was commissioned sporting a gigantic RBS emblem. Inside the building, the atrium was host to a supermarket, florist, hairdresser, and several coffee shops, accompanied by a high-end cafeteria with plentiful cooking stations and chefs.

Goodwin's followers certainly believed in Goodwin. Before the ABN Amro acquisition that led to the demise of the Bank in 2008, the annual employee engagement survey showed some of the highest levels of employee engagement in the market. However, with the acquisition almost doubling the number of the countries of operations, the RBS Group had an Achilles heel; it lacked the knowledge and experience of running a coordinated global strategy. In Germany, for example, where there were four businesses, each business, whether it was retail, corporate, or insurance, was run as a separate business. To obtain the synergies of scale required in a large acquisition meant that each country at least required a common operating platform. One key success for RBS before the acquisition had been the setup of its manufacturing or back-office division. This division managed all the back-office processes, which meant that the operating costs for the RBS Group with its diverse banking and finance portfolio were the lowest for any bank at the time. However, this only served the UK. The fragmented nature of ABN Amro, which operated in more than 20 countries, stretched the capacity of RBS and its ability to set up a platform. As the GFC hit in 2008, RBS was already flummoxed on what to do with its prize. There was no strategy in any of the countries. Once the prize was secured against its rival, Barclays, RBS imposed its RBS way of doing things. The 'Do it now' slogan was changed to 'Do it everywhere', yet staff and executives were unsure what they were required to do. The stakes for global domination were too high given the lack of capability and knowledge to manage outside of the UK.

The ability of leaders to engage in 'bad' behaviour is seen to arise from their positional power. Leadership is the exercise of power, and the quality of leadership – good, ineffective, or toxic – depends on an individual's ability to exercise power.[16] In the *Dark Side of Transformational Leadership*, Dennis Tourish[17] argues that in the business literature, leaders are described as the vanguards to guide, direct, and have a vision for change; employees are typically described as followers who should accept, obey, and follow their leaders. Tourish argues that such a position is dangerous and can lead to dictatorial tendencies. He criticizes academics that simply assume that "visionary leadership is powerful, exciting, and necessary, with leaders acting as a force for good".[18] Even influential practitioner journals such as the *Harvard Business Review* regularly publish articles on the 'secrets' of leadership, with CEOs describing their own styles of leadership. As Tourish notes, "macho imagery is rife". One edition of the *Harvard Business Review* in January 2007 dedicated to leadership showed an image of a male business executive in a suit and tie doing press-ups on a boardroom table. Leadership is shown as powerful individuals with power cajoling and coercing others to follow their vision.

In summary, "rapid business growth, increased downsizing, frequent reorganizations, mergers, acquisitions, and joint ventures have inadvertently increased the number of attractive employment opportunities for individuals with psychopathic personalities".[19]

5.3 Dysfunctional Behaviour in the Workplace

The job role that is reported to have a greater percentage of corporate psychopaths is the CEO role.[20]

In *Snakes in Suits*, two eminent psychologists identify three types of psychopaths in organizations: 'corporate manipulator', 'corporate bully', and 'corporate puppet master'.[21]

Corporate manipulators are adept at using others in their pursuit of success and power. They are deceitful, egotistical, superficial, manipulating, and prone to lying. They will not take responsibility for their actions and will lie or blame others when called to account. They are rude and callous to individuals whom they believe have nothing to offer them. They are sophisticated in being able to act or play the role in front of others and getting them to do their work. More recently, this concept has become known as the Corporate Psychopath.

Corporate bullies are much more aggressive and less sophisticated than the *corporate manipulators*. Corporate bullies rely on fear, and they bully or coerce others to do their work. They are callous to everyone except their seniors and will blame others when things go wrong. They will retain a grudge against those who call them out or do not do their bidding. While it is unclear whether the corporate bully gets any pleasure in acting vindictively, especially to more junior staff, they lack the insights or the ability to reflect on their own behaviour.

Corporate puppet masters pull the strings of others throughout the organization. These people are adept at getting others to abuse or bully others lower down in the organization. The research on this type is relatively light. However, given the role of the CEO in driving performance and defining targets, rewards, and direction, it is this role of the CEO or Director in a stand-alone unit that could succumb and act as a 'corporate puppet master'. This will be examined more closely through the experiences of the seasoned and senior executives who contributed to this book as well as secondary data from BP, Wells Fargo, and VW.

5.3.1 Measuring the Dark Side of Leadership

While it is difficult to define precise behaviours associated with the 'dark side' of leadership, there remain tools that might help measure such 'dark' behaviours. The *Diagnostic and Statistical Manual of Mental Disorders* is the key reference for personality disorders. In the most recent fifth edition, it lists ten specific personality disorders: paranoid, schizoid, schizotypal, antisocial, borderline, histrionic, narcissist, avoidant, dependent, and obsessive-compulsive personality disorder. Psychologists and psychiatrists have developed assessment tools to measure the extent of 'dark side' behaviours in 'normal people' in the workplace (see Table 5.3).

The extent to which these dark side tendencies manifest themselves depends on the individual and on the pressure within the job role or stress in the workplace.

5.3.2 Bullying in Leadership

Increased pressure for performance is linked to a greater incidence of dysfunctional behaviour. Bullying can be both subtle and/or offensive. This section will look at the dysfunctional behaviours of the 'corporate bully'. At Wells Fargo, managers and supervisors exhibited bullying behaviours by threatening to terminate the employment contracts of 'low performers', publishing the ranked order of performance as an attempt to 'name and shame' individuals, and making individuals take part in 'games' to humiliate individual achievements.[24]

According to research, 90 per cent of workplace bullies are in leadership positions.[25] More than half of US employees report that they have been

Table 5.3 Taxonomy of the Dark Side of Personality and Related Measures[22]

Dimensions[23]	*Analogous dark side tendencies among normal adults*	*Measurement Scales*		
		Hogan & Hogan (2009)	*Moscoso & Salgado (2004)*	*Schmit, Kihm, & Robie (2000)*
Borderline	Moody; intense but short-lived enthusiasm for people, projects, and things; hard to please	Excitable	Ambivalent	
Avoidant	Reluctant to take risks for fear of being rejected or negatively evaluated	Cautious	Shy	
Paranoid	Cynical, distrustful, and doubtful of others' true intentions	Sceptical	Suspicious	Intimidating
Schizoid	Aloof and uncommunicative, lacking awareness and care for others' feelings	Reserved	Lone	Intimidating
Passive-aggressive	Casual, ignoring people's requests and becoming irritated or excusive if they persist	Leisurely	Pessimistic	Passive Aggressive
Narcissism	Extraordinarily self-confident; grandiose and entitled; over-estimation of capabilities	Bold	Egocentric	Ego-centred
Antisocial	Enjoys taking risks and testing limits; manipulative, deceitful, cunning, and exploitative	Mischievous	Risky	Manipulation
Histrionic	Expressive, animated, and dramatic; wanting to be noticed and the centre of attention	Colourful	Cheerful	
Schizotypal	Acting and thinking in creative but sometimes odd or unusual ways	Imaginative	Eccentric	
Obsessive-Compulsive	Meticulous, precise, and perfectionistic; inflexible about rules and procedures	Diligent	Reliable	Micro-Managing
Dependent	Eager to please; dependent on the support and approval of others; reluctant to disagree with others, especially authority figures	Dutiful	Submitted	

exposed to bullying in the workplace.[26] Typically, bullying is downplayed and recorded as two individuals 'not getting along', which usually results in mediation as the answer. One of the challenges is that the 'victim' is perceived as weak or lacking experience. Yet research shows that this is not the case. Typically, the victim is not a poor performer, but someone who is highly capable and, as such, is likely to be a threat to the status and self-esteem of the bully.[27]

Corporate bullies tend to be considered as individual leaders or managers who typically will have influence and power over individuals. Bullying is best defined as

> intentional repeated actions that occur frequently over an extended period of time of at least six months by an individual or a group directed against an individual in the form of verbal abuse, behaviour that humiliates, threatens, and/or sabotages an individual's work production or status and there is a perceived imbalance of power.[28]

Corporate bullying is also characterized as an "intentional infliction of a hostile workplace environment"[29]: a combination of verbal and nonverbal behaviours is inflicted on an individual over a sustained period. It is the repetition over time that is used to categorize a 'corporate bully'.

Roter[30] identifies six types of corporate bullies from the direct to the indirect and from the critical to the insincere. Each type of bully will have their preferred way of operating (see Table 5.4).

Table 5.4 Types of Bully in Organizations[31]

Type of corporate bully	*Definition*
Public or Direct Bully	Uses public forums to humiliate, scream at, interrupt, ridicule, ignore, and threaten the job security of their target.
Silent or Indirect Bully	Attacks the 'target' in private while publicly coming across as pleasant and charming. Tactics include spreading rumours, talking maliciously about the target, and excluding the target from their inner circle.
Critical Bully	Tactics include finding fault, blaming others, criticizing performance, making unreasonable demands and late-night calls, and establishing unrealistic deadlines so that the 'target' is set up to fail.

Insincere Bully	Uses 'friendliness' to gain gossip and information about others and then twists or embellishes the information to instigate conflict between the target and others. These tactics may not be realized for some time. Once realized, the target will appear emotional and angry to others, while the 'friendly bully' will appear wronged by their target.
Hoarder Bully	This bully believes that 'knowledge is power'. Tactics include hoarding resources and information, ensuring that the target is excluded from meetings or decision making. The target will appear helpless and incompetent in their role.
Opportunistic Bully	This type of bully will use tactics to 'move ahead'. They will 'walk over other people' or block others from achieving their goals. They align themselves with senior management and are perceived as a 'go-getter'.

5.3.3 Bullying Tactics

Corporate bullies employ tactics that undermine and threaten their target. It is highly likely that the work experience of the target will be very different from others. Table 5.5 shows some of the tactics and examples.

Table 5.5 Bullying Tactics

Tactics	*Examples*	*Communicated as:*
Exclusion and isolation	The target is not invited to meetings or ignored; may be moved to a different unit.	You are not required at this meeting.
Creation of an uncomfortable work environment	Through gossip, rumors, verbal threats, ignoring, and isolation, the bully creates a hostile work environment.	We are going for lunch, but you need to stay and finish the work.
Unfair or destructive criticism	The bully provides feedback that is destructive, using words such as 'lazy', 'incompetent', 'inadequate'.	You are getting fat and lazy.
Blaming others for errors	The bully will look for a scapegoat to pin the blame on.	It was not my idea/ work.

(*continued*)

Tactics	*Examples*	*Communicated as:*
Unreasonable job demands	The bully will ask for work to be delivered in an unreasonable timescale or in personal time, late at night, or at weekends. The bully will request the individual to cancel any holiday or vacation to complete the work demands.	I need this urgently and you need to complete this over the weekend or cancel your holiday now.
Inconsistent application of rules	The bully applies different rules, such as timekeeping, to different individuals showing favouritism.	You don't have a life, so you need to stay late.
Threatening job security	The bully may threaten to fire the individual.	If you don't follow my rules, then you will be getting your P45.
Name-calling	Using derogatory names for individuals to belittle the individual in front of others.	You are such a slowcoach/idiot/prima donna.
Verbal or nonverbal threats	Nonverbal threats include eye rolling, smirking behind the individual's back, glaring or staring, and mocking the individual. Verbal threats include threatening to take work away, shouting, and arguing.	Watch my lips. Which part of 'no', don't you understand?
Demeaning or discriminatory comments	Comments such as about someone's size, weight, or age, and other characteristics such as sex, religion, or disability.	It's just banter. Where's your sense of humour?
Micro-managing	Constantly asking for reports or papers and making repeated changes that are relatively trivial but require the individual to stay late to make the changes.	Received typically as red-inked words and comments.
Physical threats	Making threats to the 'target' that are regarded as intimidating, such as finger pointing or threatening to physically attack an individual.	Next time, I am going to break your arms.

Adapted from Roter, A. (2017) *Understanding and Recognizing Dysfunctional Leadership*. Taylor & Francis.

Examples of bullying are recounted at all levels. The executives who contributed to this book have all held senior executive roles; some recounted their experiences of working with a toxic leader.

One senior HR executive recounted her experience through an acquisition:

> I was pretty senior and running a $300m P&L and then the PE (Private Equity) guys came in to run the group. They would have meetings which I normally should have been at; I was excluded. In the run-up to Christmas, I got this one-line email saying pull together a strategy and present on this date. The guy just flicked through my slides and threw the presentation across the table, and it went skimming off the end of the table and he said, 'This is nice to have but not a need to have'. It was anchored in a lot of student well-being as there had been a spate of suicides in the student population. I was vindicated after I left as they didn't do anything about this, and this student well-being thing became this massive media issue with drugs and all kinds of terrible ... that almost destroyed the business.[32]

5.4 The Dark Triad

Useful to our understanding of toxic leaders and leadership is the recently coined term *The Dark Triad*, which focuses on three traits – Machiavellianism, Narcissism, and Psychopathy.[33] According to experts, these personality types are the most damaging to organizations, colleagues, and stakeholders. While there are other more challenging personality types in the population and in the workplace, such as histrionic (where everything is urgent now) or obsessive-compulsive (the unrelenting demand for perfectionism), these types do not appear to inflict the same amount of damage as the Dark Triad.

The Dark Triad is critical to understanding the shadow of the organization. Some writers on leadership will typically describe the leader as *strong, clear-headed, and at times arrogant to drive through their strategy in the face of opposition*. Yet this very notion of leadership is wrong. Instead, it serves the 'dark side of leadership' very well. More recently in the academic literature, there have been discussions that certain aspects of narcissistic behaviour are regarded as 'positive'. The typical academic fashion of the idea that one must always challenge the unthinkable, misses the point. The damage and destructiveness of corporate psychopaths on organizations, on economies, and on lives and livelihoods is immense. Research needs to move away from the micro- to the macro-view. Processes need to be acknowledged and implemented that prevent the power of an organization from being placed in the hands of a Corporate Psychopath.

Psychologists note that while there is some degree of overlap behind these personality types, there are some differences. Machiavellians and Psychopaths are low in conscientiousness and exhibit self-enhancement. Machiavellianism can be described as the manipulative personality. Drawn from Machiavelli's original books are personality types that manipulate others to achieve their own ends. Narcissism is defined as grandiosity, entitlement, dominance, and superiority. Yet all three entail a socially malevolent character with tendencies towards self-promoting, emotional coldness, duplicity, and aggressiveness.[34]

Machiavellianism describes a manipulative personality by a lack of empathy, with a willingness to lie to, manipulate, and exploit others, and may take enjoyment in doing so.

Narcissism describes a personality that may appear charming initially, but narcissists have a tendency for self-enhancement and believe they are superior to others. Facets include grandiosity and entitlement.

Psychopathy describes a personality that is impulsive and thrill seeking combined with low empathy, superiority, and self-promotion. A more definitive marker is that psychopaths lack any emotion of 'guilt' and are defined as having a lack of 'conscience'. More disturbing is that psychopaths do not experience any anxiety or fear to the same extent that normal people do. That means that they do not learn by being punished, rather they will seek alternative gratification.

Some researchers have explored the dark side of personality based on the motive to elevate the self and/or harm others[35]; whereas others have focused on the dark side as negative characteristics that might emerge under stress.[36]

While there has been much work at a clinical level and knowledge generated about the nature of these traits, only some of this work has crossed over into understanding their role in the workplace. For example, research shows that *Machiavellians* are proficient at forming political alliances and cultivating a charismatic image. *Narcissistic* CEOs tend to like big and bold actions – actions that grab headlines and have large consequences. For organizations, these actions may have a positive or negative impact: big wins or huge losses. Researchers argue that organizations with narcissistic CEOs tend to fluctuate in terms of their performance and, as such, these organizations are likely to be less stable than organizations led by less narcissistic CEOs.

Hogan, the renowned psychologist, holds the view that dark personality traits are derailers.[37] In other words, a leader with dark personality traits will at some point derail – it is just a matter of time. Certain dark traits – arrogant, manipulative, demanding, authoritarian, volatile, critical – are some of the reasons that executives do derail. So how do leaders with such dark traits first gain their positions of power? Some argue that managers and leaders overlook these traits when evaluating managerial potential. However, this places the blame on managers for not being aware of or overlooking moral shortcomings, which they may be too inexperienced themselves to spot. Rather there appear to be two reasons as to why and how individuals gain positions of power and influence. One reason is that individuals with dark personality traits are extremely skilled at managing upwards. They will cultivate an image and focus on being charismatic. A second reason is that organizations can view certain behaviours as attractive to managerial potential. These can include perfectionism, being driven to succeed, and conducting hard-nosed negotiations. For example, Machiavellians seem to enjoy the combative nature of the negotiating process. Yet all three personalities of the *dark triad* are willing to use unethical tactics in negotiations.[38]

In summary, research shows that psychopaths can be extremely successful in large corporations because of their charm, manipulative nature, and remorselessness that enables them to move up the corporate hierarchy.[39] The next section of this chapter zooms in on the Dark Triad types of leadership.

5.4.1 Machiavellian Leadership

Machiavellian leaders will focus on developing two support groups: Patrons and Pawns.

Patrons are a network of typically senior leaders or those with influence in an organization. The toxic leader will actively cultivate 'friendships' and align themselves with these individuals. Patrons will be flattered and befriended to help the corporate psychopath reach more senior levels. Noticeably, the corporate psychopath will look to 'befriend' the patron, for example by engaging with them and inviting them to external social events such as playing golf or offering tickets to the theatre for a sell-out performance.

Pawns, however, are those identified as useful to the toxic leader. Typically, the pawn will be hardworking and knowledgeable, enabling the corporate psychopath to brag about delivering outstanding work due to their guidance of the pawn. Two factions will develop in the organization: (i) the 'network of supporters': patrons and pawns; and (ii) the 'group of detractors': those who realize that they have been used and manipulated or that the organization is in danger.[40]

5.4.2 Narcissistic Leadership

Narcissistic leadership in an organizational context (particularly at senior level or CEO leadership) can be translated into the following actions:

1. Engaging in strategic dynamism, that is to say, they will deliberately initiate more changes more rapidly than their non-strategic counterparts
2. Engaging in acts of grandiosity
3. Undertaking bold actions that will attract attention (significant mergers, acquisition activities, or organizational changes)

One of the very few empirical studies to explore narcissistic leadership issues at a CEO level studied the CEOs of 111 companies in the US computer hardware and software sector.[41] Using unobtrusive measures of CEO narcissism (prominence of photographs in annual reports, prominence of mentions of CEO in press releases, use by CEO of personal pronouns in interviews, and the relationship between CEO cash and non-cash compensations in comparison to that of the second-highest paid executive), the researchers gathered evidence from documents over a 12-year period. In addition, they gathered organizational performance data for these organizations for the same period. The CEO data were used to create a 'Narcissism Index'.

In analyzing the data, they found that:

1. There was a positive relationship between CEO narcissism and strategic dynamism, grandiosity, and the number and size of acquisitions
2. Narcissistic CEOs tended to undertake bold moves that attracted attention and resulted in both big wins and big losses
3. There was a positive relationship between CEO narcissism and both extreme and fluctuating organizational performance
4. The overall performance of the firms led by narcissistic CEOs was neither better nor worse than that of those led by 'non-narcissistic' CEOs

While the researchers did not (and indeed could not) distinguish between 'productive' and 'destructive' leadership, they found narcissistic leadership was not productive, particularly since the leader impact was only assessed in terms of organizational outcomes. The internal impacts on climate, individuals, commitment of others, and attrition were not considered. Yet these aspects of an organization are critical to sustained and long-term performance.

In summary, the notion that there is any form of so-called 'productive narcissism' in senior leaders that could hold potentially significant benefits to organizations in terms of achieving performance outcomes is refuted. Narcissistic leadership is damaging to an organization internally (in terms of culture, morale, and relationships), which ultimately leads to longer-term deterioration in organizational performance. The question relating to the extent to which narcissism may be a dominant cause of 'bad' leadership is not clearly answered by the current research. Certainly, in terms of short-term outcomes of leader narcissism, there is little evidence of a negative effect. However, it does appear to have a negative impact on the internal climate with a longer-term adverse impact on performance outcomes.

The authors of the 'Narcissistic CEOs' study concluded that, while they engaged in more grandiose and dramatic actions (acquisitions and strategic dynamism) and their organizations experienced dramatic performance fluctuations, in the longer term their organizations performed neither better nor worse than comparable organizations led by non-narcissistic CEOs.[42]

The notion that narcissistic leadership at a senior level is a necessity for success is refuted; performance is more volatile and riskier. The conclusion that the organizations fared neither better nor worse than competitors speaks to the impact of the leadership teams rather than to an individual leader. It is reckoned that they will mitigate the volatility of having a narcissistic leader at the helm. To deepen our understanding of the nature and impact of narcissistic leadership, it is important that further research explores the internal impact of such leadership, as well as organizational outcomes, and to understand how narcissistic tendencies develop and emerge throughout a leadership career.

Narcissism is linked to charisma and personalized use of power. Narcissistic behaviours include being self-absorbed, attention seeking, exploitative, and demanding unquestioning obedience. Narcissism has been linked to overreach in business – making ill-advised acquisitions of firms in unrelated sectors and paying more than market value to acquire them.

5.4.3 Psychopathic Leadership or the Corporate Psychopath

The corporate psychopath appears at first glance to be charming, smooth, sophisticated, and successful; unlike the criminal psychopath who shows greater anti-social tendencies or an inability to adapt to social customs. Rather this is a psychopath that has learned or adapted behaviour that will easily fit within the corporate world – and in some cases, becomes the expected behaviour. Experts have shown that this more successful psychopathic profile is able to adapt or mimic ways that fit in with society, unlike their criminal counterparts.[43]

Experts remain undecided about whether psychopaths are born or made. There is certainly evidence of both. The stark difference, however, appears to be that 'successful' corporate psychopaths have had the privilege of a good education and are typically from a middle- or an upper-class background. The criminal psychopath is typically from a lower class. Parental neglect features heavily in psychopathy but this is certainly not the whole story. Parental discord and/or neglect, low socioeconomic status, psychiatric disorders in the family, as well as alcoholism and child abuse can 'push' someone further along the psychopathic spectrum. There is also evidence of a genetic disposition to psychopathy where certain parts of the brain do not develop in the same way. Research suggests that certain parts of the brain are undeveloped or underactive in psychopaths, suggesting the lack of a conscience and the under-development of emotions and self-control.[44]

The corporate psychopath is an 'organizational destroyer'.[45] Experts reckon that psychopaths who work for organizations destroy the morale, well-being, and even the culture of the organization. They do this by lying, humiliating employees, using organizational rules to contain them, ensuring that they are disempowered by controlling budgets and resources, blaming them, taking credit for good work, and even coercing them into unwanted sexual activities.[46]

The corporate psychopath has the unnerving skill of managing upwards. The corporate psychopath's boss will typically sing their praises, whereas their colleagues and staff will find that they work for a very different persona. The corporate psychopath will treat individuals differently as required for their own success and will drop them as soon as they have served their purpose.

Corporate psychopaths are described as:

> Characteristically insincere, arrogant, untrustworthy, and manipulative in their personal style; insensitive, remorseless, shallow and blaming in their interpersonal relationships; impatient, erratic, unreliable, unfocussed and parasitic in their organizational maturity; and dramatic, unethical and bullying in their social tendencies.[47]

Corporate psychopaths like to take credit for work done. They like to show to their superiors how their teams are incompetent, whereas they are the competent leader. Employee engagement declines due to a lack of appreciation, as the coldness of the corporate psychopath shows little interest in the well-being of their teams. Employees will look to withdraw from the organization. Absenteeism rates will increase – taking a day off sick happens five times more frequently than other employees, taking longer breaks than allowed happens four times more frequently, and leaving work early happens five times more frequently.[48] If these are signs of the destructive capabilities of corporate psychopaths, then we can assume that organizations could identify and monitor these elements. For example, organizations could create a scorecard by department, unit, or team to measure such signs. This will be looked at later in the book.

Many experts and researchers note how easily corporate psychopaths can move up the corporate hierarchy and gain positions of greater power and influence. Some organizations view psychopathic executives as having leadership potential despite having negative performance reviews and low ratings on leadership and management by subordinates. This provides convincing evidence of the ability of these individuals to manipulate decision makers. Their excellent communication and convincing lying skills, which together would have made them attractive hiring candidates in the first place, apparently continued to serve them well in furthering their careers.[49]

According to one study in Australia that sampled nearly 350 white collar workers who had more than 12 years of work experience, at least one-third had worked at some time with a manager who could be classified as a corporate psychopath. It is reckoned that bullying costs the UK economy nearly £14bn per annum (2008) while corporate psychopaths cost the UK economy around £3.5bn per annum.[50] Evidence from the GFC, from the terrible environmental disaster on the Gulf of Mexico, from the lies and deceit about car emissions, from the shady dealings of banks fixing interest rates to the opening of false customer accounts, should serve as a huge warning to all. There is little doubt in the view of the experts that there are at least one per cent of employees who are likely to have psychopathic tendencies, with some experts suggesting that this might be as high as seven per cent in certain industries such as corporate banking due to the power, rewards, and prestige.[51]

Yet empirical and case studies of psychopathy in the corporate world are limited and largely confined to self-report measures of constructs related to psychopathy such as narcissism, Machiavellianism, and aberrant self-promotion. Research by industrial psychologist Paul Babiak, and criminal psychologist Robert D. Hare, found that 3.5 per cent of individuals in organizations fitted the psychopathic profile.[52]

Subsequent research found that psychopaths were **more often** found in corporate life than in a mental institution. Psychopathy was positively associated with in-house competency ratings of charisma/presentation style (creativity, good strategic thinking, and communication skills) but negatively associated with ratings of responsibility/performance (being a team player, management skills, and overall accomplishments).[53] The challenge with corporate psychopaths is that, on the surface, they appear charismatic, bold, and visionary. At times of organizational change, this type of person appears calm, rational, levelheaded, and willing to take perceived difficult decisions. Yet beneath the veneer, they lack empathy, are cold and ruthless, and seek roles that provide more power and influence:

> The persona of the high potential or 'ideal leader' is an often amorphous and hard to define concept, and executives tend to rely on 'gut feel' to judge such a complex attribute. Unfortunately, once decision makers believe that an individual has 'future leader' potential, even bad performance reviews or evaluations from subordinates and peers do not seem to be able to shake their belief. It is easy to mistake psychopathic traits for specific leadership traits. For example, charm and grandiosity can be mistaken for self-confidence or a charismatic leadership style; likewise, good presentation, communications, and impressive management skills reinforce the same picture. The psychopath's ability to manipulate can look like good influence and persuasion skills, the mark of an effective leader.[54]

Babiak and Hare continued by defining the dominant traits of a psychopath as:

- Interpersonal: the person is superficial, grandiose, and deceitful
- Affective: the person lacks remorse and empathy and does not accept responsibility
- Lifestyle: the person is impulsive, lacks goals, and is irresponsible
- Antisocial: the person has a history of poor behavioural controls and anti-social behaviour[55]

It is reckoned that people with such profiles are driven by the need for power, dominance, and prestige and will seek and secure leadership positions.[56] In many respects, this seems entirely logical given the personality characteristics that have been found to be associated with many leaders and the fact that, in many ways, leadership positions involve the exertion of power and control. The characteristics of pathological personalities do not usually appear strikingly different from those seen among *normal* individuals.

Successful business leaders are often described as being aggressive, dominant, extrovert, enthusiastic, charming, sociable, self-confident, independent, self-centred, and influential, often seeking to wield authority and restrict organizational resources. Researchers found that while business leaders were less likely to demonstrate some elements of the psychopathic personality disorder, such as physical aggression, consistent irresponsibility with work and finances, lack of remorse (antisocial), impulsivity, suicidal gestures, and so on; rather, the business leaders had learned how to coerce and influence others in a more extroverted and social way to enable them to achieve their own goals and needs.[57] While the authors found the reasons why people with a personality disorder attain positions of legitimate power and authority as perplexing, for many of those who have worked in organizations, it is of little surprise.

Two eminent psychologists found that three out of eleven personality disorders were more common in executives than in convicted criminals. The researchers interviewed and gave personality tests to senior level British executives and compared their profiles with those of criminal psychiatric patients at Broadmoor Hospital in the UK. But how did these executives manage to do so well in their careers? Three main personality disorders emerged which saw them gain a formidable set of personality characteristics:

1. Histrionic personality disorder: superficial charm, insincerity, egocentricity, manipulativeness
2. Narcissistic personality disorder: grandiosity, self-focused, lack of empathy for others, exploitative
3. Obsessive-compulsive personality disorder: perfectionism, excessive devotion to work, rigidity, stubbornness, dictatorial tendencies[58]

Corporate Psychopaths are notoriously disruptive to teamwork. At a superficial level, they will create or be part of teams that suit their purposes. However, they will look for ways to sow division and conflict. All of this is to ensure that they stand out, to be better than anyone else, and to remove any potential threat to their position. Here is an example from a real work-life situation as told to the author by a senior leader from a reputable organization:

> When Stephen arrived in the organization, he talked about the need for 'creating a spine of accountability'. Not many knew what this was, but they were keen to engage with a leader who espoused that he had vast experience in his field. During the course of three years, this leader created and recreated his leadership team. On many occasions, he changed roles, changed people, and changed the structure. In his one-to-one meetings, he would subtly criticize his peers and others in his leadership team. In one meeting, he let it be known that he liked to create division amongst his direct reports as that 'keeps them on their toes'. In one year after a strong performance by individual members of the team, he decided that everyone would receive the same performance rating – all average. He, however, ensured that his own performance rating was 'outstanding'.

These seeds of division are not always immediately apparent within the team. The corporate psychopath is like a chameleon. They will charm and befriend those with knowledge and influence. They are basically predators who prey on the easiest sources of sustenance. Corporate psychopaths are described as self-seeking, cold, and lacking empathy. This may or may not be due to abnormalities of brain function. Criminal psychopaths are known as violent and anti-social and are typically the subject of horror films. Corporate psychopaths are perceived as successful as they often hold senior positions. Yet for those impacted by a corporate psychopath, they will find them to be ruthless and lacking any kind of conscience.

Some experts have described the corporate psychopaths as 'successful psychopaths'. Why? Because the chances of being detected are slim, and the punishment is relatively mild and trivial. Individuals impacted by a psychopath will typically withdraw from the individual perpetrator by either changing job roles or leaving the organization. Raising a complaint or a grievance can lead to a 'gaslighting' experience as other colleagues may not have had the same experience. Altogether, the damage done by corporate psychopaths can be immense. Not only do they impact employees and their engagement and motivation, but they can also push loyal employees to do things that are detrimental to the organization and its reputation. As one of Donald Trump's loyal advisors and former American Vice President said, "After all the things that I have done for him. . . . "[59]

Leaders who are corporate psychopaths present the illusion of success. They come across as smooth, charming, and superficially interested in others. They come across as polished experts in how they dress and hold themselves. They will make derogatory remarks about others in a *locker room* way with those people whom they regard as useful. They may even keep a notebook to ensure they recall the names of people they feel may have wronged them. One such leader whom the author worked with would keep a small black notebook and record the name of someone who may have challenged this leader in a group meeting. Another leader who was challenged by a well-respected member of his team asked him to report to his office the following day. That day, the well-respected colleague suddenly found that he was removed from his senior role and given a new, significantly less influential role as 'Head of Special Projects'. This scenario of 'setting an example' ensured that no one else in the corporate psychopath's leadership team dare challenge him again. The impact of this behaviour left this individual stressed, bewildered, and broken. There was little option but for this well-respected colleague to leave the organization.

Corporate psychopaths can present themselves as charming, likeable, and emotionally well adjusted. They appear friendly, reasonable, and personable.

According to researchers, they will be persuasive and respond to questions with answers that reflect warmth towards others, such as family and children, and speak about loyalty. Many corporate psychopaths will present themselves as accomplished, trustworthy, intelligent, and successful. Corporate psychopaths evoke feelings of friendship and loyalty in those with whom they interact. Described as paradoxically likeable, they are very good at ingratiating themselves with people by telling them what they want to hear.[60] The personal charm and ability to manage upward enables the corporate psychopath to do well at job promotion interviews and be considered for succession planning roles. To the senior leader, they will seem loyal, hardworking, and appear better than their peers. The notion of appearing better is typically a carefully managed self-promotion campaign once inside the organization.

Corporate psychopaths are accomplished liars. They will declare knowledge of certain organizations and the way things are done. They will at times invent things to ensure that they are not exposed by their lack of knowledge and experience, especially to a senior leader. The following example comes from a real work-life experience (names and companies have been changed to protect identities):

> We were having a difficult time with senior leaders on discussing on the value of the talent management system in our organization. A senior leader wanted the process to be conflated and reduced. Many of us had concerns about the value of this process if this was allowed to happen. Jeff, the Director of the Unit, didn't want to lose face. Jeff suddenly announced that at one of his previous organizations, FinCo, an international bank, he had implemented this reduced process with great impact and implied that he had been instrumental to its success. Jeff had previously been a member of the armed forces and was known for disliking any dissent to his ideas. Yet this abrupt change in position left many in the Unit quite bewildered, and yet open to the idea that there might be a better way to be discovered. One of the team members, Sarah, was on good terms with one of the Directors at the international bank and wrote to her asking for more details on the success and learnings of this new approach. The Director replied that they had never ever considered having such a reduced approach and was curious to know why this former member of staff had conjured up this idea when it was a complete fabrication. When Jeff was confronted with this information, he denied the response of the FinCo Group HR Director. In seeking to obscure this revelation, he blamed the business for these ideas, and asked one of his loyal followers to make the issue 'go away'.[61]

The ability to detect lies and manipulations of the truth are tough lessons to learn for people who work for corporate psychopaths. Being accomplished liars enables corporate psychopaths to obtain the jobs that they want.[62] Once inside an organization, the corporate psychopath will set their sights on rising to the top. One organizational psychologist says that psychopaths tend to rise quickly in organizations because of their manipulative charisma and their single-minded determination to attain more power and status. Their intelligence and social skills enable the corporate psychopath to present a veneer of normalcy that enables them to get what they want.[63]

5.5 Toxic Leadership in the Workplace

Toxic leaders use a set of techniques, some more apparent than others. Rather than a checklist, these dimensions inform the reader of how these techniques can show up in the workplace and what they might look like. These techniques are used to control behaviour, information, thoughts, and emotions[64]:

5.5.1 Abuse of Power

The abuse of power serves personal goals. The perpetrator will use their power to reinforce self-image and enhance perceptions of personal performance. This abuse of power conceals personal inadequacies. Rules will be broken or amended to suit the perpetrator's own purposes. They will engage in corrupt, unethical, and, indeed, illegal behaviours, and use their power for personal gains.

5.5.2 Unrealistic Demands

Demands are continuous and unrelenting and will deliberately impact personal time. Taking one day's leave may result in impossible demands, with the toxic leader suddenly insisting on new work requirements and berating the individual over the phone. In one situation, a toxic leader had a large glass jar at group meetings; if someone was late, then they would have to place one dollar in the jar. Designed to make the meeting start on time, it became a way to humiliate individuals, who may have had a medical appointment for instance and therefore arrive late at the meeting. There would be no empathy for such reasons. The toxic leader typically has little respect for the time or private life of the individual and will make unreasonable demands. Individuals may end up keeping their cellphone under their pillow in fear of missing a call from the toxic leader.

5.5.3 Demand for Perfection

The toxic leader will set impossible timelines and demands. It does not matter how hard the person tries, they will be made to feel that they have fallen short; they'll feel bad and try to work even harder. During Trump's presidency, out of 24 cabinet posts, at least 46 appointees were fired or resigned – a record for a US President.

5.5.4 Control, Control, Control

Perpetrators will seek to have complete control of information – how and where it is communicated, disseminated, and consumed. Obsession with detail and perfectionism will contrive to limit subordinate initiative. This is all about controlling the subordinate to do their deeds and, in the event of challenge, they will move to castigate the subordinate with threats or by berating them in public.

Another technique is to require permission for any decisions. Decisions requiring budgetary approval for instance may be delayed or denied. This will happen over a continuous period whereby even straightforward actions will require permission. This control means that the toxic leader literally pulls all the strings. If someone goes ahead and tries to implement something, then they are likely to be called into the office, shouted at, and humiliated or threatened with being fired. Such control is also noted in leaders of cults to instil dependency and obedience.[65]

5.5.5 Them versus Us

Toxic leaders will use language to support a 'them versus us' style of approach. Toxic leaders will use one type of language for their inner circle. For example, one toxic leader shockingly described a risk-averse individual as "he's a double condom guy".[66] The language is typically base and degrading and used within the immediate circle. It is calculated that it will not be repeated, and if it is, then it is dismissed as locker-room talk. Some toxic leaders will undermine their colleague to others outside of the organization by questioning the competence of the individual. Trump used slogans such as 'lock her up' or 'build the wall' – all designed to perpetuate his 'them versus us' view of the world.

5.5.6 Enticing You In

Toxic leaders may reveal negative life stories that they utilize to inform their followers of their hardships. Toxic leaders will cultivate their background as something that requires empathy and understanding. They will actively solicit and target individuals to bring them into their 'inner fold'.

5.5.7 Divide and Rule

The toxic leader will relish putting people at odds with each other. Shrewdly, the toxic leader likes to see conflict and confusion. In her memoir *Unhinged*, Manigault Newman[67], who had worked with Trump for 14 years, described how Trump would often pit employees against each other as he did on his business television show *The Apprentice*, and observed how his face would light up.

Toxic leaders typically ask for the same work from more than one person. The individuals find out that they are doing the same work and it becomes competitive rather than collaborative. Toxic leaders may boast that they actively ensure that the individuals in their teams remain divided. Toxic leaders will have side conversations with individuals, make jokes about the others using defamatory language, or criticize individuals in meetings in a public forum. The toxic leader will ensure that their colleagues and subordinates are treated differently. This inconsistency enables the toxic leader to create a 'gaslighting' effect where individuals begin to question their own reactions and perceptions.

5.5.8 Threats

The *Wall Street Journal* described a 'culture of intimidation' at Enron. The Chief Financial Officer had an ornament on his desk with the inscription: "When ENRON says it's going to rip your face off . . . it means it will rip your face off".[68] Threatening individual job security is typical behaviour from a toxic leader.

5.5.9 Selling a Vision

Destructive leaders sell a vision of a desirable future. Such a vision will characterize the threats and insecurities of the external world and focus on personal safety by defeating adversaries and rivals. They will threateningly present a 'them versus us' storyline. Destructive leaders will be self-promoting and spend time cultivating their image, presence, and impact in front of audiences.

5.5.10 Requirement of Unquestionable Loyalty and Devotion

Toxic leaders will choose followers who do their beckoning and are 'loyal' to their requirements. Anyone who questions or offers an alternative perspective is likely to find themselves quickly placed into a different role. The toxic leader will expect absolute loyalty. Any criticism, however minor, will be viewed as dissent. The 'dissenter' will find themselves ignored, not invited to meetings, or have any connection with the toxic leader.

One Senior Executive Recounted Their Experience of a Toxic Leader[69]:

> In my previous company, we brought in this guy from another organization to be the head of this business unit. From the CV and interview, there were no signs that the person is toxic or has a toxic personality. While we were not making money, we focused on all the elements and changed the leadership and brought in this guy. I think the one thing that we forgot, which is a challenge for HR leaders, is one takes up the references that the person gives you. We never do an independent reference check. So if you think about it, then this person is going to give you names of people who are going to give positive references. We did reference checks and it all came back positive. We hired him and one month down the line we started receiving on an average every month 3 anonymous letters from local staff that he is against the local nationals and using foul language. These letters were copied to the President and HR. The HR stance was we need to go in and investigate this. Internal Audit responded that they were not going to do anything as the letters were anonymous, so they replied to the senders: please put in your name. They replied back with 'we do not trust to provide our names'. So this continued to the point that another letter is sent. It stated that 'this is getting out of hand, we cannot work with this individual, he comes in, he shouts at people, he throws things down, it is my way or the highway'. Unfortunately, the organization's viewpoint was 'he is trying to push people to perform and we would be losing money'. Then the resignations started coming. First of all the local staff started leaving and then the senior leaders also started resigning. That is when people woke up in the organization, but by that time the whole team was disengaged. Most of the talented employees had left the organization.
>
> In the end, we had to fire him, because when we started investigating him, it was very evident. He even lost his temper in front of me, 'so you guys are sitting in Head Office' and 'you have no idea what the market is and these nationals, they are only 50 per cent productive'. I then interviewed people

> who he said he loved and all of them fell into a typically 'yes sir' mentality. They wanted to keep their jobs. They mentioned that 'yes, sometimes he loses his temper, but we all do that you know. We have to deliver against objectives otherwise we will lose our bonus or lose our jobs'. So all these fear elements start coming in with a toxic leader because they use their power more than their leadership style and their setup and direction is 'my way or the highway'.

Another Senior Executive recounted her own experience (names have been changed to protect identities):[70]

> Anna had worked for her boss for four years. In her first year, she found the organization difficult to navigate. She had moved continents and left her partner and family in her home country. The new organization was unlike anything she had seen before. Her new boss told her that he had brought her into the organization to make changes. The new boss derided Anna's colleagues as being too 'comfortable' and not making the changes that he required. With these words sounding in her ears, Anna took on this mantle. In group meetings, she called out her colleagues for not making changes, and criticized their approaches. Her new boss was pleased with Anna's progress and asked her to write a guide for her colleagues so she can tell them what she needed them to do. Anna was delighted to do so.
>
> Behind Anna's back, her new boss confided in others that Anna was having a difficult transition. Anna knew it was challenging. Slowly colleagues stopped conversing with Anna and those colleagues that she had called out in meetings began to speak of her naivety in the organization. After one year, Anna went to see her boss. She said she was finding the organization difficult and that given it was only a year that she could return to her home country as she still had connections and could find an alternative job role. Her boss talked her out of resigning. He promised that he would support her and that she was the 'right' person to make the changes. Two years later, Anna was told by her boss that her contract would not be renewed. She was shattered. Her boss had continued to make promises because it would have looked bad to senior management for one of his senior recruits to resign after a year. Anna found the change in the persona to be so dramatic that she ended up seeking counselling. Just before her departure, Anna said, 'It was like he (the boss) had never known me, it is if, I am a complete stranger as he is so cold'.

It is worth noting that in Steven Hassan's: *The Cult of Trump,* the former President is described by those who worked with and for him as "mercurial, demanding absolute loyalty, alternating between praise and criticism and often pitting employees against one another".[71]

Trump as the President of the USA was notorious for firing staff who disagreed with him, ridiculing individuals on social media, proclaiming his own 'genius', and so on. Prominent psychiatrists and psychologists detailed their concerns about Trump's mental health and his fitness to serve.[72] As one psychiatrist noted,

> In Trump we have a frightening Venn diagram of three circles: the first is extreme present hedonism; the second, narcissism; and the third, bullying behavior. These three circles overlap in the middle to create an impulsive, immature, incompetent person who when in a position of power, easily becomes a tyrant.[73]

Michael Cohen, Trump's former personal attorney who admitted to fraud and perjury and was sentenced to a prison term, said, "Sitting here today, it seems unbelievable that I was so mesmerized by Donald Trump that I was willing to do things for him that I know were absolutely wrong".[74]

5.6 Is the Poison in the Person or in the Bottle?

Two researchers present an interesting perspective concerning the effect of the job role on the person.[75] They argue that a role cannot be seen in isolation, as a role is influenced by other roles in the organizational system. Employees, for example, will wait with hope or trepidation when a new CEO is appointed. Certain job roles may have a history and hold expectations about how someone is expected to behave in this role by others in the organization. Sometimes, individuals feel that they are acting out of character. Unfortunately, this is a much-neglected area of research.

However, there does appear to be a connection between certain personality characteristics and job roles. As one senior executive suggested, in an interview for this book, there are early warning signs:

> A great many CEOs have to have an element of narcissism and self-belief to get up every morning and sit there in a very public role, where you're criticised by shareholders, where your board is on your back, you've got to have a little bit of a faith in yourself. If you spot a CEO, however, whose faith is so unshakable and genuinely believes their own publicity and where they are, that's an early … that's a sign of toxicity even if they go in with the best of intentions.[76]

In the next chapter, we explore the role of followers and their role in the toxic triangle.

5.7 Summary

This chapter has explored the dark side of leadership and how it shows up in the workplace. The Dark Triad summarizes three personality types that are not necessarily mutually exclusive. Research reveals that *psychopathic*, *Machiavellian*, and *narcissistic* personality types are more prevalent in the workplace than imagined. The impact of performance pressures may accentuate and inflame toxic behaviour. Leaders are the role models in the organization; they cast a long shadow, setting an example of how others should behave, and which behaviours are tolerated. As previously noted, leadership and culture are two sides of the same coin. Organizations may inadvertently reward, select, and promote behaviours that can be defined as psychopathic with ultimately devastating consequences. The next chapter looks at the role of followers.

Notes

1 Leadership is defined here as anyone with responsibilities to manage and/or direct people, including managers and supervisors.
2 Hogan, R., & Hogan, J. (2009) *Hogan Development Survey Manual*. Second Edition. https://www.crownedgrace.com/wp-content/uploads/2016/04/Hogan-Development-Survey.pdf. Accessed 9 January 2022.
3 *Ibid*.
4 Hamel, G. (2012) *What Matters Now: How to Win in a World of relentless Change, Ferocious Competition, and Unstoppable Innovation* (1st ed.). San Francisco, CA: Jossey-Bass.
5 Tourish, D. (2013) *The Dark Side of Transformational Leadership – A Critical Perspective*. London: Routledge. p.7.
6 Furnham, A., & Taylor, T. (2004) *The Dark Side of Behaviour at Work*. London: Palgrave.
7 Kaiser, R.B., LeBreton, J.M., & Hogan, J. (2015) The dark side of personality and extreme leader behaviour. *Applied Psychology*, 641: 55–92.
8 Babiak, P., & Hare, R.D. 2006. *Snakes in Suits: When Psychopaths Go to Work*. New York: Harper Business.
9 McCall and Lombardo (1983) What makes a top executive. *Psychology Today*, 17(2): 26–31.
Furnham, A. (2010). *The Elephant in the Boardroom: The Causes of Leadership Derailment*. London: Palgrave Macmillan.
Hogan, R., & Hogan, J. (2001). Assessing leadership: A view from the dark side. *International Journal of Selection and Assessment*, 9: 40–51.
Kellerman, B. (2004) *Bad Leadership*. Boston, MA: Harvard Business School Press.
Conger, J.A. (1990) The dark side of leadership. *Organization Dynamics*, 19(2): 44–55.
Maccoby, M. (2000) Narcissistic leaders: The incredible pros, the inevitable cons. *Harvard Business Review*, 78(1): 68–78.
Kets de Vries (1993) *Leaders, Fools and Imposters: Essays on the Psychology of Leadership*. San Francisco, CA: Jossey Bass.
10 Interview with Senior Executive, November 2021.

11 Whicker, M.L. (1996) *Toxic Leaders: When Organizations Go Bad*. Eugene: Quorum Books.

Lipman-Blumen, J. (2005) *The Allure of Toxic Leaders: Why We Follow Destructive Bosses and Corrupt Politicians – and How We Can Survive Them*. Oxford: Oxford University Press.

Walton, M. (2007) Leadership toxicity – An inevitable affliction of organizations. *Organisations & People*, 14(1): 19–27.

Schmidt, A.A. (2008) Development and validation of the toxic leadership scale, Masters Thesis, University of Maryland.

Watt, S.R., Javidi, M., & Normore, A. (2017) *Increasing Darkness: Combining Toxic Leadership and Volatility, Uncertainty, Complexity and Ambiguity (VUCA)*. Long Beach: California State University.

Singh, N., Sengupta, S., & Dev, S. (2019) Toxic leadership: The most menacing form of leadership. In M. Brandebo & A. Alvinius (Eds.), *Dark Sides of Organizational Behavior and Leadership*. London: IntechOpen. p. 150.

Morris, J.A. (2019) Understanding Coping Strategies and Behaviours of Employees Affected by Toxic Leadership. *Walden Dissertations and Doctoral Studies*. 6359.

Milosevic, I., Maric, S., & Loncar, D. (2020) Defeating the toxic boss: The nature of toxic leadership and the role of followers. *Journal of Leadership and Organizational Studies*, 27(2): 117–137.

Einarsen, S., Aasland, M., & Skogstad, A. (2007) Destructive leadership behaviour: A definition and conceptual model. *The Leadership Quarterly*, 18(3): 207–216.

Thoroughgood, C.N., Sawyer, K.B., Padilla, A., & Lunsford, L. (2018) Destructive leadership: A critique of leader-centric perspectives and toward a more holistic definition. *Journal of Business Ethics*, 151: 627–649.

Christie, A., Barling, J., & Turner, N. (2011) Pseudo-transformational leadership: Model specification and outcomes. *Journal of Applied Social Psychology*, 41(12): 2943–2984.

12 Carucci, R. (2018) 3 Ways Senior Leaders Create a Toxic Culture. *Harvard Business Review*. 1 May 2018.

13 Bass, B.M. & Riggio, R.E. (2006) *Transformational Leadership* (2nd ed.). Mahwah, NJ: Lawrence Erlbaum Associates Publishers. p.3.

14 Rosenzweig, P. (2007) Misunderstanding the nature of company performance: The halo effect and other business delusions. *California Management Review*, 49(4):6–20.

15 Collins, J., & Porras, J.I. (1994) *Built to Last*. New York: William Collins.

Collins, J. (2001) *Good to Great – Why Some Companies Make the Leap and Others Don't*. New York: HarperCollins.

Collins, J. (2009) *How the Mighty Fall*. Jim Collins.

Collins, J., & Hanson, M.T. (2011) *Great by Choice: Uncertainty, Chaos, and Luck – Why Some Thrive Despite Them All*. Grand Island, NE: Cornerstone.

16 Kets de Vries, M.F.R. (1993) *Leaders, Fools and Imposters – Essays on the Psychology of Leadership*. Hoboken, NJ: Jossey Bass, p.22.

17 Tourish, D. (2013) *The Dark Side of Transformational Leadership* (1st ed). London: Routledge.

18 Tourish, D. (2013:4).

19 *Ibid.*
20 Connell, C. (2015) Psychopaths Among Us. *iWitness News*. https://www.iwnsvg.com/2018/01/25/psychopaths-among-us/. Accessed 9 January 2022.
21 Babiak & Hare (2006).
22 Kaiser *et al.* (2015).
Hogan & Hogan (2009).
Moscoso, S., & Salgado, J.F. (2004) "Dark Side" personality styles as predictors of task, contextual and job performance. *International Journal of Selection and Assessment*, 12: 356–362.
Schmit, M.J., Kilm, J.A., & Robie, C. (2000) Development of a global measure of personality. *Personnel Psychology*, 53: 153–193.
23 *The Diagnostic and Statistical Manual of Mental Disorders* is the key reference for personality disorders. In the most recent fifth edition, it lists ten specific personality disorders: paranoid, schizoid, schizotypal, antisocial, borderline, histrionic, narcissist, avoidant, dependent, and obsessive-compulsive personality disorder.
24 van Rooij, B., & Fine, A. (2018) Toxic corporate culture: Assessing organisational processes of deviancy. *Administrative Sciences*, 8(23): 1–38.
25 Lewis, S.E. (2006) Recognition of workplace bullying: A qualitative study of women targets in the public sector. *Journal of Community and Applied Social Psychology*, 16(2): 119–135.
26 Namie, G., & Namie, T. (2009) US workplace bullying: Some basic considerations and consultation interventions. *Consulting Psychology Journal: Practice and Research*, 613: 202–219.
27 Roter, A.B. (2017) *Understanding and Recognising Dysfunctional Leadership: The Impact of Dysfunctional Leadership on Organisations and Followers*. London: Routledge.
28 Einarsen, S., & Raknes, B. (1997) Harassment in the Workplace and the Victimisation of Men, Violence and Victims. *Journal of Scientific Research*, 12: 247–263.
29 Yamada, D.C. (2000) The Phenomenon of 'Workplace Bullying' and the Need for Status-Blind Hostile Work Environment Protection. *Georgetown Law Journal*, 88:84.
30 Roter, A. (2017) *Understanding and Recognizing Dysfunctional Leadership*. New York: Taylor Francis.
31 Roter, A. (2017) *Understanding and Recognizing Dysfunctional Leadership*. London: Taylor Francis.
32 Interview with Senior Executive, November 2021.
33 The Diagnostic and Statistical Manual of Mental Disorders (DSM; latest edition: DSM-5-TR, published in March 2022) is a publication by the American Psychiatric Association (APA) for the classification of mental disorders using a common language and standard criteria.
34 Experts also note the overlap as follows: a. Machiavellianism with psychopathy; b. Narcissism with psychopathy and c. Machiavellianism with narcissism.
35 Paulhus, D.L., & Williams, K.M. (2002) The dark triad of personality: Narcissism, machiavellianism and psychopathy. *Journal of Research in Personality*, 36: 556–563.
36 Hogan & Hogan (2001).

37 Check out Hogan's psychological assessment measuring the dark side of leadership: https://www.hogandarkside.com/.
38 Boddy, C. (2013) *The Corporate Psychopath – Organizational Destroyers*. London: Palgrave Macmillan.
39 *Ibid.*
40 Babiak & Hare (2006).
41 Chatterjee, A., & Hambrick, D.C. (2007) It's all about me: Narcissistic chief executive officers and their effects on company strategy and performance. *Administrative Science Quarterly*, 52(3): 351–386.
42 *Ibid.*
43 *Ibid.*
44 https://www.med.wisc.edu/news-and-events/2011/november/psychopaths-brains-diff. Accessed on 26 June 2022.
45 *Ibid.*
46 Babiak & Hare (2006).
47 Boddy (2013) p.5.
48 Boddy (2013).
49 *Ibid.*
50 *Ibid.*
51 Babiak & Hare (2006).
52 *Ibid.* p.193.
53 Babiak & Hare (2006).
54 *Ibid.* pp.190–191.
55 Babiak & Hare (2006).
56 Kernberg, O.F. (1979) Regression on organizational leadership. *Psychiatry*, 42(1): 24–39.
57 Board, B.J., & Fritzon, K. (2005) Disordered personalities at work. *Psychology, Crime & Law*, 11(1): 17–32.
58 *Ibid.* pp.17–32.
59 Pence, M. cited in Jacobs, E. (2021) Furious Pence to GOP pol after Capitol siege: 'After all I've done for him'. *New York Post*. https://nypost.com/2021/01/07/pence-to-gop-pol-after-capitol-siege-after-all-ive-done/. Accessed 9 January 2022.
60 Clarke, J. (2007) *The Pocket Psycho*. Australia: Random House.
61 Recounted to the author, 2017.
62 Kirkman, C.A. (2005) From soap opera to science: Towards gaining access to the psychopaths who live among us. *Psychology and Psychotherapy*, 78: 379–396.
63 Babiak & Hare (2006).
64 Hassan, S. (2020) *The Cult of Trump*. New York: Free Press.
65 *Ibid.*
66 Interview with Senior Executive, December 2021.
67 Manigault-Newman, O. (2018) *Unhinged. An Insiders Account of the Trump White House*. New York: Gallery Books.
68 https://www.wsj.com/articles/SB1030320285540885115. Accessed 6 June 2022.
69 Interview with Senior Executive, November 2021.

70 Recounted to the author in 2017. Pseudonyms have been used.
71 Hassan (2020).
72 Lee, B.X. (2017) *The Dangerous Case of Donald Trump: 37 Psychiatrists and Mental Health Exerts Assess a President*. New York: Thomas Dunne Books.
73 *Ibid.*
74 *Ibid.*
75 Chapman, J., & Long, S. (2009) Role contamination: Is the poison in the person or the bottle?. *Socio-Analysis*, 11: 53–66.
76 Interview with Senior Executive, December 2021.

6 Susceptible Followers

6.1 Introduction

Toxic leadership and toxic workplace cultures are major risks to organizational performance and to the welfare of employees in the workplace and broader society. Toxic workplace cultures cost an estimated $223bn over the five years prior to 2019.[1] While it is important to better understand toxic leadership and how to spot it in organizations, there is also a need to look at the broader context and the range of stakeholders involved. Books on toxic leadership are quick to focus on destructive leadership behaviours and the consequences they have for organizations and their cultures. However, recently more attention has been paid to the role of other parties, specifically followers and their interaction with leadership processes and working environments.

In a pragmatic sense, leaders require followers to be able to call themselves 'leaders'. In cases of toxic leadership, followers have historically been framed as innocent bystanders and passive recipients of the leader's vision and behaviour, or 'susceptible followers'.[2] This stereotypical view of followership is due to a lack of consensus around what followership means and its relationship to leadership.[3] This must not undermine the impact that toxic leadership and culture may have on employees, organizations, and their effectiveness. Instead, it is important to shed light on how such toxic leadership behaviour comes to be through a more holistic understanding by bringing followers into the conversation – for example, how employees, managers, and boards, and the roles they may (or may not) play assist in the development of 'bad' leaders and cultures in different contexts.

6.2 Leadership and Followership

In research and practice, questions have been raised surrounding traditional approaches that frame leadership as top-down and hierarchical in nature.[4] As a result, our understanding of followership is often framed through the lens of

DOI: 10.4324/9781003330387-9

leaders and leadership. Let us review three approaches to how followers have historically been framed in leadership research[5]:

(i) The leader-centric view
This view supports the idea that leaders are the opposite of followers; they hold power and the ability to directly influence followers to achieve objectives. This typically portrays followers as passive bystanders who 'follow' and 'receive' leadership influence and respond wilfully without much resistance or challenge. The foundations of modern business management (Taylorism, Fordism, and scientific management) are built upon this premise and the need for 'lazy workers' to be managed. This long-standing perspective reinforces our understanding of followers as 'subordinates'.

(ii) The follower-centric approach
Follower-centric approaches gained prominence in response to leadership-centred views and focused on the part of the follower in the creation of leaders and leadership. In this view, leadership is viewed as socially constructed by followers as a means for them to understand the organization, its purpose, and direction through what has been classed as 'The Romance of Leadership'.[6] This idea was developed through shared assumptions about what is real and not real in the social life of organizations. Followers create narratives around their leaders, dependent on what they need them 'to be'.

(iii) Relational view
This understanding of leadership posits that the relational dynamics are key; for example, through leader-member exchanges and how leaders and followers collaborate to produce quality work and organizational outcomes. This view is also present in the 'toxic triangle',[7] whereby toxicity in organizations is a result of destructive leaders, susceptible followers, and conducive environments.

These perspectives highlight how our understanding of followers has been shaped by the leadership process and the relationships between leaders and followers.

Early definitions of followership discussed the term as similar to 'subordinate', emphasizing the role of hierarchy and defining followers in terms of 'what they do' instead of 'who they are'.[8] Much of modern social history is shaped by hierarchical and authoritarian portrayals of leaders in power[9] and the view that humans are intrinsically motivated to lead in the 'fight to survive'.[10] This hierarchical nature is also present within contemporary organizations, which causes followers to face dilemmas on how to react to toxic behaviours and misconduct due to their place in the 'pecking order'.[11] This narrative misleads via stereotypes of how the actions and decisions of leaders overshadow, and are seemingly more important than, the follower, with followers being framed as passive or easily conforming. For example, Kellerman describes this as "subordinates who have less power, authority, and influence than do their superiors, and who therefore usually, but not invariably, fall into line".[12] There is cause for challenging this definition and turning the spotlight onto how organizations can foster environments which allow for "proactive, autonomous, and ethically responsible followers".[13]

Some of the earliest contemporary commentators on the topic of followership discuss the importance of the followership role. In his *Harvard Business Review* (1988) article[14] "In Praise of Followers", Robert Kelley raises this preoccupation with and dominant focus on leadership in organizations as odd, due to the fact that more people could be classed as 'followers' rather than leaders. Kelley points out that what distinguishes leaders from followers is the need for leaders to have a stronger desire to articulate a vision, compared with the more humble followers who pursue their goals without harm to others.

One way that the leader-follower relationship has been reconstructed over recent years is how leader and follower roles come to be recognized in organizations, and the relational nature in which they depend on one another, interact, and even change over time. Researchers have explored how leadership and leader-follower relationships develop in organizations, and how these roles are mutually claimed and 'granted' in working environments.[15] This fits well with the premise of this book of how toxic conditions develop in organizations and what roles leaders and followers play.

6.3 Expectations of Followership

The way in which a follower should behave has been central to much research. One researcher suggested that followers should be characterized based on five components, termed "courageous followership"[16]:

- The courage to assume responsibility for themselves without an expectation that the leader will provide security or opportunities for growth
- The courage to serve a leader by assuming new or additional responsibilities
- The courage to challenge by voicing any discomfort, or when the policies and behaviour of the leader conflict with a personal sense of what is right
- The courage to participate fully in transformation and change
- The courage to leave the leader or the organization and withdraw all support, even with high personal risk

These beliefs on the role of the follower are assumed in most organizations. These assumptions were developed into a model that defined two key underpinning behaviours for effective followership: 'the courage to support' and 'the courage to challenge the leader's behaviour or policies'. In this framework,[17] four kinds of followers are defined:

1. Resource – low support, low challenge. Will do enough to retain position but no more
2. Individualist – low support, high challenge. Will speak up when others are silent, but voice is marginalized and perceived as chronically critical
3. Implementer – high support, low challenge. Leader values this style, but a risk that follower will not voice caution
4. Partner – high support, high challenge. Assumes full responsibility for own and leader's behaviour and acts accordingly

So how do followers see themselves? One study[18] found that followers tended to align themselves to one of the following three categories:

1. Passive followers who are loyal, supportive, and obey their leaders' directives
2. Active followers who provide 'opinions' when given the opportunity, but remain obedient and loyal regardless of whether or not they are in agreement with the leader
3. Proactive followers who are willing to constructively challenge their managers if needed

6.4 Followership and Toxic Leadership

Despite a plethora of books teaching followers how to cope with bad, sad, or mad leaders, there are few studies that look at understanding how followers cope with toxic leadership. Toxic leadership, as we discussed in the previous chapter, describes leaders who engage in consistently negative behaviours, from bullying, manipulating, intimidating, micromanaging, and arrogance to unethical and abusive behaviour.

Typically, followers who find themselves working for a toxic leader will employ two strategies: 'avoidance' and 'seeking emotional support'. Yet one study found that both these strategies led to increased stress.[19]

In another study, followers reported six leadership behaviours that they perceived as harmful. These behaviours all had an impact on the individual's psychological state and emotional and physical health – see Table 6.1 for examples of harmful leadership behaviours.[20]

In dealing with a toxic leader, followers have sought various coping strategies that included avoidance and support-seeking. These are detailed in Table 6.2.

Table 6.1 Examples of Harmful Leadership Behaviour

Behaviours	*Described as …*
Manipulating	Creating conflict: *she has her favourites*, use of deception/lying: *he presented my presentation as his to the Board, replacing my name with his*, and professional misconduct: *he had personal relationships with several female staff members below his level.*
Intimidating and bullying	Autocratic management style: *my way or the highway*; belittling staff: *swearing and using intimidating language*; *if an employee spoke up against the manager, he would target them and systematically try to get rid of them.*
Abusive or emotionally volatile	Abuse, tantrums, and threatening behaviour.
Narcissistic	Arrogant behaviour: *constantly seeks and needs praise, must win at all costs.*
Micromanaging	Fault-finding, controlling: *he had to know what I was doing every minute of the day.*
Passive aggressive	Ignores or refuses to take action: *the leader agreed to take action and then later negated on this.*

Adapted from Webster, V., Brough, P., & Daly, K. (2014) Fight, flight or freeze: Common responses for follower coping with toxic leadership. *Stress and Health Journal*, 32: 346–354.

Table 6.2 Followers' Coping Strategies

Coping strategies	*Actions*
Problem solving/ direct communication	Confronting the leader/undertaking health and well-being activities
Support-seeking	Mentor or colleague, family, and friends
Avoidance of contact	Taking leave, resigning, seeking a transfer, ignoring the leader
Reframing	Cognitive restructuring, treating it as a problem project
Information-seeking	Professional advice, self-education, reading
Submission	Accepting the problem
Self-reliance	Regulating emotions and behaviours
Helplessness	Feelings of helplessness, despair, and insecurity
Delegation	Feelings of shame, self-blame
Ingratiation	Flattery of toxic leaders to appease their behaviour

Adapted from Webster, V., Brough, P., & Daly, K. (2014) Fight, flight or freeze: Common responses for follower coping with toxic leadership. *Stress and Health Journal*, 32: 346–354.

6.5 Followership in Toxic Cultures

As discussed, toxic leaders and toxicity in organizations are detrimental to organizational functioning. Since leaders do not exist without followers, it can also be assumed to some degree that toxic leaders might not exist without toxic followers. To better understand toxicity in contemporary organizations, the followers of toxic leaders should be examined, a focus which has received very little attention in both research and practice. This section explores different types of followers. Research into toxic leadership has found the followers mimicking and mirroring organizational leaders' behaviours. The presence of corporate psychopaths has an insidious effect and trickles into the subconscious. Neuroscientists found that some neurons mimic or mirror the neurons in other people's brains, and this can trigger empathetic feelings.[21]

One effect of having toxic leaders in the workforce is reported to be the withdrawal of effort, energy, and commitment to an organization by other employees. Other researchers have found that employees who perceived their supervisors to be abusive were most likely to leave their jobs.[22]

Corporate psychopaths create a toxic workplace environment typified by conflict, bullying, disruption, increased workload, low levels of job satisfaction, and higher than necessary organizational constraints.[23] Researchers describe toxic leaders as immoral, ruthless, demeaning to others, forceful, deceptive, self-serving, predatory, and manipulative. Researchers have found that employees who experience a toxic leader are more likely to take sick leave, even when not sick. There is a correlation between poor management and sickness absence.[24] The underlying cause of absenteeism relates to low morale, poor communication, low job satisfaction, and a feeling of not being appreciated. Staff will resign and leave an organization as a means of withdrawal.[25]

More concerning is that one bad leader can 'infect' others. One researcher found that social pressures within organizations from peers or leaders who are dishonest can force employees to 'fit in' with others' dishonesty, and in turn become dishonest themselves.[26] As one senior HR practitioner commented[27]:

> I think there is nothing more dangerous than a committed disciple, and as I said, in the same way in which leadership magnifies, it magnifies and amplifies, so if people respond to the adverse behaviours and culture created by leaders and are seen to be rewarded or favoured because of that, then that amplifies...

One of the leading frameworks in the literature surrounding toxicity in organizations is the Toxic Triangle, which highlights the factors involved in destructive leadership, including the role of 'susceptible followers' and the reasons underpinning why certain types of followers are vulnerable to abusive leaders.

6.6 Susceptible Followers

According to eminent researchers,[28] 'destructive leadership' combined with 'susceptible followers' ultimately leads to the destruction of the organization. It is not suggested that all 'bad' leadership behaviours will lead to the destruction of the organization. Rather that certain types of followers may be more *susceptible* than others, and that does not include all followers. Followers are separated into two camps: 'conformers' and 'colluders'; "Conformers comply with destructive leaders out of fear whereas colluders actively participate in a destructive leader's agenda".[29] Conformers are more likely to be submissive and unlikely to enact destructive behaviours, while colluders will actively engage with a destructive leader's mission. The attention to ideal followership behaviours has been heavily influenced by business ethics and corporate social responsibility. The two types of follower behaviours described focus on what has become known as 'crimes of obedience', where followers conform or collude, and these behavioural types are described as more typical in toxic organizations.

Observers argue that people who are ambitious for status and power may be willing to follow their leader if it suits their personal agenda. Similarly, if the leader extols the same values or even a vision, this may also lead to greater collusion. Other observers note that individuals whose beliefs are consistent with those of the destructive leaders are likely to commit to their cause. These types of followers can be described as **'colluders'**.

Other researchers point to immaturity on the part of the followers. Freud, for example, argued that in a crowd, people's superegos collapse and are replaced symbolically by the leader. The leader then becomes the 'guide' for the individuals' actions. In other words, deference leads to conformity. There is a 'natural' tendency for people to obey authority figures, as well as to emulate or align with 'higher status' individuals. These followers can be described as **'conformers'**.

In a study in a public university in the United States, researchers supported these definitions. Table 6.3 summarizes the definitions and examples of followership.

In another study[32] exploring the impact of how a conducive environment and susceptible followers influence toxic leadership behaviours in the US Air Force, a researcher found that susceptible followers have a direct influence on toxic leadership behaviours. The researcher found that the most harmful indicators of susceptible followers were those displaying the 'colluder' role. The collusive behaviours were ambition, greed, lack of impulse controls, and Machiavellian tendencies. This confirms that susceptible followers are a key part of the toxic triangle.

Table 6.3 Definitions and Examples of Followership

Follower type *subtype*	*Thumbnail definitions*	*Taxonomy*[30]	**Examples** [31]
Conformer Lost Soul	Low self-esteem individual who desires clarity in direction and if given support by a leader, will become a loyalist.	a. Well-recognized follower b. Drawn to leaders who can offer them a sense of belonging, clarity, and direction c. Prone to dependence, vulnerability, and manipulation in attempt to gain leader acceptance.	Faculty member who can be counted on to publicly support the president any time a perceived attack is made upon the president; announces awards given to the president to the campus via e-mail.
Conformer Bystander	The fearful who avoid the leader but will support the leader publicly or back down to avoid retribution.	a. Passive and motivated by fear b. May be more independent and private.	Faculty member who is known to oppose the policies and practices of the president, but in his role as a department chair, says nothing publicly to defy the administration. Staff employee who is known to fear for their job and supports elements of the president's agenda in public.
Conformer Authoritarian	Law and order individual, seeks structure, and readily accepts authority figures.	a. Differs from lost souls: supports hierarchical structures and unconditional support of leader b. Willingness to live up to expectations of role instead of seeking approval	Former top-level administrator, retired shortly before new president was installed, joined the new president's informal cabinet; tells questioning administrators, faculty, or staff that they should support the president 'because they are the president'.

Colluder Acolyte	True believer in the toxic leader's agenda	a. Opposite of lost souls: clear sense of self b. Recipient of the leader's vision due to their goal internalization motivation/goal identification c. True believer: the leader knows best and is expert.	Top-level administrator who has expressed agreement with the agenda of the president; widely believed to have assisted in surveillance of employees. Faculty member appointed by the president to serve as a top-level administrator despite being perceived as having limited qualifications; is seen as fulfilling the hand-in-glove requirement.
Colluder Opportunist	Toxic 'leader in waiting', supports the leader, capitalizes on opportunities to secure political, financial, or social gain	a. Views their link to destructive leaders as means for personal success and financial, political, or professional outcomes b. Driven by rewards, even for bad behaviour (exchange) c. Believes the leader holds valuable resources and valuable outcomes.	Supports administration in multiple public events, is rewarded with substantial remuneration for a key campus-wide committee position; is named interim upper-level administrator despite being perceived as having limited qualifications for the position.

In terms of the conducive environment, two factors mitigated against 'susceptible followers' and their 'negative behaviours': (1) proactively managing change by enabling individuals to develop a level of resilience to unpredictability; and (2) ensuring that all employees are treated equitably and shown no signs of favouritism.

6.7 Positive and Negative Followers

The scant literature that exists on followership has largely focused on the positive outcomes of followers, or on how followers receive destructive leadership. There remains the issue of negative follower behaviour, that is, followers who exhibit immoral values, lack of care for colleagues, and enact purely self-serving behaviours that support toxic environments. The behaviours of negative and positive followers are defined in Table 6.4.

While there is evidence that toxic leaders exploit their followers' psychological desires and fears,[34] there is also evidence that certain 'followers' can display

Table 6.4 Thody's Typology of Positive and Negative Behaviours[33]

Negative followers		*Positive followers*	
Behaviours:	*Roles played:*	*Behaviours:*	*Roles played:*
Alienated	Communicator Distorter	Independent	Coordinator
Isolated	Saboteur	Active passive	Mentee/ Apprentice
Passive	Toxic creator	Entrepreneurial	Disciple
Dependent		Loyalist	Gatekeeper/Filter
Observer		Exemplary/ Exceptional	Partner/Comrade
Reluctant		Interdependent	Toxic handler
Sheep		Transactional	Second in command
Machiavellian			Rescuer
Plateaued			Muse
Survivor			
Yes-people			
Sycophants			

negative and toxic behaviours and have the potential to enact 'shady strategic behaviour':[35]

> Susceptible, willing followers emerged rapidly and conspired to aid the leader in inculcating strong, corporate culture.[36]

These actions show that followers can contribute, embed, and reinforce a toxic culture by their own behaviours. They can choose to distort information, mock peers and colleagues, or choose to praise the leaders while in their presence but do the opposite when with other colleagues. Described as sycophants, yes-people, and Machiavellian, such followers focus on their own needs. In such situations, the follower may be highly competitive in order to show the leader and senior management the quality of their work, and they may at times claim work that is not their own.

Organizational Citizenship Behaviours (OCBs) are behaviours that describe employees who want to go the extra mile. They refer to employees who act to support the broader social and psychological environment and who are considered discretionary, as well as going over and above their job description. Employees who are pressurized into engaging with OCBs experience more stress and work-family conflicts, as well as other personal costs. Studies reveal that OCBs are often linked to the expectation that 'going the extra mile' or 'collaborating with colleagues' will earn the employee a promotion. For some followers, 'going the extra mile' is not altruistic but self-serving, enabling the individual to enhance personal image or impress management. Such individuals may selectively engage with highly visible OCBs to facilitate their own personal success.[37]

What if 'followers' are guided by the wrong values or lack a moral compass and compassion? What if followers scored high on 'dark triad' traits? Researchers exploring these questions found that followers with 'dark triad' traits were (i) likely to have negative effects on fellow colleagues and on the organization, and (ii) failed to pursue shared objectives, preferring to pursue their own interests.[38]

As discussed in the previous chapter, the 'dark triad' is a constellation of three traits: narcissism, Machiavellianism, and psychopathy. While these traits can overlap, they are distinguished as follows:

- Narcissism has a strong sense of entitlement, self-importance, and a strong need for power
- Machiavellianism is defined as having a calculating and deceitful interpersonal style
- Psychopathy is described as a lack of empathy, with a reckless and manipulative style

While the last chapter looked at the Dark Triad in respect to leadership, how the Dark Triad traits are likely to show up in followers will now be examined. Followers who scored highly in Dark Triad personality traits are likely to have self-serving preferences. Their actions will be aimed at achieving their own self-interested goals, which can be harmful or negative to others.

6.7.1 Narcissistic Followers

Narcissists have a need to shine in the workplace. They are likely to make career choices that enable them to do so. In terms of OCBs, they are likely to use the behaviours that serve their own interests.

Narcissists use two different ways to do this: using charm of admiration (being self-assured, dominant, and expressive) and aggressiveness towards rivals (annoyed, hostile, and socially insensitive).

While narcissistic leadership is characterized by overconfident decision making, volatile leadership performance, and poor management, narcissistic followers tend to overestimate themselves. They are more likely, for instance, to overclaim their influence by name dropping. They are more likely to take credit for someone else's work. They will also proclaim themselves as creative. All these will reinforce their grandiose self-belief. More worryingly, narcissists do not feel bound by rules.

Providing feedback to a narcissist follower can be challenging. This type of follower will see any feedback, unless overly positive, as negative. In response, the narcissistic follower is likely to respond in a hostile way and look to devalue the feedback or seek to undermine the leader.[39] Narcissistic followers will seek out others in the organization where they can bask in their glory.

Narcissistic followers will question a supervisor's authority if it enables them to gain recognition. This type of individual can have a disastrous impact on colleagues, who may find themselves lured into an erratic lifestyle (too much socializing or substance abuse) or even seduced into a romantic relationship (short-term).

6.7.2 Machiavellian Followers

Machiavellian followers will be politically oriented and seek ways to maximize situations where they will personally benefit. They are unlikely to be 'team workers' in that they will distrust others and will seek to control the influence of others. Knowledge may be viewed as a source of power and, as such, the

Machiavellian follower will seek to control access to this knowledge. This may result in misrepresenting the knowledge if it helps them to control and retain their power.

Bullying at work and Machiavellian traits are closely related but only when the Machiavellian individual is in a position of power: in other words, in a role where they can 'get away with it'. There is a strong correlation between self-related work commitment and Machiavellianism, and a negative relationship between commitment to the team, supervisor, or even the organization.[40]

6.7.3 Psychopathic Followers

Psychopathic followers tend to have a short-term focus and disruptive tenure. They have a penchant for lying to gain immediate rewards, and they display recklessness and fearlessness. They can be perceived as charismatic due to their strong ability at impression management. Such followers enjoy rivalry and pitting individuals against each other. They are unafraid to cross moral boundaries. Psychopathic followers are likely to thrive in organizations that require a rational, emotionless behavioural style, a strong achievement focus, and a willingness to take risks. Even breaking rules may be perceived by others as challenging the status quo.

Overall, psychopathic followers will look for opportunities to obscure their own performance by creating chaos (Table 6.5).

Table 6.5 Red Flag Behaviours for each of the Dark Triad Traits (Adapted from Schyns, Wisse, and Sanders)[41]

Red Flag Behaviours	*Narcissism*	*Machia-vellianism*	*Psychopathy*
Overclaiming their contribution to the organization and taking credit when such credit is not merited	x		
Showing behaviour (e.g., proactivity) in ways that serve to promote themselves	xx	x	
Becoming aggressive after negative feedback and devaluing the feedback source	xx		

(*continued*)

Red Flag Behaviours	*Narcissism*	*Machia-vellianism*	*Psychopathy*
Treating valued members of the organization as trophies, and differently from those they do not perceive as adding to their own positive self-views	xx		
Demonstrating a self-oriented perspective combined with the employment of a 'choose your battles' mindset		xx	
Keeping knowledge to themselves as a source of power and influence		xx	
Making use of manipulation tactics to reach strategic goals		xx	
Choosing competition over cooperation		x	xx
Making fast, short-term focused decisions without accounting for the possible negative consequences for others			xx
Making big, bold, and risky decisions that are not restrained by organizational rules or knowledgeable, respected insights	x		xx
Criticizing co-workers to impact their emotional well-being and divert their attention from the job role			xx
Seducing co-workers to live a 'wild' life or seducing then into a sexual relationship		x	xx

Note: xx = main behaviour, x = secondary behavior

6.8 Toxic Followers Working for Toxic Leaders

The idea that toxic followers could be working for toxic leaders has only recently been explored. Machiavellians are manipulative and deceitful individuals willing to utilize any strategy or behaviour needed to attain their goals. One study[42] explored what occurs when Machiavellian employees have a

Machiavellian leader with the same negative, manipulative disposition. Machiavellian employees have a negative worldview and are likely to trust their leaders less. When Machiavellian employees have Machiavellian leaders, their trust in their leader significantly decreases, and their level of stress significantly increases.

6.8.1 Other Types of Followers

This chapter has focused primarily on the 'susceptible' or 'toxic' follower as this type is a key enabler within toxic cultures. It would be remiss not to discuss other types of followers. Other types of followers have been categorized as those individuals who stand up to the leader and those who do not. This is simplistic. Some argue that courageous followers will stand up to leaders as they assume that the leader wants to hear their voice.[43] In contrast, others argue that certain leaders do not want to listen or even hear any such voices. While we might wish to embrace the assertions to be a courageous follower, the circumstances reveal that many employees face considerable risk when speaking up.

As one senior executive interviewed for this book noted[44]:

> I think that point on followership is really important because you either have to be very brave, if you are a follower and you see bad behaviour and you challenge it, then you might be ostracized and marginalized or made to feel uncomfortable.

6.8.1.1 The Quiet Resistance

The literature is silent on what practitioners label as the 'quiet resistance'. The 'quiet resistance' defines an individual as one who can see some of the damage and harm that emanates from a toxic leader. This damage and harm might be at a macro level. For example, at one organization, the CEO decided to undertake post-employment screenings as a result of a single case across more than 100,000 employees. After a period of time, a director sought to deflect this approach by arguing for a more proportionate response but was overruled by the CEO. The outcome resulted in some reputational damage to the director.

In my interviews for this book, some of the senior executives described 'quiet resistance' as an alternative strategy:

> You can learn to navigate these dysfunctional toxic cultures almost as a matter of survival, and then what happens is you find you're actually good at it. Right? So that doesn't mean you're morally bad, it doesn't mean you participate, it doesn't mean you support it, but you work your way around

> it, and you're well remunerated for it. And then you think, well, okay, this is life. I know the question you're going to next, is do I have personal experience of this: Yes, I do, yes, I do, yes, I do. I was in my early to mid-thirties, we'd just had our child, I had a mortgage, I had commitments, and I worked for a toxic company, toxic culture, (with a) brutally nasty CEO. His henchwoman, if you like, was the head of HR. So, there's your supposed guardian actually in cahoots. Of course, I used to do my fantasy perusing of the job boards and the papers for the next job, but the sad fact of the matter was I'd also worked out how to minimize the damage, navigate my way around, be actually quite effective as an executive.
>
> You understand what turns on these psychopaths and what keeps them going. I'll give you a simple example: there was one guy who would come up with the most grandiose schemes, and you were absolutely on the way out if you said no. The way around it was to instantly applaud it, 'Brilliant! How visionary.' Stop the person in their tracks, and then say, 'Leave this with me, so exciting, leave this with me,' and then you go away and you load up all the risks, and you bring it back to this guy to point out where, if things go wrong, he'd be on the hook. Not you. Some of it was ludicrous, like something out of a cheap pantomime, saying: 'What a brilliant idea, and here's a plan, of course there's a risk, if this goes wrong, goes really badly, wow, it could look really bad for you, but I love your bravery.'[45]

And

> I'd add a third category that was the quiet resistance. So, I don't think everyone was a colluder, and there were and are still, people who think that they can do good from inside as well, but they pick their battles.[46]

6.8.1.2 The Survivor

The survivor is defined as an individual who manages to keep their head down to 'survive'. The survivor seeks to do the best job they can. This type of follower may have certain skills that enable the individual to keep their job role and can speak up when necessary.

Senior executives interviewed for this book talked about survivors in terms of those who accept some bad behaviours as a necessary evil in the workplace:

> You would have read the descriptions of the daily meetings where everyone took it in turn to get a beating, and that is the survival element there where you go, 'I am glad it is her go or his go today and not my go'. For the majority of people, it was 'I have a job and I do my job to the best of my abilities . . . so, is it my responsibility to worry about those blokes in the ivory tower up there that are good, bad or indifferent?' Because on the ground it probably doesn't make much difference on a day-to-day basis.[47]

> I think there was just this culture of fear and like 'I am really glad (name) is the one getting it in the neck'. So, everyone just went down beneath the parapets … It seemed it is easier to feel targeted when you are the victim, but there seemed to be a gender aspect with it. The female leader seems to attract some more of the scorn, more scornful behaviour than the male.[48]

More research is needed to understand the role of followers in toxic cultures. To date, the research is focused on susceptible followers, and it would be enlightening to learn more about the other types of followers mentioned here. Being a follower does not mean being overly committed to the leader, as the follower may not possess the voice or the resources to be able to challenge the leader successfully. Followers may carry out the leader's commands but do so grudgingly. They may also seek to remove the destructive leader.[49] These forms of resistance may present a way to dilute, mitigate, and survive within a toxic culture.

6.9 Summary

As discussed, no matter how clever or devious, the leader cannot achieve toxic results on their own. To achieve a toxic agenda, a leader requires "the assistance of susceptible followers and a conducive environment".[50] There remains a question as to when 'non-susceptible followers' will no longer tolerate the behaviour or the 'madness' that they've been subject to or observed, at which point these individuals will resign and, by doing so, leave a greater preponderance of 'susceptible followers' behind. This increasing proportion of 'susceptible followers' is likely to be a significant tipping point to embedding toxicity, as described in Part 1, as an organization moves towards Stage 4: Cult of Singularity (see Figure 4.2).

In summary, research has shown that people respond more quickly to negative behaviour than positive behaviour. In the hands of a destructive or toxic leader, the overall working environment will be corrupted.

The next chapter will explore the third dimension of the toxic triangle: *the conducive environment*.

Notes

1 Society for Human Resource Management (2019) https://www.shrm.org/about-shrm/press-room/press-releases/pages/shrm-reports-toxic-workplace-cultures-cost-billions.aspx. Accessed 27 June 2021.
2 Pelletier, K.L. (2010) Leader toxicity: An empirical investigation of toxic behaviour and rhetoric. *Leadership*, 6(4): 373–389.

3 Ulh-Bien, M., Riggio, R.E., Lowe, K.B., & Carsten, M.K. (2014) Followership theory: A review and research agenda. *The Leadership Quarterly*, 25(1), Feburary.
4 Bass, M., & Stogdill, R. (1990) *Handbook of Leadership: Theory Research and Managerial Applications*, (3rd ed.). New York: The Free Press.
5 Ulh-Bien, et al. (2014) Followership theory: A review and research agenda. *The Leadership Quarterly*, 25(1), Feburary.
6 Meindl, J., Ehrlich, S., & Dukerich, J. (1985) The romance of leadership. *Administrative Science Quarterly*, 30(1): 78–102.
7 Padilla, A., Hogan, R., & Kaiser, R.B. (2007) The toxic triangle: Destructive leaders, susceptible followers and conducive environments. *The Leadership Quarterly*, 18: 178–194.
8 Hersey, P., & Blanchard, K. (1982) *Management of Organizational Behaviour* (2nd ed.). Englewood Cliffs, NJ: Prentice Hall.
9 Baker, S. (2007) Followership: The Theoretical foundations of a contemporary construct. *Journal of Leadership and Organizational Studies*, 14(1): 50–60.
10 Dawkins, R. (1976) *The Selfish Gene*. Oxford: Oxford University Press.
11 Uhl-Bien, M., & Carsten, M. (2007) Being ethical when the boss is not. *Organizational Dynamics*, 36: 187–201.
12 Kellerman, B. (2008) *Followership: How Followers are Creating Change and Changing Leaders*. Boston, MA: Harvard Business School Publishing. p. xix.
13 Thoroughgood, C.N., Padilla, A., Hunter, S.T., & Tate, B.W. (2012) The susceptible circle: A taxonomy of followers associated with destructive leadership. *The Leadership Quarterly*, 23: 897–917.
14 Kelley, R. (1988) In praise of followers. *Harvard Business Review*, 66(6): 142–148.
15 DeRue, D.S., & Ashford, S.J. (2010) Who will lead and who will follow? A social process of leadership identity construction in organizations. *Academy of Management Review*, 35: 627–647.
16 Adapted from Chaleff, I. (2008) Creating new ways of following. In R. Riggio, I. Chaleff & J. Lipman-Blument (eds.), *The Art of Followership: How Great Followers Create Great Leaders and Organizations*, pp. 67–87. San Francisco, CA: Jossey Bass.
17 The authors provide a rich account of the literature on followership. *See* Crossman, B. and Crossman, J. (2011) Conceptualising followership – a review of the literature. *Leadership*, 7(4): 481–497.
18 Carsten, M., et al. (2010) Exploring social constructions of followership: A qualitative study. *Leadership Quarterly*, 21: 543–562.
19 Yagil, D., Ben-Zur, H., & Tamir, I. (2011) Do employees cope effectively with abusive supervision at work? An exploratory study. *International Journal of Stress Management*, 18(1): 5–23.
20 Adapted from Webster, V., Brough, P., & Daly, K. (2014) Fight, flight or freeze: Common responses for follower coping with toxic leadership. *Stress and Health Journal*, 32: 346–354.
21 Goleman, D., & Boyatzis, R. (2008) Social intelligence and the biology of leadership. *Harvard Business Review*.
22 Tepper, B.J. (2000) Consequences of abusive supervision. *The Academy of Management Journal*, 43(2), 178–190.

23 Boddy, C. (2013). *The Corporate Psychopath – Organizational Destroyers*. London: Palgrave Macmillan.
24 Buzeti, J. (2021) The connection between leader behaviour and employee sickness absence in public administration. *International Journal of Organizational Analysis*, 30(7), 1–19
25 Clarke, J. (2005) *Working with Monsters: How to Identify and Protect Yourself form the Workplace Psychopath*. Sydney: Random House.
26 Boddy (2013).
27 Interview with HR Director (2) (October 2021) by the author.
28 Padilla, Hogan, & Kaiser (2007).
29 Padilla, Hogan, & Kaiser (2007). p. 183.
30 Adapted from Thoroughgood, C.N., et al. (2012) The susceptible circle: A taxonomy of followers associated with destructive leadership. *The Leadership Quarterly*, 23: 897–917.
31 Adapted from Pelletier et al. (2019).
32 Beightel, R. S. (2018). How a Conducive Environment and Susceptible Followers Influence Toxic Leadership Behaviours in the Air Force: An Examination of the Toxic Triangle Theory. Theses and Dissertations. https//scholar.adit.edu/etd/1832
33 Thody, A. (2003) Followership in education organizations: A pilot mapping of the territory. *Leadership and Policy in Schools*, 2: 141–156.
34 Lipman-Blumen, J. (2004) *The Allure of Toxic Leaders*. Oxford: Oxford University Press.
35 Schyns, B., Wisse, B., & Sanders, S. (2019) Shady strategic behaviour: Recognizing strategic followership of dark triad followers. *Academy of Management Perspectives*, 33(2), 234–249.
36 Pelletier, K.L., Kottke, J.L., & Sirotnik, B.W. (2019) The Toxic Triangle in Academia: A case analysis of the emergence and manifestation of toxicity in a public university. *Leadership*, 14(4): 421.
37 Bolino, M.C., Klotz, A.C., Turnley, W.H., & Harvey, J. (2013) Exploring the dark side of organizational citizenship behaviour. *Journal of Organizational Behaviour*, 34: 542–559.
38 Schyns, B., Wisse, B., & Sanders, S. (2019) Shady strategic behaviour: Recognizing strategic followership of dark triad followers. *Academy of Management Perspectives*, 33(2): 234–249.
39 *Ibid.*
40 *Ibid.*
41 *Ibid.*
42 Belshak, F.D., Muhammad, R.S., & Den Hartog, D.N. (2018) Birds of a feather can butt heads: When Machiavellian employees work with Machiavellian leaders. *Journal of Business Ethics*, 151: 613–626.
43 Chaleff, I. (2009) *The Courageous Follower: Standing up to & for Our Leaders*. Oakland, CA: Berrett Koehler Publishers.
44 Interview with Senior Executive, October 2021.
45 Interview with Senior Executive, December 2021.
46 Interview with senior Executive, November 2021.

47 *Ibid.*
48 Interview with Senior Executive, 2 November 2021.
49 While the authors (Padilla et al., 2019) on the Toxic Triangle explore the concept of susceptible followers, they tend to gloss over key historical facts. In the case of Hitler and the rise of Nazism in Germany in the 1930s, the Nazi party secured around only one-third of the votes. In addition, a number of assassination attempts were made on Hitler throughout his tenure.
50 Thoroughgood, et al. (2012:901).

7
Conducive Environments

7.1 Introduction

Let us now explore the third element of the toxic triangle: a conducive environment.[1]

A toxic workplace environment is recognized as one that is characteristic of unfavourable experiences that poorly affect employees.[2]

This third domain in the toxic triangle envelops leaders and followers and their interactions. A conducive environment is described as one without *checks and balances*, or where the organization is *tolerant of toxic behaviours* of its leader or leaders.[3] It is asserted that toxic leaders will not survive or succeed in positive working environments.

In studies that examined corrupt organizations, there were justifications for the actions and behaviours. These included that corrupt organizations or toxic working environments perceived themselves as fighting a war, with the 'end justifying the means'. Security and loyalty to the cause are paramount. Non-corrupt behaviours are then punishable as deviant and 'not one of us'.[4]

There are four elements that are significant in creating a conducive environment for a toxic leader and for susceptible followers. These factors include instability, perceived threats, favouritism, and an absence of checks and balances.

7.1.1 Instability

Instability refers to the lack of certainty or predictability in the organization. Making change and setting a new vision or business restructuring with redundancies and job losses all create a degree of instability across the organization. Yet as seen in Chapter 5, leadership theory is dominated by the idea that to be a 'leader', there needs to be a vision and that this needs to be delivered in a unitarist way. Some critics have pointed to the dangers of transformational

DOI: 10.4324/9781003330387-10

leadership that dictates a shared vision and goals to motivate employees to realize these goals, while simultaneously leaders having the power to reward, punish, and fire employees for not conforming to the said goals. These critics argue that 'transformational leadership' centralizes power, providing for increased authority and dominance. Proponents of transformational leadership argue that personal and organizational goals need to be aligned to achieve a common unitary purpose, and in so doing, employee commitment is heightened.

In the interviews for this book, when asked how and why cultures become toxic, one senior executive commented on the consequences of focusing on financial or performance results:

> There are two or three elements to that. One is when you want to achieve results, it could be numbers, it could be market share, it could be any financial element, then the focus is only on that element and not on the overall organization, (or) moving forward as a team. It starts bringing that tough competitiveness in people because they need to deliver and they want to prove themselves. It is a natural outcome that people start becoming toxic or start bullying people or you get this done for me or else. You know that when that 'else' word comes then you know it changes the dynamics. It is a very fearful word and a lot of leaders, apparent leaders, or supposed leaders use it.[5]

Chapter 5 discussed the dominance of this type of leadership thinking and the fact that power is a frequently unacknowledged variable in organizational theory. Creating instability or initiating a transformation agenda can enable leaders to enhance their power by advocating radical change to restore order and equilibrium. Turbulence within the organization and its surrounding environment makes toxic leadership much more probable as followers are likely to see a strong figure to 'steady the ship'.[6] In my working experience, it is rare to find a newly appointed Chief Executive who does not embark on a new change initiative. Boards should pay careful attention to any proposed change agenda that could upset the status quo and vigorously question the value of such initiatives for all stakeholders.

The pressure for performance may include instability, and perceived threats will enable a conducive environment. Organizations embarking on change, or constantly changing in terms of organizational structures and reporting lines, are at risk of creating a conducive environment. This is not to say that change should never happen, rather the point is that the risks and impact of the change need to be fully addressed prior to the implementation.

Instability may also include high levels of turnover or absenteeism or significant work demands, leading to a long-hours working culture and presenteeism.

7.1.2 Perceived Threats

Perceived threats can be threats of reduced funding, threats from a perceived competitor, or the threat of reduced shareholder value. These may also manifest in instability and loss of jobs and/or compromises in rewards.

The point is that there does not have to be an actual threat, merely the perception of one. Leaders can perpetuate the perception of a threat.

In one study within a public university, the researchers reported on widespread bullying that led to perceived threat. Employees who complained to the HR department found they were subsequently called in by their supervisor-perpetrator, who would then report that no further action would be taken on the complaint. HR management was perceived as carrying out the orders of senior management, leading to breaches in confidentiality. Fear of retribution for raising concerns or grievances can also be categorized as a perceived threat.[7]

A senior executive pointed to a threat of when people are scared to speak up:

> A (toxic) culture is where people are scared, and scared of speaking their mind. I think that is the baseline of toxicity, where a culture is not conducive to listen to employees, and that is also the birth of non-inclusion, and that is where subgroups of the organization may feel left away or a set of people may feel left away. Now when you hesitate to speak up your mind, when you hesitate to take any initiative, when you hesitate three or four times before expressing your opinion at a table or in a meeting or in front of your boss, that is the beginning of a toxic culture.[8]

7.1.3 Favouritism

The relationship that followers have with their supervisors can impact their access to rewards, opportunities, and resources within the organization. Studies have shown that when followers are within the 'in-group', they will identify with and report less about the leader's toxic behaviours than when they are on the outside. Moreover, followers on the outside of the leader's group are more likely to file grievances due to the toxic behaviours compared with those in the favoured group.

One senior executive interviewed for the book described a type of favouritism:

> We have had a couple of dreadful cases where in one (work team) an individual did commit suicide. You could never quite prove it, but it looked like it happened at work, and the atmosphere at work might have been part of that. Again, in micro-cultures I think it can happen when it becomes very insular. I think all you need is a couple, and you have to be careful how you phrase this, but people that are poisonous characters, quite malevolent and quite sneaky in the way that they are, and that generates a culture … often

> I have seen this, and I will give an example, where you can get one really unreasonable and poisonous character and (they are) very powerful, so others coalesce around that individual because they are trying to be with the 'in' crowd and not in the 'out' crowd. So in essence they tolerate and accept and play up to those bad behaviours as they are desperate to stay in the 'in' crowd and not be exiled to the 'out' crowd.[9]

Another senior executive spoke of being either 'in' or 'out' of favour:

> (In my previous organization) some were told 'look, people screw up', and some people are out of favour whilst others aren't out of favour as long. My parallel would be the court of the king in the medieval courts, you'd be the flavour of the month and then you wouldn't. I remember going on another one of the senior leadership things, meet the HR Leadership Team (HRLT), I was invited and I was told by one of the HRLT, and it was early on in my time there, 'we like you', so the flip of that is 'we don't like you', isn't it? Not we really think you are good or we respect your abilities, no, we like you or we don't like you.[10]

7.1.4 Absence of Checks and Balances

In the original article on the Toxic Triangle, there is an assumption that a conducive environment can be enabled where there is a lack of checks and balances. The assumption is that corporations that lack independent board oversight allow individuals or parties to usurp power. In addition, the authors note that managerial discretion allows for destructive leaders to abuse their power, and this is more likely in senior job roles where there is less supervision or accountability (other than to the Board). The authors note: 'Effective institutions, systems stability, and proper checks and balances, along with strong followers, will tend to trump attempts to take over the system'.[11]

Yet with the organizations that were explored in Part 1, all had respectful and solid Boards, and some of the organizations were subject to external regulation as well. Corporate Boards are expected to review the top executive and to evaluate his or her performance with regard to the organization's success. Unfortunately, Boards have been occasionally poor at oversight in this regard. Top executives may also select and appoint the Board members and are given great latitude in managing resources and people.[12]

At a strategic level, the role of the Board is a significant influencer in this role. The role of the Board as 'critical friend' is there to ensure good governance and regulate the behaviour and ambitions of the senior executive.

Since the Global Financial Crisis, the role of the Board has been questioned. New requirements have been added in the latest UK Corporate Governance Code, with principles for Board directors (see Table 7.1).

Table 7.1 Financial Reporting Council: The UK Corporate Governance Code, July 2018[13]

(A) A successful company is led by an effective and entrepreneurial board, whose role is to promote the long-term sustainable success of the company, generating value for shareholders and contributing to wider society.
(B) The Board should establish the company's purpose, values, and strategy, and satisfy itself that these and its culture are aligned. All directors must act with integrity, lead by example, and promote the desired culture.
(C) The Board should ensure that the necessary resources are in place for the company to meet its objectives and measure performance against them. The Board should also establish a framework of prudent and effective controls, which enable risk to be assessed and managed.
(D) In order for the company to meet its responsibilities to shareholders and stakeholders, the Board should ensure effective engagement with, and encourage participation from, these parties.
(E) The Board should ensure that workforce policies and practices are consistent with the company's values and support its long-term sustainable success. The workforce should be able to raise any matters of concern.

Boards are expected to assess the basis on which the company generates and preserves value over the long term. In addition, the Board should assess and monitor culture and ensure that policy, practices, and behaviours are aligned with the company's purpose, values, and strategy. The Board should question and seek assurances that corrective action has been taken by management.[14] Organizations should also have mechanisms for whistleblowing, enabling individuals to raise grievances against their line managers without fear of retaliation. Moreover, the Chair should be independent, and the roles of the Chair and Chief Executive should not be exercised by the same individual.

Moreover, the diversity of Boards was acknowledged as critical to the effective functioning of a Board.

As one senior executive noted:

> I think the more homogenous the Board is, the more likely you are going to get people who are compliant followers. That is why I think diversity of teams is so important, because through diversity of opinion and thought, the more likely that you are going to (listen to) people who will express

> different views and are less likely to be blind followers ... (which) is what you want to try and avoid. You want criticism and challenge to be encouraged, and that tends to happen where there is more diversity ... so I think diversity is one of the solutions around that one.[15]

And noting the importance of the Board as key to the culture of the organization:

> The Board (needs to) continuously evaluate the people's agenda. The Board needs to look at engagement scores, whistleblowing, 360-degree feedback for senior leaders – all of that is going to be driven by the Board. In effect, the Board is saying: 'We are here, and we are keeping an eye on you, and you need to behave in the values which we stand for'. So, Boards can actually play a very crucial role in setting a compliance methodology and other elements around that, which can ultimately avoid a toxic culture or start to have a more positive culture. At the end of the day, the Board needs to decide what kind of organization they need to be, and once they have defined that, you know culture will start to come out of that.[16]

7.2 Cultural Values

In the toxic triangle, cultural values are addressed as part of the conducive environment. Cultural values provide a shorthand for how to behave within an organization, what is valued and what is not. Some authors have proposed that 'dark' leaders will emerge when there is a need for stability and structure, offering easy solutions to complex problems. However, as seen in Part 1, the norms shape the values under pressure.

Values that may have articulated 'driven for results' can be interpreted in a cajoling way to a more bullying and demanding set of expectations. Uber illustrates how its values were used to justify 'bullying' and 'boorish' behaviours.

Cultural values can be manipulated under the direction of a destructive leader and embedded by susceptible followers. The way things get done can be rapidly changed. For example, strategic decisions that rely on collaboration among various units or departments can be hastily circumvented, or by convening responses with extremely tight deadlines, or appointing 'cronies' to nod through agreement. Similarly, the consequences of speaking out can result in being replaced or removed altogether, leading to a fearful culture.[17]

Post the ABN Amro acquisition, RBS changed the meaning of certain corporate values and statements such as: 'do it now' to 'do it everywhere' – the 'it' was never defined but the statements surfaced a more demanding and relentless management expectation.

Vignette 7.1 Working in a Conducive Environment? The Case of BrewDog[18]

In 2021, former employees of the craft beer giant BrewDog accused the company of operating under a culture of fear. Around 61 former members of staff signed the document.

Extract from the letter:

> To the CEO: It is with you that the responsibility for this rotten culture lies. Your attitude and actions are at the heart of the way BrewDog is perceived, from both inside and out. By valuing growth, speed and action above all else, your company has achieved incredible things, but at the expense of those who delivered your dreams.
>
> In the wake of your success are people left burnt out, afraid and miserable. The true culture of BrewDog is, and seemingly always has been, fear. You go on LinkedIn and claim the buck stops with you, but do you have the guts to look at the team you have built around you and admit that the overwhelming majority of them are quietly afraid that their next mistake could be their last at BrewDog? In the last few weeks, the silence has been deafening – this is not the time to try and quietly wait things out.
>
> Now, for those of you still working at BrewDog.
>
> You have a choice. The next time you are pressured into doing something against your will, or working in such a way that it will affect your mental health, push back. It is absolutely not worth it. The only reason BrewDog has become what it is, is that under immense pressure, good people have done bad things to achieve the job set before them, in such a way that benefits only the company. Being told to ignore health and safety guidelines? Don't. Someone's demanding you send beer to an event in the USA by bypassing customs? Nope.

At the time of writing, a BBC investigation showed that Scottish beer giant BrewDog sent multiple shipments of beer to the US in contravention of US federal laws.

Staff at its Ellon brewery told the BBC they were put under pressure in 2016 and 2017 to ship beer with ingredients that had not been legally approved. One US-based importer said they had been deceived by BrewDog. At the time of writing, BrewDog CEO James Watt admitted to "taking shortcuts" with the process. A BBC investigative programme revealed that staff at the Ellon brewery in Aberdeenshire knew that two of its flagship products, Elvis Juice and Jet Black Heart, contained extracts which would not be approved in the US.

One former worker told the investigation: "The pressure was enormous. 'Just make it happen', that was the culture. It was clear to us this was coming from the top – from James [Watt]". Another said: "We were continually told to ship beer to the USA, despite everyone knowing the beers hadn't been approved. Everyone was worried they'd be [fired] if they didn't do what was asked".

US Treasury officials from the Alcohol and Tobacco Tax and Trade Bureau (TTB) were given false information on at least five occasions during a six-month period, which meant that potentially hundreds of kegs of beer were sent with incorrect labelling – a violation of TTB laws.

7.3 Measuring a Conducive Environment

Measuring the extent of a conducive environment can provide insights into the culture of an organization. Unlike an engagement survey that explores the motivation and commitment of employees, this type of survey addresses the way things get done in the organization.

Surveys can reveal elements of toxicity or whether toxicity is more embedded across the organization. As many of the senior executives interviewed for this book noted, the value of a survey is its helpfulness in identifying units or departments where there might be a toxic leader, as well as providing a macro-level assessment. Table 7.2 proposes questions that can be used in an employee survey using the Likert Scale (5-point rating scale from 'strongly agree' to 'strongly disagree').

7.4 The Pressure of Performance on Individual Behaviour

As discussed in Chapter 4, the pressures of performance raise expectations for the individual as well as organizations. Performance management, goal setting, and management by objectives are well established as levers to drive outputs. Performance pressures have been attributed to be the primary cause of corporate misconduct, such as the financial fraud at Wells Fargo where employees told regulators that they had felt extreme pressure to open as many accounts as possible to meet sales targets.[20]

Table 7.2 Survey Questions to Measure Toxic Work Environments

Toxic work environment characteristics	*Survey Questions* [19]
Instability	I have a clear understanding of the organization's goals
	I know what is expected of me in the workplace
	I have a clear understanding of the direction that senior management is leading the organization
	The senior management team clearly communicate the strategic priorities
	I understand how my work contributes to the goals of the organization
Culture	Senior leadership creates a culture of openness and trust
	Diverse perspectives are valued in my (organization)
	I feel encouraged to find better ways of doing things
	The management empower staff to do their best
	Colleagues collaborate effectively across different units/departments
	My supervisor or someone at work seems to care about me as a person
	In the last year, I have had opportunities to learn and grow
	I have the chance to use my strengths every day
	My job makes good use of my skills
Perceived threat	I am afraid to make a mistake
	Mistakes are not tolerated
	There is someone at work who encourages my development
	In the last seven days, I have received recognition or praise for doing good work

(*continued*)

Toxic work environment characteristics	*Survey Questions*
Ethics	I can report unethical behaviour without fear of reprisal
	I am treated with respect and dignity at this organization
	My manager acts with honesty and integrity
	Undesirable behaviours are not tolerated
	I am held accountable for my actions at work
Favouritism	My manager deals fairly with everyone
	Management deals fairly with everyone
	Changes (e.g., promotions, reassignments) in my unit are made on an objective job-related basis
	My performance is evaluated fairly
Absence of checks and balances	Internal processes and procedures enable me to deliver high-quality services to our clients
	My manager keeps me informed about changes affecting the unit and our work
	At work, my opinions seem to count
	My colleagues (fellow employees) are committed to doing quality work
	I have the resources to do my work right
	Work pressures in my job are at an acceptable level

Performance pressure, while boosting outcomes, comes at a price. Research shows that when people are under greater performance pressures, they are more likely to engage in behaviours such as theft, fabricating their CV, and lying.[21] More recently, researchers have asked whether performance pressures also encourage employee Unethical Pro-organizational Behaviour (UPB) – behaviour that is conducted in the name of serving and protecting their employing organization. Here, a moral justification would be used to rationalize such behaviour on the grounds that it will promote and protect the interests of the organization. The concept of performance pressure means any factor or combination of factors that increases the importance of performing well. This pressure is focused on the successful delivery of a performance target or meeting customer satisfaction metrics rather than the pressure of time or in the face of a crisis. In the work environment, performance pressures typically result from the reward systems as well as from individual managers who are able to observe, evaluate, and reward (or sanction) performance.

Greater pressure leads to an increase in employee unethical behaviour that can violate societal values, laws, or regulatory standards. These unethical behaviours are typically rooted in the desire to be 'pro-organization' rather than being 'pro-self' and are couched in the belief that the intent is to benefit the organization. For example, employees may engage in cheating, misleading, or lying if it results in boosting sales or profits or the overall reputation.

People, however, have their own moral compass and generally know right from wrong. So how can performance pressures lead to such unethical behaviour? In truth, the pressure of performance can lead people to make such unethical choices by 'disengaging moral reasoning'. Individuals may say that "the order came from above" or "it's above my paygrade" as a way to displace moral responsibility. In addition, individuals may utilize moral justification techniques. Moral justification would include misrepresenting customer satisfaction scores or forging results to provide benefit for the good of the organization.

Performance pressures through objectives, goal setting, and targets are constant. Rewards are typically contingent on performance delivery. Meeting these targets is seen as critical, not only to retain employment, but also for career success. Researchers exploring the impact of performance pressures on individual behaviours found a surprising insight; individuals with highly creative and divergent mindsets, coupled with a low moral compass, were far more likely to engage in unethical behaviours. This has three implications in the workplace. First, managers need to be mindful of the 'dark side' of performance pressure and take a more balanced view of achieving high performance. Second, talent selection and development should combine criteria for morality with creativity. Third, feedback channels for employees to express concerns about performance targets, combined with training, support, and development, should be used to foster an ethical culture.[22]

7.5 Performance Management Systems

Performance management systems are universally designed to measure performance and are often linked to rewards. After the Global Financial Crisis, more weight was placed on how an individual delivered their results as opposed to a sole focus on the results alone.

Yet performance management systems are one of the significant contributors to toxic cultures. The traditional 'performance-based' systems feature the following:

- It is individually focused
- The manager is required to provide feedback and a performance rating
- The rating scale is typically on a scale of 5, from unacceptable to outstanding
- The rating scale may impose a bell-shaped curve (normal distribution curve) so that most employees will receive a '3' or satisfactory rating
- The rating scale will inform end-of-year bonuses or other rewards

Given that, organizations can spend a significant amount of time on performance management systems. Deloitte (UK), for example, found that they were spending up to 2 million hours per annum (Table 7.3).[23]

Performance management is not based on behavioural science or psychology. It is a mathematical model that alleges to increase productivity and the ability of

Table 7.3 The Key Steps in Performance Management

Overview	*Brief description*
The desired output step	This is the annual cycle of goal-setting where objectives are typically cascaded down the organization
The 'in-group' step	Feedback is gathered on the individual's performance by the manager, from clients, or colleagues
The assessment step	Each manager will assess their direct reports and provide a 'grade'
The comparison step	All rating grades are reviewed across the function and the organization to determine the relative position and fit within the normal distribution curve
The consequences step	The ratings will inform talent management process and potential promotion, or they will inform an improvement plan to rectify poor performance and may result in dismissal

employees by retrospectively grading the employee. Organizations in the US, UK, and even the Middle East have adopted this traditional approach.

One researcher suggested that by firing the bottom ten per cent, organizations could improve their productivity. However, this was seen to be, at best, a one-off event. Organizations adopt performance management as they regard it as 'best practice'. Yet some organizations are questioning the value of a performance management system that yields little commercial value, exhausts significant management time, and disengages many employees. We are now witnessing the trend that removes ratings and even the annual reviews.

So how does performance management, or more specifically, the ratings distribution curve, contribute to toxic cultures? In four ways:

1. Performance management is individualistic: it is highly competitive by design and pits individuals in the same team against one another
2. Performance management is psychologically and inherently biased: it takes no account of the rater and their psychological profile and how this influences the rating. One study involving more than 4,000 managers showed that a 61 per cent variance in ratings was due to individual perceptions and revealed more about the Rater than the individual being rated[24]
3. Performance management is contextual to the job role: the idea that a scientist can be evaluated using the same rating scale as a sales manager is naïve
4. Performance management is analytically weak: it is too simplistic to analyze performance on a single annual rating

One study[25] showed that there were unintended impacts over time; these included:

- Organizational disaffection
- Lowered trust in managers' intentions
- Lowered employee assessments of manager competence and fitness to lead
- Emergence of 'visibility' syndrome rather than output
- Short-term work prioritized over long-term impactful work
- Highly effective employees refusing challenging assignments or promotions on the grounds it might impact their rating
- People stopped helping each other

Yet the idea of performance management and forced ranking has persisted. The Harvard Business Review[26] published an article saying that a forced ranking on an ad hoc basis would improve the performance of the organization; the author argued that the bottom ten per cent should be shown the door and the top 20 per cent should be rewarded. However, the author noted that this could have a detrimental effect on morale. In addition, the idea of a forced ranking assumes firstly that the management is able to have a clear and consistent view of individual performance, secondly that people can be easily replaced, and thirdly that underperformance can only be dealt with by a forced ranking scenario.

Microsoft's forced distribution ranking system was blamed for creating a toxic culture in the early 2000s that stifled innovation and led to backstabbing of colleagues. This forced distribution or 'stack ranking' divides employees into a certain percentage of top performers, average performers, and underperformers. The UK's Civil Service rankings, for example, were fixed at 25 per cent (top), 65 per cent (average), and 10 per cent (underperformers), respectively, until the system was reformed a couple of years ago.

In many organizations, line managers will assign provisional grades and then attend 'calibration' meetings with other managers to agree on the forced distribution and the individual ratings. Some managers will try to set their own parameters, such as if an individual received an outstanding rating one year, then they could not receive the same the following year. Others might decide to award low ratings to part-time or new employees as perversely 'they are easier to sacrifice'.

7.6 The Negative Consequences of Performance Management Systems

First, the forced distribution does not recognize individuals who are part of high-performing teams. Individual high performers in these teams will be forced into an average rating or worse. Second, it is counterproductive to team working and collaboration as it does not recognize that work is delivered through and with others. Third, job roles and knowledge are widely variable within the organization and the selection of the best candidates is then undermined by the forced distribution. In summary, one way of embedding a toxic culture is to implement a forced distribution performance management system.

There has been a focus on 360-degree feedback as part of the performance review. Although some organizations have moved away from this approach to incorporate it as part of leadership development and learning, caution needs to be exercised when the general tone of upward feedback is about ingratiation. People may not feel free to speak openly or tell the truth to those in power, even in situations that may be regarded as anonymous. When ingratiation and flattery are directed at the CEO, evidence suggests that this acts to support strategic persistence by encouraging senior leaders to become overconfident in their strategic judgement.[27]

Neurobiologists studying traders' risk-taking noted that the Central Bank's actions designed to increase a sense of certainty were a significant factor in the financial collapse in 2008.[28] This sense of certainty worked to lower the perceived threat to traders and increased their dopamine levels, which, in turn, increased their preparedness to take unacceptable risks. Keeping to a level of uncertainty constrains risky behaviour. Overly complimentary feedback to a CEO thereby negates the possibility that leaders will notice and act on their strategic judgement or acknowledge poor organizational performance or risks.

Objective-setting can be useful for the job holder and the team to consider areas or targets that they are able to achieve in the year. Yet the focus on the short-term and the cascade of objectives and targets has been misused in organizations, such as Wells Fargo. This top-down cascade of objectives is sold on the basis that everyone is aligned in the organization. However, critics note that firstly, it is too focused on the short term and is detrimental to the long-term health of the organization; secondly, it ignores the substantial evidence that flexibility in the job role is critical to organizational productivity; and thirdly, effective performance is undermined by the top-down control model of work.

7.7 Bullying

Let us turn to bullying and how, if left unchecked, it contributes to the conducive environment and the spread of toxicity.

Workplace bullying is a phenomenon that exists around the globe in a range of industries and organizations. The International Labour Organization (ILO) states that bullying has become so widespread that it represents the greatest threat to success in the workplace.[29]

Workplace bullying differs from workplace conflict in that it consists of unwelcome conduct that has an intimidating, punishing, or frightening effect and infringes upon an employee's personal dignity, self-esteem, and life opportunities. When they occur, these acts can be characterized as uncivil or disrespectful workplace behaviour. When such behaviours become a pattern over a prolonged period of time and occur consistently, this is defined as workplace bullying.

Bullying can include a range of behaviours that manifest physically, verbally, and/or through body language and can be characterized as direct action or a lack of action:

- Repeated hurtful remarks or attacks or making fun of someone's work or someone as a person (including any aspect of their identity)

- Excluding someone or stopping them from working with people or taking part in activities that relate to their work
- Psychological harassment including intimidation, belittling, or humiliating comments
- Holding back information which someone needs in order to do their work properly
- Pushing, shoving, tripping, or grabbing someone
- Initiation or hazing – making someone do humiliating or inappropriate things in order to be accepted
- Physical, verbal, or written abuse, including via email or social media[30]

At Rio Tinto, when asked in a survey about whether the individual who had experienced bullying in the last five years had chosen to make a formal or informal complaint, two-thirds said no. A further question asked why the individual had chosen NOT to report the incidence of bullying; most responded that they believed it would have a negative consequence on their career or that it would not make a difference.

The qualitative research into Rio Tinto exposed stories about bullying and the degree to which it had become normalized:

> I have personally witnessed bullying behaviours [from] very senior people, and have had other people share their same experiences [in relation to] very senior people. I am not confident that anything will change until we see some changes in the known bullies in our organization. I have struggled over my time in Rio to be able to talk about this – without feeling like I will be told to 'toughen up' and 'that's just life in a global miner'. If we are really serious about this, we need to look more deeply at some of the individuals.

And

> [The manager] constantly demeans her team members' skills and experience, ignores feedback and undermines team cohesion. I consider myself most fortunate not to have to work for, or with her – but my team members are clearly impacted. Measurable outcomes of her behaviours include very high staff turnover, difficulty in recruiting replacement resources, and the actions of her own team to avoid interacting with her... I have raised this... but the feedback is that as a permanent member of staff, there is little that can be done.

And

> I have seen . . . a senior manager in my team have numerous people complain about him. I have seen him bully and harass others, and yet Rio Tinto

> continues to push his career. I don't think he is an outlier for the business either. For some managers of Rio Tinto, being driven and bullying their subordinates as a result of this drive is all too common, and [Rio Tinto] seems to reward those who do it, putting them on the right career path.

And

> When [bullying] comes from an employee to employee ... one can speak up, but mostly it comes from the top (managers/supervisor). It becomes difficult to stand up because of an abuse of power.[31]

In my conversations with senior executives, many related their own personal experiences of bullying in different organizations. Some had chosen to leave the organization; others noted the impact on their own mental health. These cases related to the manipulation of corporate data, to withholding critical health and safety information. The behaviours included verbal abuse and threatening language. In one case, the individual had to use the threat of law relating to Health and Safety officials:

> "I don't want to talk to you. You can just report me for bullying if you want." He screamed it in the middle of an open plan floor on an executive suite . . . HR were pretty poor and they always did investigations so that they would always blame the complainant. I mean very few complaints were upheld. HR always just hunted down anyone putting in a grievance. So, I said, "I'm not putting in a grievance". It's beyond that. Because this is actually against the law to bully a health and safety advisor on health and safety grounds. It's actually against the law to do that. So, I'm going to just go straight to the Chief Executive.[32]

> (This senior executive) asked a question and I said I started my sentence with "I understand that" and he just jumped down my throat and said, "I don't want someone who (expletive) understands that. I want someone who knows, and if you're not the (expletive) person then find me someone who does".[33]

Bullying is pervasive. Research into bullying in one global organization found that one in two people had experienced bullying, including exclusion, in the last five years. Bullying is counter to a psychological safety culture. Sexual harassment is described by laws and statutes around the world as conduct of a sexual nature which is unwanted, unwelcome, and has the purpose of being intimidating, hostile, degrading, humiliating, and offensive.

See Table 7.4 for examples and types of bullying tactics:[34]

Table 7.4 Bullying Tactics (Adapted from Roter, 2017)

Tactics	*Examples*	*Heard to say*
Exclusion and isolation	Not invited to meetings or ignored; may be moved to a different unit	You are not required at this meeting
Creation of an uncomfortable work environment	Through gossip, rumours, verbal threats, ignoring, and isolation, the bully has created a hostile work environment	We are going for lunch, but you need to stay and finish the work
Unfair or destructive criticism	Bully provides feedback that is destructive, using words such as lazy, incompetent, and inadequate	You are getting fat and lazy
Blaming others for errors	Bully will look for a scapegoat to pin the blame on	It was not my idea/ work
Unreasonable job demands	The bully will ask for work to be delivered in an unreasonable timescale or in personal time, late at night or at weekends. The bully will request the individual to cancel any holiday or vacation to complete the work demands	I need this urgently and you need to complete this over the weekend or cancel your holiday now
Inconsistent application of rules	The bully applies different rules, such as timekeeping, to different individuals, showing favouritism.	You don't have a life, so you need to stay late
Threatening job security	The bully may threaten to fire the individual or make statements, saying that 'you had better prepare yourself for a brown letter'.	If you don't follow my rules, then you will be getting your P45
Name-calling	Using derogatory names for individuals to belittle the individual in front of others	You are such a slowcoach/idiot/ prima donna/
Verbal or non-verbal threats	Non-verbal threats include eye rolling, smirking behind the individual's back, glaring or staring, mocking the individual. Verbal threats include threatening to take work away, shouting, arguing	Watch my lips Which part of 'no', don't you understand?

Demeaning comments	Demeaning comments such as about someone's size and weight, or age and other characteristics such as sex, religion, disability.	It's just banter. Where's your sense of humour?
Micro-managing	Constantly asking for reports or papers and making repeated changes that are relatively trivial but require the individual to stay late to make changes	Received typically as red-inked words and comments
Physical threats	Making threats to the 'target' that are regarded as intimidating, such as finger pointing or threatening to physically attack an individual.	Next time, I am going to break your arms

7.8 Rewarding Toxic Behaviours

> Toxic rock stars are a cancer on company culture. Leaving them in a position of power reveals what the company truly values: profits over people.[35]

Many people will recognize the scenario at work of a high performer or a leader who is also a bully that delivers results but creates a toxic environment. These people labelled as 'toxic rock stars'[36] have a detrimental impact on diversity and inclusion as well as attrition. Yet in too many organizations, the power wielded by a toxic rock star is promoted by others. Typically, the HR department is regarded as ineffectual in its lack of response, and they are blamed for their inadequate response. Herein lies the challenge. The HR function is a support function. As such, it does not have the mandate to fire senior executive leaders. Although as we will see in the next chapter, there is strong reason for the HR function to deliver organizational justice for the sake of promoting a positive and healthy culture.

The challenge for organizations is balancing the short-term desire for results with the longer-term need for a healthy and positive workplace. While shareholders demand revenues, there has also been an increasing demand for sustainability. David Owen, a former British politician and a neurologist by training, has written about a personality disorder he had observed among political and business leaders, a disorder that he calls the Hubris Syndrome. This syndrome is characterized by recklessness, inattention to detail, overwhelming self-confidence, and contempt for others. All of which can result in "disastrous leadership and cause damage on a grand scale". The Syndrome is a "disorder of the possession of power, particularly power which has been associated with overwhelming success, held for a period of years, and with minimal constraint on the leader".[37]

In describing risk-taking on the trading floor, one researcher showed how physiology mixed with lax risk management systems and a bonus system that rewards excessive gambling can produce a volatile banking scenario.[38] The researcher concluded that bonuses and employment security should be calculated over a longer period of time with a focus on prudent rather than reckless risk-taking.

7.9 The Impact of Harassment and Bullying

Rio Tinto, one of the largest and most successful mining companies in the world, has faced a number of harassment and bullying claims and recently commissioned an independent report on its corporate culture. Rio Tinto employs more than 45,000 people, with nearly 80 per cent male. A new CEO, Jakob Stausholm, commissioned the report on the psychological safety and workplace culture and the degree to which they both aligned with Rio Tinto's institutional values.

The report was based on a robust methodology involving qualitative and quantitative data. This included a survey completed by around 10,000 people and more than 100 'group listening sessions', as well as confidential one-to-one sessions and written submissions.

The report found[39]:

- Bullying was systemic, experienced by almost half of the survey respondents
- Sexual harassment and everyday sexism occurred at unacceptable rates
- Racism was common across a number of areas
- Employees did not believe that the organization was psychologically safe, which impacts their trust in the reporting systems
- Harmful behaviour occurred from and between employees, managers, and leaders, including senior leaders
- Unique workplace features, such as the hierarchical, male-dominated culture, created risk factors
- A capability gap in leading and managing people existed across many levels of the organization, particularly on the frontline
- People, policies, and systems were not properly embedded or 'lived' across the organization

- Harmful behaviour was often tolerated or normalized
- Harmful behaviour by serial perpetrators was often an open secret
- Employees believed that there was little accountability, particularly for senior leaders and so-called 'high performers', who were perceived to have avoided significant consequences for harmful behaviour

The report illustrated that the culture, on the whole, is positive. Employees talk about being proud to work at the organization:

> Let me start by saying that I truly believe Rio Tinto as a business has its employees' best interests at heart and is probably the best business to be a part of.[40]

Others noted that the culture depended on the manager:

> You can work years at Rio and have nothing but a positive experience, but then you get a bad manager and your world completely changes.[41]

7.10 The Impact of Harmful Behaviour on Corporate Reputation

A study conducted by *Harvard Business Review*[42] found that the publication of poor corporate behaviour resulted in a decline of share price. For example, Hewlett-Packard's stock fell almost nine per cent following reports that the former CEO had a personal relationship with a female contractor. Corporate reputation, or the way in which external stakeholders see a business, is also intrinsically linked to good organizational culture. The impact of harmful behaviour on corporate reputation can be significant and long lasting, with shareholders frequently reacting negatively to news of misconduct.

To examine how corporations handle allegations of CEO misbehaviour, the authors[43] conducted an extensive review of news media between 2000 and 2015. They identified 38 incidents where a CEO's behaviour garnered a meaningful level of media coverage (defined as more than ten unique news references) and categorized these incidents as follows:

- 34 per cent involved reports of a CEO lying to the board or shareholders about personal matters, such as a drunk driving offence, undisclosed criminal record, falsification of credentials, or other behaviour
- 21 per cent involved a sexual affair or relations with a subordinate, contractor, or consultant.

- 16 per cent involved CEOs making use of corporate funds in a manner that is questionable but not strictly illegal
- 16 per cent involved CEOs engaging in objectionable personal behaviour or using abusive language
- 13 per cent involved CEOs making public statements that are offensive to customers or social groups

Yet Boards treated these incidents inconsistently. Nearly half of the companies faced an unexpected governance issue, such as an unrelated legal claim or bankruptcy. The consequence of CEO misconduct can reverberate across the organization. The answer: when the CEO engages in misconduct, the Board has an obligation to investigate the matter, take proactive steps to ensure that it is properly dealt with, and that the corporate reputation, culture, and long-term performance are not damaged.[44]

The International Labour Organisation Treaty recognizes the right of all employees to work free from violence and harassment, and it came into force in June 2020. Similarly, the UN Guiding Principles on Business and Human Rights sets out guidance for nation states and companies to prevent, address, and remedy human rights abuses committed in business operations.

As we have discussed, organizational culture is a powerful asset that can attract talent, customers, and investors to the organization, or conversely, drive them away.

7.11 Summary

We have explored the concept of a conducive environment by examining how people are managed within an organization as a way of understanding the context of a conducive environment, from the selection of senior leaders to how certain practices, such as 'forced distribution curves' on performance ratings, can serve to embed toxicity. Such forced distribution curves have all the hallmarks of toxicity: lacking empathy, pitting colleagues against each other, and encouraging negative behaviours. We also explore how cultural values can be manipulated to become complicit enablers of toxic cultures. Finally, we have explored how bullying if left unchecked can spread toxicity and harm the corporate reputation.

In summary, the contributing factors of susceptible followers and toxic leaders combine to create a conducive environment. Knowing this, we will now explore effective solutions and preventative remedies.

Notes

1 Campbell, J-L., & Goritz, A.S. (2014) Culture corrupts! A qualitative study of organizational culture in corrupt organizations. *Journal of Business Ethics*, 120: 291–311.
2 Anjum, A., Ming, X., Siddiqqi, A.F., & Rasool, S.F. (2018) An empirical study analysing job productivity in toxic workplace environments. *International Journal of Research and Public Health*, 15: 35.
3 Hogan, R., & Kaiser, R.B. (2007) The toxic triangle: Destructive leaders, susceptible followers and conducive environments. *The Leadership Quarterly*, 18: 176–194.
4 Campbell & Goritz (2014).
5 Interview with Senior Executive, November 2021.
6 Pelletier, K.L., Kottke, J.L., & Sirotnik, B.W. (2019) The toxic triangle in academia: A case analysis of the emergence and manifestation of toxicity in a public university. *Leadership*, 14(4): 405–432.
7 Pelletier, et al. (2019).
8 Interview with Senior Executive, November 2021.
9 Interview with Senior Executive, October 2021.
10 Interview with Senior Executive, October 2021.
11 Padilla, A., Hogan, R., & Kaiser, R.B. (2007) The toxic triangle: Destructive leaders, susceptible followers and conducive environments. *The Leadership Quarterly*, 18: 176–194.
12 Pelletier, et al. (2019).
13 https://www.frc.org.uk/getattachment/88bd8c45-50ea-4841-95b0-d2f4f48069a2/2018-UK-Corporate-Governance-Code-FINAL.PDF. Accessed 18 June 2022.
14 Financial Report Council. (July 2018) The UK Corporate Governance Code.
15 Interview with Senior Director (6) 4 November 2021.
16 *Ibid.*
17 *Ibid.*
18 https://www.punkswithpurpose.org/dearbrewdog/. Accessed on 19 January 2022
19 Adapted from various employee engagement survey questions.
20 Corkery, M. (2016) Bank is fined for setting up sham accounts. *New York Times*, September 9.
21 Furnham, A., & Taylor, J. (2004) *The Dark Side of Behaviours at Work*. London: Palgrave Macmillan.
22 Chen, M., & Chen, C.C. (2021) The moral dark side of performance pressure: How and when it affects unethical pro-organizational behaviour. *The International Journal of Human Resource Management*. DOI: 10.1080/09585192.2021.1991434.
23 Buckingham, M., & Goodall, A. (2019) Reinventing Performance Management, *Harvard Business Review*.
24 *Ibid*.
25 McBriarty, M.A. (1988) Performance appraisal: Some unintended consequences. *Public Personnel Management*, 17(4): 421–434.
26 Grote, D. (2005) Forced ranking: Making performance management work. *Harvard Business School*, 14 November 2005.

27 Wilde, J. (2016) *The Social Psychology of Orgaizations*. London: Routledge.
28 Coates, J. (2012) *The Hour Between Dog and Wolf: Risk-Taking, Gut Feelings and the Biology of Boom and Bust*. London: Harper Collins: Fourth Estate.
29 Hodgins, M., MacCurtain, S., & Mannix-McNamara, P. (2020) Power and inaction: Why organisations fail to address workplace bullying'. *International Journal of Workplace Health Management*, 13(3): 265–290.
30 https://www.riotinto.com/-/media/Content/Documents/Sustainability/People/RT-Everyday-respect-report.pdf, p. 32. Accessed 1 February 2022.
31 *Ibid.*, p. 36.
32 Interview with Senior Executive, 9 November 2021.
33 Interview with Senior Executive, 15 October 2021.
34 Roter, A.B. (2017) *Understanding and Recognising Dysfunctional Leadership: The Impact of Dysfunctional Leadership on Orgaisations and Followers*. New York: Routledge.
35 Purushothaman, D., & Stromberg, L. (2022) Leaders, Stop Rewarding Toxic Rock Stars. *Harvard Business Review*, 20 April 2022.
36 *Ibid.*
37 Owen, D., & Davidson, J. Hubris Syndrom: An acquired personality disorder? A study of US Presidents and UK Prime Ministers over the last 100 years. *Brain*, 132(5), 1396–1406.
38 Coates (2012).
39 https://www.riotinto.com/-/media/Content/Documents/Sustainability/People/RT-Everyday-respect-report.pdf. Accessed 1 February 2022.
40 *Ibid.*, p. 19.
41 *Ibid.*, p. 20.
42 Larcker, D., & Tayan, B. (2016) We studied 38 incidents of CEO Bad behavior and measured their consequences, *Harvard Business Review*. 9 June 2016.
43 *Ibid.*
44 *Ibid.*

Part III

How to Build and Sustain a Healthy Workplace Culture

8
How to Build and Sustain a Healthy Workplace Culture

8.1 Introduction

In this chapter of the book, we explore how organizations can build and sustain a healthy workplace culture. There are seven key levers that need to be orchestrated to provide a remedy for toxicity. The RESPECT approach sets out the seven levers.

- Realign corporate values and measure engagement, inclusion, and respect
- Enable psychological safety and support employees to speak up
- Strengthen and enable leadership to act as role models
- Promote and align HR policies and processes
- Elevate well-being
- Call out toxic behaviours
- Transform career development and learning through the growth mindset

In Chapter 9, there is a framework for action that can be adapted for implementation in your organization.

8.1.1 Defining a Healthy Workplace Culture

A healthy workplace culture has been defined in different ways over time. Much of the focus to date has been on employee engagement. Yet with an estimated 63 per cent of employees not engaged or actively disengaged in 2021, we need to understand the reasons behind this disengagement. Too much of the employee engagement approach has been about 'flag-waving' rather than fully understanding what the data reveals.

A healthy workplace culture is more than 'employee engagement'. A healthy workplace culture can be characterized as having the following elements: high trust, respect for differences, an appreciation of emotional expression and

DOI: 10.4324/9781003330387-12

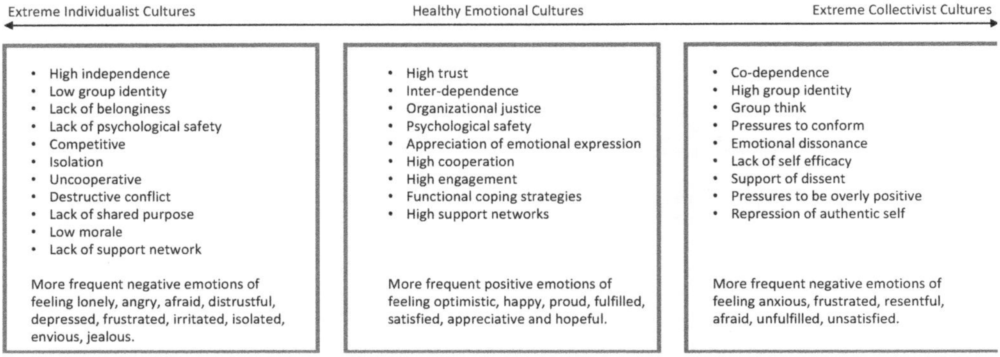

Figure 8.1 Conceptualization of a Healthy Emotional Culture (Adapted from Hartel, C.E.J., 2008[2])

psychological safety, high levels of cooperation, support networks, interdependence, organizational justice, inclusion, and engagement. This would include the prevalence of more positive emotions such as feeling appreciated and valued as well as being fulfilled, happy, satisfied, and optimistic.

To build a healthy emotional culture, organizations need to measure the quality of relationships between leaders and followers. HR or employment policies are a key lever in creating a positive work environment. These policies need to be consistently applied to all, irrespective of rank or status, to ensure there is organizational justice. Research shows that one key benefit of a healthy emotional culture is that people learn best in positive emotional and social environments, which is key to improved organizational performance (Figure 8.1).[1]

In exploring the link between emotions and organizational culture, researchers have observed two extreme stages where toxic emotions are experienced by individuals. These two extremes are defined as 'extreme collectivist cultures' and 'extreme individualistic cultures'.

8.1.1.1 Extreme Collectivist Cultures

Cultures that advocate extreme collectivism suppress individuality as they seek to mould an employee to a single 'template'. Employees will repress their personality styles at work and will not be able to reveal their authentic selves in the workplace; this may cause anxiety and frustration. For example, in one study[3] it was found that women who were compelled to adopt feminine display rules that required them to suppress negative emotions and simulate positive emotions at work suffered from emotional dissonance. Repression of negative emotions has been linked to heart disease and suppressed immune functioning.

At a macro-level, extreme levels of collectivism may discourage whistleblowers, as there is an overwhelming desire to conform and belong. This 'need to belong' has been shown in many studies to result in individuals hiding their true feelings in the desire to belong to the group.

8.1.1.2 *Extreme Individualistic Cultures*

In contrast, overly individualistic cultures are defined by excessive independence that makes it difficult for employees to identify with the organization. Employees may not be encouraged to form relationships with others and may feel isolated, lonely, and vulnerable as there are little to no support networks. In one study, highly individualistic work cultures were found to be characterized by a climate of fear and a lack of social support.[4]

In both cultures, individuals can experience a dissonance with their own emotions that is psychologically distressing. In such situations, we can expect to see high absenteeism, depression, and disengagement.

The organizational culture has the power to act as an invisible control mechanism. For an employee, the first few months of joining a new organization are about learning how to behave and react. Researchers have described these behaviours as 'emotional display rules' – defined as the socially desirable emotions in a given context. In this sense, individuals will adapt and manage their emotions to make them consistent with the situation or the environment. In its extreme, the term 'emotional labour' is used. Here, emotional labour is linked to the concept of display. These display rules dictate the emotions that can be expressed, when, by whom, and to whom. Any individuals who deviate from culturally accepted display rules, such as not laughing at inappropriate jokes at the expense of others, may find themselves subject to negative social sanctions.[5] The extent to which a person is disengaged from their own self-identity can be psychologically demeaning. Research indicates that the dissonance between a person's emotions and their ability to express those emotions within a culture can lead to physical symptoms and illnesses such as asthma, breast cancer, and coronary heart disease.[6]

8.2 Realign Corporate Values and Measure Engagement, Inclusion, and Respect

It is increasingly recognized that corporate culture is critical to any organization in delivering long-term success. The Financial Reporting Council (FRC),[7] the regulatory body of auditors, accountants, and actuaries, talks about the need to promote good governance throughout the organization and promote a healthy culture. To do this, they argue, requires attention to three important issues:

- Connect purpose and strategy to culture – the company's purpose should reflect the values and not operate in isolation
- Align values and incentives to encourage behaviours that are consistent with the company's purpose
- Assess and measure how culture is reported

Understanding the elements of a conducive environment is a key part in building a healthy workplace. Identifying the elements and areas of toxic culture in an organization enables leaders to take action and set expectations. Surveys to measure employee engagement have led to a cottage industry to measure the extent of positivity that employees feel, if are they proud to work for the organization, and what do they tell their friends and family; there are few surveys that acknowledge and assess the 'negative' side of the organization. To have a complete understanding of a culture, organizations need to measure both aspects: engagement and disengagement.

Let us look at the reasons that employees disengage with the organization and decide to resign. Research on the 'Great Resignation', a phenomenon captured in 2021 when, between April and September 2021, more than 24 million American employees left their jobs, was an all-time record.[8]

In analyzing 34 million online employee profiles to identify US workers who left their employer for any reason (including quitting, retiring, or being laid off) between April and September 2021, researchers found that toxic culture was ten times more likely to be the cause than compensation and benefits.[9]

The research showed that while resignation rates were high on average, they were not uniform across companies. Attrition rates ranged from less than two per cent to more than 30 per cent across companies. While the industry sector did explain part of this variation, there was also significant variation within an industry sector. For example, the researchers noted that companies with a reputation for a healthy culture, such as Southwest Airlines, Johnson & Johnson, Enterprise Rent-A-Car, and LinkedIn, experienced lower-than-average turnover during the first six months of the Great Resignation. And more innovative companies, including SpaceX, Tesla, Nvidia, and Netflix, experienced higher attrition rates than their established competitors. To illustrate, the researchers found that employees were 3.8 times more likely to leave Tesla than Ford, and more than twice as likely to quit JetBlue than Southwest Airlines.[10]

The researchers found that there were four main reasons for resignation:

1. Job insecurity and reorganization: The authors suggest that poor career prospects and job insecurity contributed significantly to employees leaving of their own accord
2. High levels of innovation and potential burnout: The researchers found that when employees rate their company's innovation, they are more likely to speak negatively about work-life balance and a manageable workload
3. Failure to value and appreciate employees: The researchers identified that when organizations failed to appreciate the efforts of their employees, they were more likely to leave
4. Recognizing the importance of well-being: Employees were more likely to resign when organizations did not protect their health or well-being

In further research on 1.3 million Glassdoor reviews from US employees who worked in 500 companies, a sample of large organizations from 40 industries, researchers analyzed the negative comments. The researchers found that there were five 'toxic culture attributes' that contributed to undermining the organizational culture.

The 'Toxic Five' attributes are defined as:

1. **Disrespectful:** Lack of consideration, courtesy, and feeling disrespected at work had the largest negative impact on an employee's overall rating of their corporate culture and is strongly linked to how employees describe a toxic culture
2. **Non-inclusive:** Inequity, cronyism, and nepotism were also linked strongly to a toxic culture. Managers playing favourites, such as promoting their friends or hiring those from the same college, all led to employees feeling excluded. In addition, the lack of a fair and inclusive environment for specific demographic groups – such as gender, race, sexual identity and orientation, disability, and age – is considered a predictor of a toxic culture
3. **Unethical:** Lack of regulatory compliance, unethical behaviour, and dishonesty were identified as features of a toxic culture. These included descriptions of dishonest behaviour as 'sugar-coating', making false promises, deceiving, and lying
4. **Cutthroat:** Around ten per cent of employees in the sample criticized the lack of collaboration or uncooperative colleagues or organizational silos. Around one per cent described the workplace as 'dog-eat-dog' or 'stab each other in the back'. When employees talked about colleagues actively undermining one another, the researchers found that this strongly predicted a negative culture score
5. **Abusive:** Although one-third of respondents mentioned their manager in the review, just 0.8 per cent described their manager as abusive

The leading predictors for employee retention suggest that there are three key factors: The first key factor is offering later career opportunities – 2.5 times more predictive of retention than compensation. The second key factor is offering remote work options – 1.5 times more predictive than compensation. The third factor is providing corporate social events as a way to strengthen connections between team members.[11]

8.2.1 Values

Organizations will typically describe their organizational culture by using a set of values. These values are statements that typically reflect four to five values. These corporate values are typically found on an organization's website, on recruitment advertising, in a code of conduct, or in the annual reports, yet seldom are they measured.

8.2.2 Consensus on Values

According to research, there are nine culture values that are most often found across a wide range of organizations.[12] By analysing 1.2 million reviews of large companies in the US in Glassdoor using Natural Language Processing (NLP) methodology, the authors found remarkable similarities in the 'values' that the organizations want their employees to practise on a day-to-day basis. Three-quarters of organizations publish an official statement of the corporate culture listing specific values such as respect, integrity, collaboration.

In frequency order, the culture values from the Culture 500 study[13] are set out in Table 8.1.

This list echoes similar findings in another report which identified the values most valued by FTSE 100 Companies (see Figure 8.2).[14]

Table 8.1 Most Frequently Cited Values Across a Wide Range of Organizations

Value	*Definition*
Agility	Employees can respond quickly and effectively to changes in the marketplace and seize new opportunities
Collaboration	Employees work well together within their team and across different parts of the organization
Customer	Employees put customers at the centre of everything they do, listening to them and prioritizing their needs

Diversity	Company promotes a diverse and inclusive workplace where no one is disadvantaged because of their gender, race, ethnicity, sexual orientation, religion, or nationality
Execution	Employees are empowered to act, have the resources they need, adhere to process discipline, and are held accountable for results
Innovation	Company pioneers novel products, services, technologies, or ways of working
Integrity	Employees consistently act in an honest and ethical manner
Performance	Company rewards results through compensation, informal recognition, and promotions, and deals effectively with underperforming employees
Respect	Employees demonstrate consideration and courtesy for others, and treat each other with dignity

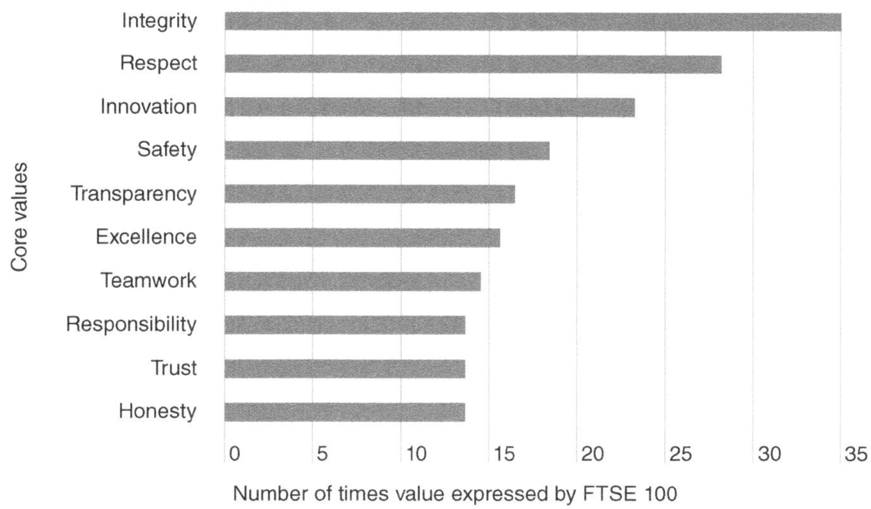

Figure 8.2 The Values Most Valued by FTSE 100 Companies

Simply adopting formal values statements is not enough. In order to have an impact on behavioural outcomes and influence the way business is done, values need to be embedded in the company:

- Reflected in the purpose, strategy, and business model of the company
- Translated into expected behaviours

- Widely and consistently communicated, including through codes of ethics/conduct
- Reinforced through recruitment, performance management, and reward processes
- Integrated within the different functions, processes, and operations in the business

Key bodies such as the FRC ask Boards to continually question senior leadership and to evaluate the Board's effectiveness in ensuring alignment with values and behaviours (see Table 8.2 for questions for Boards).

Table 8.2 Questions for Boards (Adapted from the FRC Report 2016)

Values and behaviours	
How are we demonstrating that the board's behaviour reflects the behaviour that we expect throughout the company? Are we leading by example?	Has the company made a public commitment to the values?
Are we clear about the values and behaviours that we expect when recruiting new executives?	What behaviours are being driven when setting strategy and financial targets?
Do we hold the Chief Executive to account when we see misalignment?	How are we challenging 'group think' and testing key decisions for cultural alignment?
Are we discussing culture in sufficient depth at board meetings?	Are we seeing evidence of sub-cultures in the business that could undermine the overall culture?
How are we taking account of culture in our Board Effectiveness reviews?	What percentage of time is spent on financial performance management versus behavioural performance management? Is the balance right?
How can we ensure that we consider the impact on culture in all the decisions that we take?	What is the organization telling the outside world about what it stands for and how it conducts its business?

8.2.3 Measure Values

According to McKinsey,[15] there are four building blocks of change: role modelling, fostering understanding and conviction, developing talent and skills, and reinforcing with formal mechanisms (see Figure 1.2).

This framework, discussed earlier in the book, is useful for practitioners to consider how to evaluate their values and how effectively they are embedded within the organizational culture.

Employee surveys can measure the extent that the corporate values have been embedded in the organization. To do this, the engagement survey should ask several questions, and measure these on the 5-point Likert scale ('strongly agree' to 'strongly disagree'). Taking on board that there is consistency in the values mentioned in annual reports and on corporate websites, Table 8.3 proposes a set of engagement survey questions to test the extent that employees are engaged with the most reported culture values.

Each of the values is tested in the following way:

- Do I see it in my leaders?
- Do I have the skills and knowledge?
- Is it reinforced by the policies and procedures?

8.2.4 Drivers of Employee Engagement

The strongest driver of engagement is a sense of feeling valued and involved, according to Institute for Employment Studies (IES) research. The engagement model they developed shows the main drivers of employee engagement and focuses on measures that increase perceptions of involvement in, and value to, the organization.

These are:

- employees are involved in decision making
- the employer demonstrates concern about employees' health and well-being
- senior managers show employees that they value them
- employees feel able to voice opinions
- good suggestions are acted upon
- employees have the opportunity to develop their jobs
- managers listen to employees

Table 8.3 Engagement Survey Questions to Test Culture Values

	I see it in my leaders (role model)	*I have the skills and knowledge*	*It is reinforced by policies and procedures*
	See	*Demonstrate*	*Reinforcement mechanisms*
Innovation	Typically, my manager will find better ways of doing things	In my day-to-day work, I am encouraged to find better ways of doing things.	Our policies and processes encourage us to look for new ways of doing things
	Senior leaders encourage innovation over efficiency		
Entrepreneurship	Typically, my manager encourages me to take informed risks	In my day-to-day work, I can take informed risks	Our policies and processes encourage us to be entrepreneurial
	Senior leaders demonstrate entrepreneurship		
Agility	Typically, my manager responds quickly to change	In my day-to-day work, I can respond quickly to changes in the marketplace	Our policies and processes enable us to respond quickly to change
	My senior leaders demonstrate agility		
Passion for winning	Typically, my manager encourages competition	In my day-to-day work, I compete with colleagues	Our polices and processes encourage us to compete with each other
	My senior leaders encourage competition over collaboration		
Frugality	Typically, my manager reduces costs to deliver our work program	In my day-to-day work, I can reduce costs to deliver my work	Our policies and processes encourage us to reduce costs at every opportunity
	My senior leaders reduce cost at every opportunity		

Efficiency	Typically, my manager works efficiently	In my day-to-day work, I work as efficiently as possible	Our policies and processes enable us to work efficiently
	My senior leaders encourage efficiency over innovation		
Consistency	Typically, my manager treats everyone consistently	In my day-to-day work, I treat others consistently	Our policies and processes ensure everyone is treated consistently
	My senior leaders treat everyone consistently		
Action oriented	Typically, my manager makes decisions in a timely manner	In my day-to-day work, I make decisions in a timely manner	Our policies and processes enable decisions to be made in a timely manner
	My senior leaders make decisions in a timely manner		
Collaboration	Typically, my manager encourages colleagues to share information	In my day-to-day work, I share knowledge with colleagues within (organization)	Our internal policies and processes encourage collaboration across the organization
	My senior leaders encourage collaboration over competition		
Customer centric	Typically, my manager prioritizes the needs of customers/clients at every opportunity	In my day-to-day work, I prioritize the needs of my customers/clients to inform my work	Our policies and processes enable us to deliver high-quality services for our clients/customers.
	My senior leaders prioritize client needs at every opportunity		
Quality	Typically, my manager encourages me to deliver my best work	In my day-to-day work, I have the skills and knowledge to deliver my best work	Our policies and processes enable us to deliver their best work
Execution	My manager is held accountable for results	In my day-to-day work, I am held accountable for results	Our policies and processes ensure we are all accountable for results

IES[16] produced a list of the main drivers of employee engagement among staff in an NHS organization, with each one rated for its degree of importance. In descending order, these drivers were:

- training, development, and career
- immediate management
- performance and appraisal
- communication
- equal opportunities and fair treatment
- pay and benefits
- health and safety
- cooperation
- family friendliness
- job satisfaction[17]

Most of the proprietary questionnaires used by consultancies to measure levels of engagement tend to focus on views of management behaviour and leadership. West Bromwich Building Society has used Hemsley Fraser's 9 Factors Going the Extra Mile Commitment Survey since 2000.[18] It contains 36 questions, including: "Does your manager treat people in a way that makes them feel valued?" and "Are work meetings effective and valuable?" BT's annual CARE (Communications and Attitude Research for Employees) survey includes the following statements, with employees indicating whether or not they agree: "My manager actively promotes safe working behaviours" and "My manager is supportive if I have to take time off for home/family emergencies". DIY retailer B&Q has used the Q12 survey from Gallup since 2000; according to the market research organization, Q12 focuses on the 12 'universal' employee needs that, when met, evoke strong feelings of engagement, including aspects that can be influenced by supervisors, such as recognition and communication.[19]

Essentially engagement measures what employees say about the organization: *I would recommend this organization as a great place to work*; whether they will stay with the organization: *I feel a strong sense of belonging to this organization*; and whether employees will go the extra mile and strive for the success of the organization: *The organization motivates me to go beyond what I would in a similar role elsewhere*.

Despite the potential advantages of an engaged workforce, the CIPD[20] found that almost two-thirds of UK employees are either just partly engaged or totally disengaged with their work. Although the UK tends to fare better than some other developed economies such as Australia and the US, the CIPD figures still suggest that a large proportion of workers are either uncommitted or not entirely devoted.

This has caused a level of discomfort within organizations and within the practitioner community. Much focus has been on having the right rewards or other interventions to improve engagement.

Yet engagement surveys can be misleading as they tend to show a partial picture of the organization. It is senior leadership after all that determines the questions to be asked and who will be selected to complete the survey.[21]

8.2.5 Measure Engagement . . . and Disengagement

Let us now look at the use and value of surveys and other diagnostic tools. In understanding culture, one of the key insights is diagnosis. Over the past 15 years, there has been a fanfare for organizations to conduct employee engagement surveys. These are designed to show just how motivated employees are and, so it follows, that such motivation will lead to better organizational performance. Indeed, there has been a wealth of publications in this arena.

According to one study, revenue in organizations with high levels of engaged employees is six per cent higher than in those with a less engaged workforce,[22] while US research found that increasing an individual's level of engagement can improve their performance by up to 20 per cent and reduce the probability that they will leave by 87 per cent.[23]

Engagement questions tend to focus on 'measuring' engagement. These questions will typically use the 5-point Likert scale from 'strongly agree' to 'strongly disagree':

- I am proud to work at (name of organization)
- I would recommend this (name of organization) as a great place to work
- (Name of organization) is the best place to work in (industry sector)
- (Name of organization) inspires me to do my best work
- I feel a strong sense of belonging to (name of organization)
- (Name of organization) motivates me to go beyond what I would in a similar role elsewhere

> An engaged employee is one who is willing and able to contribute to company success. It is not a measure of happiness or satisfaction but the extent to which a person puts discretionary effort into their job, beyond the required minimum to get the job done, in the form of extra time, brainpower or energy. It's about going the extra mile.[24]

8.2.6 Measuring Disengagement

Nearly eight years after the Global Financial Crisis, the Financial Services Culture Board (FSCB) was set up in 2015 to help raise standards of behaviour and competence in the banking sector. The impetus to create a professional body for banking in the UK resulted from a Parliamentary Commission. This private sector body is funded by membership subscriptions. Their first goal was to establish an Assessment Framework that would allow member firms to gauge progress in managing culture.

Importantly, the framework asks 36 core questions which are both positively phrased and negatively phrased.

There are nine categories, with each category providing a list of questions. In total, around one-third of the questions are negatively phrased (see Table 8.4).

Table 8.4 The FSCB Assessment Framework 36 Core Questions

Honesty
I believe senior leaders in my organization mean what they say.
In my organization, I see instances where unethical behaviour is rewarded.
My colleagues act in an honest and ethical way.
It is difficult to make career progression in my organization without flexing my ethical standards.
Respect
At my work, I feel that I am treated with respect.
At my work, people seek and respect different opinions when making decisions.
In my organization, both Risk and Compliance are respected functions.
In my organization, we are encouraged to follow the spirit of the rules (what they mean, not just the words).
I believe my organization puts customers at the centre of business decisions.
Openness
In my experience, people in my organization are truly open to review and feedback from external sources.
In my organization, people are encouraged to provide customers with information in a way that helps them make the right decisions.
In my experience, people in my organization do not get defensive when their views are challenged by colleagues.
In my organization, I am encouraged to share learnings and good practices with others.
If I raised concerns about the way we work, I would be worried about the negative consequences for me.

Accountability

In my experience, people in my area clearly understand the behaviour that is expected of them.

I believe senior leaders in my organization take responsibility, especially if things go wrong.

I see people in my organization turn a blind eye to inappropriate behaviour.

I see people in my organization try to avoid responsibility in case something goes wrong.

I feel comfortable challenging a decision made by my manager.

Competence

In my experience, people in my organization have the skills and knowledge to do their jobs well.

In my role, I am encouraged to continually learn new skills and improve my role-specific knowledge.

I am confident in the ability of people in my area to identify risks.

Reliability

When my organization says it will do something for customers, it gets done.

I see the people I work with go the extra mile in order to meet the needs of our customers.

When people in my organization say they will do something, I can rely on them getting it done.

Resilience

In my experience, people in my organization are good at dealing with issues before they become major problems.

My organization focuses primarily on short-term results.

I often feel under excessive pressure to perform in my work.

Working in my organization has a negative impact on my health and well-being.

Responsiveness

I believe that my organization responds effectively to staff feedback.

Our internal processes and practices are a barrier to our continuous improvement.

I believe that my organization responds effectively to customer feedback.

I believe that my organization encourages innovation in the best interests of our customers.

I have observed improvements in the way we do things based on lessons learnt.

Shared purpose

My organization's purpose and values are meaningful to me.

There is no conflict between my organization's stated values and how we do business.

Key:

Positively phrased questions *Negatively phrased questions*

Note: Shaded texts are questions to test toxicity in the organization.

The FSCB Survey asked 24 firms to complete the Assessment Framework, with an overall response from more than 45,000 employees across these firms. Results from the 2021 Survey[25] across all the participant member banks show both some interesting and some disturbing results:

- 90 per cent said that 'people in my area clearly understand the behaviour that is expected of them'
- One in seven people (15 per cent) said that the organization turns a blind eye to inappropriate behaviour
- 32 per cent[26] do not believe senior leaders in their organization take responsibility when things go wrong
- 24 per cent said that 'working in my organization has a negative impact on my health and wellbeing'
- 43 per cent felt 'under excessive pressure to perform in my work'
- 26 per cent disagreed with the statement that 'people in my organization do not get defensive when their views are challenged by colleagues'
- 26 per cent feared that if they raised concerns about 'the way we work', they would be personally worried about the consequences

The FSCB summarized these findings by saying that 94 per cent of colleagues felt accepted by colleagues at work but 14 per cent were worried about judgements made about their ability based on stereotypes relating to their identity

Table 8.5 Questions to Measure the Levels of Toxicity

Disrespectful	I am treated with respect and dignity in the workplace
	Diverse perspectives are valued in the workplace
Non-inclusive	My manager likes to play their favourites
	My manager deals fairly with everyone
Unethical	I can report unethical behaviour without fear of reprisal
	My manager acts with honestly and integrity
Cut-throat	The work environment is uncollaborative
Abusive	I would describe the culture as toxic
	Undesirable behaviours are not tolerated

or background, with five per cent feeling excluded by unfair treatment, cliques, and other factors.

In every organization, there will be pockets of toxicity or micro-cultures. Teams, units, and departments can have their own micro-cultures. These may not reflect the overall organizational culture. Leaders have the opportunity to identify these pockets through a survey. Table 8.5 lists suggested questions that have been used in various engagement surveys in SME and international organizations to identify pockets of toxicity, which relate to the 'five toxic culture attributes' defined earlier in the chapter. These questions are best evaluated using a 5-point Likert scale response from 'strongly agree' to 'strongly disagree'. Using demographic and comparative data by unit and departments will enable an organization to see the 'red flags' of toxicity.

8.3 Enable Psychological Safety and Support Employees to Speak Up

Psychological safety has developed as a concept in recent times. According to Edmondson, essentially psychological safety is about the effectiveness of team learning, with the focus on the process rather than the outcome:

> Fast-paced work environments require learning behavior to make sense of what is happening as well as to take action. With the promise of more uncertainty, more change, and less job security in future organizations, teams are in a position to provide an important source of psychological safety for individuals at work. The need to ask questions, seek help, and tolerate mistakes in the face of uncertainty – while team members and other colleagues watch – is probably more prevalent in companies today.[27]

Writing for the *Harvard Business Review*, Tim Clark argues that agility does not work without psychological safety. Agile management practices are best defined by the way the team can challenge themselves and interact to solve complex issues. To harness this intellectual friction, Clark states that the team relies on psychological safety to have a collaborative dialogue. High psychological safety, Clark argues, elicits a performance response with innovation as the goal, whereas low psychological safety elicits a fear response with survival as the goal. "When team members stop asking questions, admitting mistakes, exploring ideas, and challenging the status quo, they stop being agile".

More recently, the concept of agility has impacted the HR function. As organizations have moved to a team-led approach combined with a need to develop and deploy talent more quickly, the HR processes have required a radical rethink. As a result, organizations are reconsidering how they manage performance and evaluate talent. This has raised certain questions:

- What skill sets are critical and how best to develop them?
- What is the balance of buying talent versus building talent?
- How best to reward people?
- How best to facilitate learning?
- How best to target the right kind of career experiences to advance individual capability?

As described in the previous chapter, many organizations are moving away from annual performance reviews and annual performance ratings. As individuals are increasingly working in teams, often on different projects with different leaders for a shorter time, an annual performance appraisal looks to be increasingly anachronistic.

The real value of the appraisal process is feedback. As human beings, we have an instinctive desire to learn and get better at what we do. The discipline of the annual performance appraisal process provided that feedback – on at least an annual basis. More recently, organizations across many industries have switched to more frequent performance feedback, including retail (Gap), big pharma (Pfizer), insurance (Cigna), consumer products (P&G), and accounting and consultancy (the Big Four firms).

8.3.1 From Evaluating to Coaching

So how has this changed the performance appraisal? Feedback has become more immediate and bespoke. For example, Regeneron Pharmaceuticals, a fast-growing bio tech company, has tailored its feedback cycle based on the employee groups. Research scientists crave metrics and are keen on assessing competencies, so they meet their managers twice a year for competency evaluations and milestones reviews. Client-facing groups receive feedback from customers in their assessments. In total, Regeneron have four distinct appraisal processes which are all about reinforcing the need for continual feedback.

The role of the manager is critical in adopting agile talent practices, and as such investing in managers' coaching skills is paramount. At Cigna, the training includes short weekly videos, peer-to-peer feedback, and 'learning sprints' where supervisors can engage in sessions to reflect on and test-drive new skills on the job. The key is about sharing ideas and tactics through these learning cohorts.

Moving supervisors away from judging employees to coaching is seen as important for the culture and the sustained growth of the organization. P&G have invested heavily in training supervisors on how to establish employees' priorities and goals, how to provide feedback about contributions, and how to align employees' career aspirations with business needs and learning and development plans.

8.3.2 Multidirectional Feedback

In healthy cultures, multidirectional feedback is encouraged to enable every individual to receive constructive and timely feedback. The Mitre Corporation not-for-profit research centres took steps to build on their confidential employee surveys and focus groups to uncover the issues that people wanted to discuss with their managers. However, the organization found that it was difficult to get subordinates to give feedback. The concern by subordinates was whether the leader was readily open to feedback. Similarly at the World Bank, 360-degree appraisal reviews were collated for the senior management to provide written anonymous texts to provide feedback on what the individual does well and what could be better.

A law firm in Scotland has implemented their own 360 appraisal process on their managers and leaders, where the HR manager sends out a questionnaire and collates the data. The survey asked three questions:

1. When (the manager) is at their best, what do they do and what do you experience?
2. When the manager is not at their best, what do you see and what do you experience?
3. If you can identify two development themes for this individual, what would they be and why?

This firm comprises around 300 partners and staff; the data help to identify around ten development interventions for the coming year based on the feedback.

Other organizations have sought to institutionalize discussions using a 'five conversations' framework. J&J, for example, use this five conversations framework over a 12-month period that includes: goal setting, career discussion, mid-year appraisal, year-end appraisal, and a compensation review.

While upward feedback from employees to supervisors and leaders is valued within agile organizations, it takes a lot of work as people are not used to voicing their opinions about management. Hence, psychological safety is critical to enabling a healthy workplace.

8.3.3 Speaking Up

Providing speak up and whistleblowing policies leads to an increased level of trust in organizations.[28] Trust is key in having a healthy workplace culture. Enabling employees to speak up using independent channels ensures that concerns can be raised. Anonymity for the whistleblower and the seriousness with which management treats the whistleblowing concerns are essential for its effectiveness. However, it is difficult to measure the success of this approach. There need to be additional ways that individuals can raise ethical or bullying concerns – and that can include asking questions in the engagement survey (see Table 8.1).

Many organizations will publish a code of conduct or ethics. This code will detail specific policies on whistleblowing, for instance, or on gifts and hospitality, the latter being a policy designed to ensure that employees may not succumb to any form of potential bribery by setting standards and expectations.

8.4 Strengthen and Enable Leadership to Act as Role Models

"Leaders must embody the desired culture (especially the Chief Executive) embedding this at all levels and in every aspect of the business".[29] This is quoted from the FRC which regulates auditors, accountants, and actuaries and sets the UK's Corporate Governance and Stewardship Codes. The FRC recognizes that a healthy culture generates value, and that poor behaviour can be exacerbated when companies come under pressure.

Public and private bodies all note the critical importance of how leaders behave and what they do. The CIPD say:

> Culture is much more about people than it is about rules. Codes of conduct are a baseline; a culture is created by what you do rather than what you say. The alignment and consistency of behaviours of leaders, and how they communicate through words and actions is the essential starting point.[30]

The leaders and managers at all levels are the role models of the culture. Yet so too are the members of the Board. As the FRC noted in their report:

> For boards, culture starts with their behaviour in the boardroom. Employees need to see that the leadership is held to account and to the same standards as the rest of the organisation. 'Leading by example' was one of the themes most often emphasised by chairmen when speaking about the board's influence on culture. For example showing respect to senior managers who present to the board. Several chairmen spoke of managers evaluating the board's behaviour and many emphasised behaviour as important. When chairmen were asked how much attention they give to setting the tone through leading by example, 58 per cent said 'we do enough for now' and 36 per cent answered 'some – but we could do more'.[31]

The Chief Executive is seen to have the most influence over the culture of the business. It is the Chief Executive who sets expectations and drives behaviour and change throughout the organization. Chief Executives need to be visible and communicate constantly with the organization through meetings, events, messages, webcasts, and video. In the FRC report, several Chief Executives emphasized the importance of being approachable and accessible to customers and employees. Communications from the Chief Executive can have a significant effect on behaviour; consistent, regular, and open communication of simple messages are key to building trust and encouraging the desired behaviours. A number of Chief Executives found sharing stories of good and bad culture (from the business) was effective in demonstrating expected behaviour.[32]

In Edmondson's research on psychological safety, she notes the critical role of team leaders as key enablers in setting out the beliefs and behaviours for work teams (see Table 8.6), noting both positive and negative examples.

8.4.1 Train, Promote, and Develop Leadership Capability

As we have seen in previous chapters, the role of the line manager has a significant impact on setting the expectations for behaviours and standards. The

Table 8.6 Learning Behaviours and Beliefs in Work Teams (Adapted from Edmondson, A., 1999)

Beliefs about the team interpersonal context
Members of this team respect each other's abilities
Members of this team are interested in each other as people
In this team, you are not rejected for being yourself or stating what you think
Members of this team believe that other members have positive intentions
Team behaviours
Seeking or giving feedback
Making changes and improvements (versus avoiding change or sticking with a course for too long)
Obtaining or providing help or expertise
Experimenting
Engaging in constructive conflict or confrontation

training and development strategy and associated programmes should reflect the corporate values in how these values should be lived in the organization. Experiential learning, roleplaying, and conversation games are all useful ways to discuss how the values are lived in realistic management situations. Leadership styles need to align to the values, and being explicit about the behaviours that the organization regards as positive versus negative is useful in setting out expectations.

One senior executive interviewed for this book explained how his organization set clear expectations regarding its zero-tolerance approach to any forms of discrimination in the workplace:

> So I think having very clear leadership, really stating your position on policies and how you want to be as a company ... it creates the right framework in which to change. So you would have seen that my backdrop is about black history month around diversity and inclusion, yet we are still predominately white male but we know how important it is right now for (our organization). We are going through a programme called Stand Up for Race (and) all 42,000 employees are going through briefing sessions around issues regarding race and discrimination and, in a nutshell, there are like four to five videos done by actors for a couple of minutes each. They all describe different but real situations that have happened in this organization. You know someone perhaps is isolated because (of their ethnicity). So there are five different situations talked through by actors and we run facilitated sessions of about an hour with groups of employees to talk through those, and

> the reason we are doing that is that we had two or three really ugly employment tribunal cases which highlighted some glaring gaps in the way that we approach some race discrimination cases. So our executive leadership team took the decision that actually it was of such significance that we wanted to run these sessions right across the company to get people thinking about it and also to be really explicit that as a company we don't want to be any part of that.
>
> For example I have run a couple of those sessions in areas where they have asked me, as they thought they might have trickier audiences. I did one in Preston where there had been a couple of tribunal cases, and it was really interesting running it for frontline staff and it generated a really good debate. Some were like: 'yes, I'm now being discriminated against as I'm a white bloke', but we actually had a really mature debate. Whether someone still within themselves thinks it is political correctness and woke or whatever, there is a bit of me that doesn't care as they have had to go through that session. So even if they still believe that, what they will know is that as a company, that is not acceptable. So that is a big investment to run that but it makes a big statement, and I sometimes think that making big statements is also really, really important.[33]

Succession planning is a key part to reinforcing the values and culture. As we have observed in this book, narcissistic personalities will seek out positions of power and influence. Some selection methods such as interviews will play to the strengths of the narcissist, indeed, the very traits that we associate with a great leader, described as 'bold and strong-willed' and to be able to challenge conventional wisdom.

In one research paper reviewing the literature on narcissistic leaders encompassing 150 studies, two professors concluded that a narcissistic leader can destroy an organization; they argue that narcissistic leaders are:

> Individuals whom corporate boards tend to select as CEOs, especially in times of upheaval, when the status quo is failing. They're adept at self-promotion and shine in job interviews. Then, once they're in power, we find out who they really are. Sometimes they're as good as their promise. But many turn out to be not just confident but arrogant and entitled. Instead of being bold, they're merely impulsive. They lack empathy and exploit others without compunction. They ignore expert advice and treat those who differ with contempt and hostility. Above all, they demand personal loyalty. They are, in short, raging narcissists.[34]

In identifying successors, it is recommended that organizations examine a wide range of data including 360 appraisals and engagement survey data, as well as undertaking psychometric tests such as Hogan. These will provide a much richer assessment of the individual and an understanding of both the bright side and the potential dark side, and help make the right succession planning decision.

8.5 Promote and Align HR Policies and Processes

The HR function can play an important role in embedding the culture and values in the organization. Aligning the policies and processes is a critical step as we have seen in driving culture.

The FRC recommends that Boards work closely with the HR function to create the appropriate organizational culture. Boards tend to focus more on remuneration through the Remuneration Committee rather than aligning strategic human resource management practices relating to selection, training, leadership development, and talent management with the appropriate organizational culture. As one Chief Executive noted:

> People and succession come up too rarely at boards. There should be more focus on the top 100, developing the mix and spending time with the leadership group. It's about having a pipeline of talent. You have to be clear about succession and have a strategy.
>
> Adam Crozier, Chief Executive, ITV[35]

The 'elephant in the room' is the role of HR. In some organizations, the role operates at the executive level, enabling the function to influence and embed the values and culture. In other organizations, the HR function remains a support function with little agency or power.

The dominating mantra from the HR profession has been the urgency for HR to have a 'seat at the table', in other words, be a member of the executive team. In that drive, some of the senior executives interviewed expressed concern that HR had focused or sided too much with the role of the employer and negated its role as an 'employee champion'. The role of the employee champion is considered by Ulrich,[36] as one of the four key value roles of HR. The other three include administrative expert, strategic partner, and change agent. By negating the role of employee champion, the HR function would lose its gravitas and influence in being an agent for change, as it was effectively compromised.

One senior executive interviewed for this book was particularly damming but echoed the thoughts of others:

> Our profession has not covered itself in glory … at all, it has not covered itself in glory. Let's look at examples of toxicity. The whole Me Too movement has uncovered some of the most repulsive, revolting behaviour that has perpetuated over decades. The very definition of toxicity in that

> context. Where has HR been in all this? I'll tell you where, mostly on the side of the perpetrator trying to protect the company. HR has not covered themselves in glory there at all. That's because the role of HR within a company and the relationship of the CEO is fraught with danger, because on the one hand you (HR) are there to execute on the side of capital. On the other, you are supposed to represent your people. Most of the time HR has opted to stay on the side of capital. How many HR people have stepped up to actually actively report a toxic CEO or fellow member to the board? The third piece, even more damning I think, is that you could argue that HR is actively contributing to toxicity.[37]

Many of the senior executives interviewed for this book argued that the HR function needed to strengthen its role as one representing 'organizational justice'. This raises questions about how this can be achieved and what the profession needs to do to enable this role and build capability with its members.

8.5.1 Embedding Values through HR Policies and Processes

While there are many HR policies and processes, the most impactful relate to selection, promotion, performance management, and reward (we look at disciplinary and related policies under 'Rooting Behaviours' later in this chapter). As line managers are critical to the implementation of these processes, these processes serve to identify to employees the behaviours necessary for promotion or for higher rewards.

Even before someone is hired into your organization, they will attend an interview or selection process that reveals a significant amount about the corporate culture. The level of engagement and how the assessment is conducted will reveal whether this is a warm, personal, and collegiate organization or whether it is a more impersonal, cog-in-the-wheel approach.

Communicating values and expected behaviours starts early in the process and will influence the type of candidates who are attracted to work for your organization. The induction process, performance management, and training and development should also reflect the values. For example, in one organization with the value 'collaboration', they would reward individuals through targeted bonuses or have a leader board charting the individuals who had received the most positive feedback comments. HR practitioners should continually challenge themselves and ask the following questions:

- What value does this process add to the success of the organization?
- To what extent is this policy and process aligned to our corporate values?

In one of the interviews for this book, a senior executive explained how a graduate recruiter in Australia would put candidates through an intense selection process to identify any potential toxic behaviours:

> The recruiter who ran graduate recruiting was fantastic at weeding out people who showed any signs of fast becoming toxic leaders in the future ... And she was like a hawk, watching. She was brilliant at saying, 'Do you know what? I know that person aced the case study; I know that person is seen as the driver, but you know what? Late at night I've seen what they do; I've seen them take credit for work that other people are putting in; I've seen them bully people into keeping quiet; I've seen them manipulate.' And if it was too far to the extreme, she'd say, 'I'm sorry, I'm not, I'm not putting this person through.'[38]

Remuneration practices are often criticized as a driver of poor behaviours. We have previously discussed in the last chapter the challenges created by some traditional performance management systems which tie bonus payments to achieving individual objectives. This can lead to non-collaborative and highly individualistic behaviour:

> Most companies measure individual performance against objectives. In future more companies will measure individual behaviour against a standard.
>
> John Stewart, Chairman Legal & General (until 01.06.16)[39]

Adherence to values and expected behaviours is important in retaining a healthy workplace culture. Key decisions on who is promoted or terminated will speak to the organization's values and drive the expected behaviours across the organization.

The 20th-century focus on performance management is about control and command. According to the vast majority of HR textbooks in the field, performance management is linked to the strategic direction of the organization, and then objectives are cascaded from the top and down through the organization. This is an annual exercise that results in an annual individual appraisal and an overall performance rating. Organizations would typically link a bonus payment to the performance rating. As we have seen, many organizations have sought to decouple the bonus payment from the performance rating. The reason unsurprisingly is that individual behaviours are reported to be competitive and undesirable in the desire to be awarded the top rating and highest bonus. This financial model of incentivization has been shown to be costly in terms of performance and human motivation.

Some organizations are moving away from this traditional performance management system. Deloitte, one of the Big4 management consultancies, changed its approach to performance management in 2016. Prior to the change, Deloitte set objectives for its 65,000 employees. During and at the end of the year, the manager and their staff member would meet to review how well these objectives were being met. The evaluations were then factored into a single rating arrived after 'lengthy consensus meetings'. By its own reckoning, Deloitte calculated that it was spending two million hours per annum on this performance management system. Its new performance management system no longer includes the 360-degree feedback, the once-per-year appraisal reviews, or cascaded objectives. Instead, Deloitte asks team leaders four questions about the individual employee at the end of each project or quarterly. These four questions have proved to be far more informative on succession planning, development paths, and promotion.

The four questions that Deloitte asks are[40]:

1. Given what I know of this person's performance, and if it were my money, I would award this person the highest possible compensation increase and bonus (*measures overall performance and unique value to the organization on a five-point scale from 'strongly agree' to 'strongly disagree'*)
2. Given what I know of this person's performance, I would always want him or her on my team (*measures the ability to work well with others on the same five-point scale*)
3. This person is at risk for low performance (*measures problems that might harm the customer of the team on a yes-or-no basis*)
4. This person is ready for promotion today (*measures potential on a yes-or-no basis*)

The authors of this new performance management system argue that all too often individual performance is brought down to a single number, and that these ratings seldom reflect the complexity of particular work. By using this new system, they have concentrated on the richness of the data rather than the simple. In their research at Deloitte, they identified 60 high-performing teams involving more than 1,200 employees across the organization. In addition, they had a control group of nearly 2,000 employees. They conducted a survey and found that there were three items that correlated best with high performance for a team:

1. My co-workers are committed to doing quality work
2. The mission of our company inspires me
3. I have the chance to use my strengths every day

Of these three items, the third was the most powerful across the organization.

In optimizing HR policies and processes to align and embed values, here are some questions that leaders should ask:

- How well are our values and expected behaviours embedded in all our HR policies and processes, from selection to development to performance management to reward?
- Do we continually listen to our employees and enable them to speak up using different channels?

8.6 Elevate Well-being

In many organizations, working long hours equates to career success. In one study, two business school professors found that people are hired on the basis of promise, but over time the less competent or those with less time to put into their work are weeded out. At higher organizational levels, differentiation is based mostly on motivation and effort – hours – as there are few remaining differences in capability. Over time, the competition for promotion and recognition results in employees becoming complicit in the long work hours culture. Even when organizations have flexible working and paid holidays, employees will be pressured to respond to emails or take calls even when legitimately on leave from the office.

In *Dying for a Paycheck*, Jeffrey Pfeffer explores the health effects of long work hours – the costs are alarming. There are a number of effects from sleep deprivation to drug abuse, from exacerbation of work-family conflict to lack of time for exercise and relaxation. A study[41] of around 7,100 British civil servants aged between 39 and 62 without any known heart disease found that over a ten-year period, people who worked ten hours per day were about 45 per cent more likely to have suffered a heart attack and those who worked 11 hours per day were 67 per cent more likely than those who worked eight hours per day. Other studies also show a positive correlation between hours worked per week and poorer health, increased mortality, increased injury rates, and more illnesses.[42]

A study by the OECD compared the hours worked per person in OECD countries between 1990 and 2012 and the GDP created per hour worked. The study revealed that productivity is highest when people spend fewer hours working. There is significant evidence that productivity declines when longer hours are worked:

- During World War I, a study was undertaken to increase the productivity of munitions plant employees. It was found that the optimum number of hours per week was around 48. Below that, productivity would fall, and above that, productivity would also *fall*[43]

- In one study exploring 18 industries in the US, researchers found that overtime lowers average output per hour. A ten per cent increase in overtime resulted in a 2.4 per cent decrease in productivity[44]
- From 2015 to 2017, Sweden conducted a trial of a shorter work week. Nurses at a care home worked only six hours for five days a week. The results were fewer sick hours, better health and mental well-being, and much greater engagement for patients in their care. Activities for patients actually increased by more than 85 per cent than in the longer working week[45]

The costs of poor management practices and toxic cultures significantly impact health outcomes and costs. Researchers have found the following:

- More than 120,000 deaths per annum and approximately five to seven per cent of annual health care costs are associated with and may be attributable to how US companies manage their workforces[46]
- Employees who view their workplace as unfair are 35 per cent to 55 per cent more likely to suffer from major disease[47]
- Incremental health care costs from toxic workplaces were $16bn in the US in 2008.[48]
- 61 per cent of employees said that workplace stress had made them sick, and seven per cent said that they had actually been hospitalized[49]

The link between long hours and productivity is negative; in fact, long hours are damaging. Yet organizations seek loyalty and commitment from their employees. As such, they actively regard those who work through their vacations or holidays or work long days and weekends as highly productive when that is not the case. Long hours lead to fatigue, poor decision making, and being less creative and reflective.

8.6.1 Flexible Working Arrangements

To change the culture and move away from long hours and a potential dog-eat-dog environment, organizations should set expectations for work time and downtime. In 2021, Portugal took the step to ban bosses texting or emailing staff after hours as part of new laws dubbed ‘right to rest’. Other countries in Europe have or are exploring the ‘right to disconnect’. France adapted its Labour Code in 2015 after a report on the impact of digital technologies on labour. The introduction of this law followed a study that showed that one in three workers were using professional digital tools (smartphones) outside of work hours and that two in three workers wanted more controls and rules to regulate against this. Employers who fail to include the right to disconnect in France are liable to criminal prosecution punishable by up to a year in prison or a fine.

Italy, Slovakia, and Germany are all tackling the right to disconnect through legislation or by strongly encouraging organizations to implement these policies. Volkswagen implemented a policy in 2011 stating that it would stop email servers from sending emails to the mobile phones of employees between 6pm and 7am. Other German companies such as Allianz Telekom, Bayer, and Henkel all have similar policies in place to limit the amount of digital connection employees have after work hours.[50] In 2013, Germany's employment ministry banned its managers from contacting staff after hours as part of a wider agreement on remote working. It was done in order to protect the mental health of workers.[51] In 2014, automobile company Daimler introduced a software called "Mail on Holiday" that its employees could use to automatically delete incoming emails while they were on vacation. This was done to allow Daimler's employees the opportunity to get a break and come back to work refreshed.[52]

At the time of writing, in the UK more than 3,000 employees at 60 companies will trial a four-day working week. In what is seen as the largest study of its kind in the world, this change in working pattern will mean that employees will work their fulltime hours in four days. Flexible working arrangements, which have been around for many decades, are having a revival post-pandemic.

8.6.2 Create a Sense of Community

To create a sense of community, many organizations have strengthened their employee value proposition by offering their employees volunteer opportunities to help not-for-profit organizations. The offering, of one to up to five days per annum, can bring together organizational teams to contribute to the community and strengthen their relationships. One survey found that around nearly eight out of ten people who had volunteered felt healthier and less stressed.[53]

In healthy workplaces, employees feel valued and recognized. Discussions about the future and career progression matter. All the evidence shows that irrespective of national culture, as human beings we have a strong desire to learn and progress in life.

8.6.3 The Business of Well-being

There is an ever-growing 'well-being' business that takes an 'individualistic' approach. Fix the individual, make them fitter and healthier, it follows that so too the organization will be fit and healthy as well. The corporate well-being market is now estimated to be $20.4bn in the US and is forecast to grow to $87.4bn by 2026.[54]

The well-being agenda not only includes health (physical and mental) but can also include financial management and community initiatives. The Future Workplace 2021 HR Sentiment survey found that 68 per cent of senior HR leaders (of which 40 per cent were CHROs) rated employee well-being and mental health as a top priority. However, the CIPD survey in 2022 found that this had declined in importance and that most organizations were tackling working when ill (presenteeism) and found that this was much higher for those working from home (WFH) (81 per cent versus 65 per cent among those in the workplace). Line managers were found to often lack the skills required, with less than two-fifths of HR respondents saying that managers were competent to have sensitive discussions, with even fewer capable of spotting signs of poor mental health.

Well-being is much more than an individual concern. Well-being is a structural issue for organizations. Organizations are recommended to offer employee assistance programmes as well as measure absenteeism and long-term sickness.

WFH has both positive and negative outcomes. The positive outcomes include:

- Lack of distractions from colleagues, especially in open-plan offices
- Lack of commuting and the opportunity to take more exercise
- Opportunity to control environmental factors such as location of work, temperature, humidity, air quality

The negative aspects include:

- Decreased physical activity – such as lack of walking between meetings
- Extended hours of screen exposure leading to fatigue, headaches, and eye-related issues
- Lack of face-to-face interactions contributing to social isolation and depression
- Blurred work-life boundaries, making it difficult to detach from work and juggle carer responsibilities

- Some organizations installed surveillance measures, such as measuring an employee's number of keystrokes per hour to ensure the individual is 'working'

Researchers reckon that the pandemic has led to a 'watershed' moment regarding where work gets done. The learning has been that many white-collar jobs, such as lawyers, accountants, consultants, technologists, and office workers, can be done remotely. Gratton[55] identifies the following changes:

- Workers' digital skills accelerated dramatically out of necessity
- Bureaucracy has declined because of ruthless prioritization due to shift in remote work
- Flexibility has become a reality as employers have recognized that employees can still get their work done
- People have struggled to separate work and home
- Remote working has highlighted the importance of human connection, especially for younger staff

Gratton believes that organizations need to tailor what work looks like and where work gets done based on the unique purposes and values of the organizations. However, there are as many questions as answers. Much of our office experience may need to be radically re-thought, where offices become more about collaborative experiences.

Organizations need to balance two perspectives: individual well-being and organizational well-being. Too little attention is placed on the latter. In the FSCB survey of more than 70,000 employees across 24 organizations, 'resilience' scored the lowest across all the measures, with one in four employees saying that working for their organization had a negative impact on their health and well-being, and one in five employees saying that the organization's focus is primarily on short-term results. Organizations should measure and publish their score on questions relating to how employees feel they are appreciated and valued as well as other metrics such as absenteeism and turnover.

8.6.4 Elevate Well-being Questions Using the 5-Point Likert Scale

- My manager, supervisor, or someone at work seems to care about me as a person
- I feel valued and appreciated
- I feel my work-life balance is about right
- I often feel under excessive pressure to perform my work
- My organization focuses on short-term results

8.7 Call Out Toxic Behaviours

Calling out toxic behaviours means taking action on those perpetrating harmful behaviour. As we have seen, identifying this behaviour in individuals over a period of time can be problematic. Leaders displaying sociopathic behaviours may appear and behave differently with other people.

More recently, organizations have taken to publishing policies on bullying and harassment. These policies make explicit the kinds of behaviours that will not be tolerated in the organization. The CIPD publishes guidance on the responsibilities of employers and employees:

> Employers should put in place a robust and well-communicated policy and guidance that clearly states the organization's commitment to promoting dignity and respect at work ... Employers and individuals can be personally ordered to pay unlimited compensation where discrimination-based harassment has occurred, including the payment of compensation for injury to feelings. Prosecution can arise under criminal as well as civil law.[56]

Bullying and harassment policies are specific on the types of behaviour regarded by the organization as unacceptable. The policies will state that such behaviour is likely to lead to disciplinary action and potentially dismissal, irrespective if it happened in a work situation or not.

Harassment is defined as unwanted conduct that intentionally or unintentionally violates a person's dignity, or creates an intimidating, hostile, degrading, humiliating, or offensive working environment for them. Harassment can take many forms, such as verbal harassment (crude language, offensive jokes, suggestive remarks, malicious gossip, offensive songs); nonverbal harassment (sexually suggestive posters/calendars, pornographic material, graffiti, offensive emails, text messages, wolf-whistles); physical harassment (unwanted touching, patting, pinching, brushing against another person, assault); pressure for sexual favours (to gain a job or promotion) or victimization (because the individual rejected this pressure); and isolation or non-co-operation and exclusion from social activities due to a reason related to gender, ethnicity, etc.

Examples of behaviours that are typically listed in a bullying and harassment policy will include the following:

- Shouting or swearing at someone
- Ignoring or deliberately excluding a person
- Persecution through threats and installing fear
- Spreading malicious rumours
- Constantly undervaluing effort
- Dispensing disciplinary action which is totally unjustified
- Spontaneous rages, often over trivial matters

Examples of less obvious bullying include:

- Deliberately withholding information or supplying incorrect information
- Deliberately sabotaging or impeding work performance
- Constantly changing targets without good reason
- Setting an individual up to fail by imposing impossible deadlines
- Removing areas of responsibility and imposing menial tasks
- Unreasonably blocking applications for holiday, promotion, or training

In addition, the policies will also contain the behaviours that would constitute sexual harassment. Conduct 'of a sexual nature' includes a wide range of behaviour, such as:

- Sexual comments or jokes
- Displaying sexually graphic pictures, posters, or photos
- Suggestive looks, staring, or leering
- Propositions and sexual advances
- Making promises in return for sexual favours
- Sexual gestures
- Intrusive questions about a person's private or sex life or a person discussing their own sex life
- Sexual posts or contact on social media
- Spreading rumours about a person
- Sending sexually explicit emails or text messages
- Unwelcome touching, hugging, massaging, or kissing

Cyberbullying has become more prevalent in recent years. This form of bullying would involve the use of the internet, email, or phone to send, post, and display images that are intended to hurt or embarrass another person.

The National Bullying Helpline provides support to anyone who believes that they may be a victim of bullying or harassment. They also provide a useful summary to support individuals to recognize the signs of 'gaslighting':

- A lack of openness and transparency. This may be with immediate line management in a one-on-one relationship, or it may be at corporate level involving an entire Executive Board and/or a business owner
- A reluctance to minute meetings or draw up file notes. We should not assume this is down to a lack of management skills. It could be intentional and therefore far more serious
- Refusal to follow policies unless it suits the business. For example, reluctance to acknowledge a verbal employee complaint or investigate a formal

grievance but at the same time applying a forceful approach to performance management and disciplinary policies

- Drip-feeding information or failing to provide full facts (which we have historically described as 'setting a person up to fail') or repeatedly rescheduling meetings or withholding important information
- Moving goalposts or changing elements of an employee job description without first engaging in discussion or making reference to a change-management policy
- Springing surprises, that is, calling last-minute meetings but failing to share data or advise in advance what the purpose of the meeting is and what the likely outcomes may be
- Knee-jerk suspensions over minor issues where a discussion or an informal meeting would have resolved any misunderstanding
- Instant dismissals without following due process
- Failure to carry out fair and thorough grievance or disciplinary investigations and deciding in advance of an investigation that an employee's complaint will not be upheld (i.e.: pre-determined outcomes). Warning signs include a refusal to appoint an independent, impartial workplace investigator in grievance and disciplinary cases
- Undermining behaviour intended to destroy an employee's confidence. For example, open criticism or alleging that others have complained where, in fact, there is no evidence of any complaint[57]

The CIPD publishes a useful guide for line managers who may need to deal with bullying and workplace conflict.[58]

Although individuals are encouraged by organizations to speak up, the reality, as we have seen, is that many choose not to do so. The reason: fear of losing their job, fear of being ridiculed for raising concerns or not being listened to, and hope that the situation might go away.

Organizations and leaders would do well to use the engagement survey as a way of identifying potential areas of bullying and harassment (see Table 8.1 for questions that test toxicity).

8.8 Transform Career Development and Learning through the Growth Mindset

In late 2021, nine out of ten HR directors in the UK were concerned about employee attrition, and rightly so, as research shows that one in four employees plan to leave their jobs in the next three to six months.[59]

Linked to this was the failure by organizations to develop their employees and actively manage career development. Current approaches to career and talent management fail both employers and employees. In a study of more than 8,000 employees and leaders, Gartner found that three in four organizations considered that they would face a capability gap in the next three to five years. Yet 70 per cent of employees were dissatisfied with career opportunities in their organizations. The researchers found that improving career satisfaction added an additional two to five per cent in revenue and profit by increasing employee engagement. In addition, eliminating an internal skills shortage generated an additional five to eight per cent annual increase in revenue and profit.[60]

How do career frameworks and management have an impact on making a healthy workplace? The transparency and clarity of career development is a key factor. Clarifying the expectations and sharing how someone can progress is key to engagement.

8.8.1 Career Management at the World Bank Group

In 2014, the World Bank Group embarked on restructuring their organization with a move away from the regional model to a global organizational structure. The impact was significant. New job roles were created, new ways of working were introduced, and a ten per cent reduction in the workforce was implemented to reduce operating costs. This was an organization that had not changed in more than 20 years. The impact of these changes reverberated across the organization and, in the following years, annual staff surveys showed a significant decline in engagement.

One of the key areas contributing to this descent was the lack of career development and the opportunity for personal development and growth. In an organization with 15,000 staff across 140 countries and headquartered in Washington DC, the average tenure was ten years, which typically resulted in one promotion.

Senior leaders recognized that the design and implementation of the new organizational structure had fundamentally shifted the understanding of how to navigate a career in the World Bank. The new global practices model was built on technical knowledge. For managers and leaders who had taken on Country Director or Manager roles where they managed a portfolio of programmes working at senior levels with the respective government, this meant that they feared their technical knowledge was being diminished. The Bank initially sought to rectify this gap in technical capability by buying in expertise. When it was recognized that the Bank needed to address the overall talent and career management strategy, a new unit was set up sponsored by the Managing Director.

The new Career Management Unit set about reviewing key challenges such as: how to deploy staff and respond effectively to pandemics and political crises with speed and agility, as well as how to navigate a career in the World Bank. To respond to these questions, the Career Management Unit invited business leaders to attend a weekly Career Advisory Panel that was chaired by two directors.

The work was deliberately delivered in phases. The first phase set out the principles of the new approach. The deliberations showed that the 'free market approach' to career management, where individuals were invited to apply for roles (advertised internally and sometimes externally), did not work. The process to appoint a Country Manager, for example, would take on average six months. The free-market approach is typically the way most organizations promote their employees. The organization 'hopes' that the employee will be able to develop and gain the right kind of career experiences in the organization. Typically, this does not happen. Individuals can sometimes become deskilled over time if they remain and there is little to no change in their job role.

In the case of the World Bank, the first phase resulted in agreeing on three principles that would serve to inform the approach to career management.

The principles are set out in Figure 8.3 and are summarized as follows:

1. Promote shared responsibility for career management with an emphasis on strategically managed careers. This principle was about moving away from

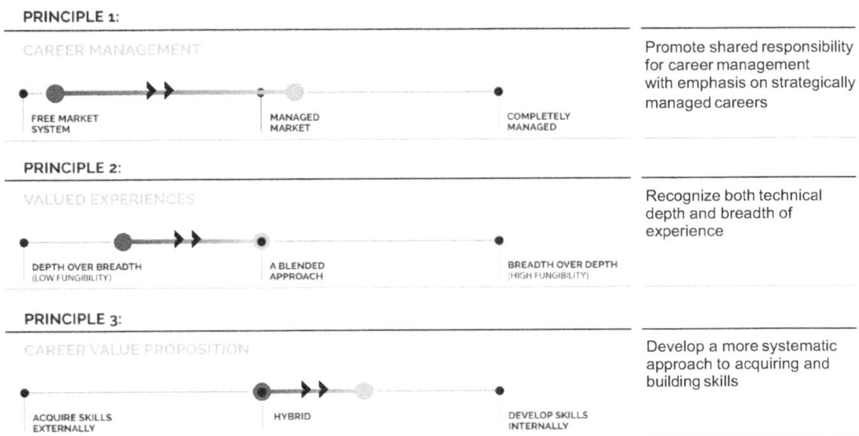

Figure 8.3 Principles of Career Management at the World Bank

a free-market approach with the emphasis on the individual to manage their own career, towards a managed market approach

2. Recognize both technical depth and breadth of expertise. The change in the organizational structure had unbalanced the recognition given to broader job roles such as Country Managers or Country Directors. These roles are responsible for millions of dollars to fund infrastructure or education or engineering projects in developing countries. This principle set out to recognize that a more blended approach was valuable
3. Develop a more systematic approach to acquiring and building skills. The organization had sought to hire senior leaders to run the new global practices. These global practices were set up by their technical domain, such as education or financial markets. They were designed to share knowledge and learning in the technical area and to apply this learning across the developing world. This principle recognized that the Bank needed to develop and invest in its own people

Once the principles were agreed at senior levels, Communications set out the next phase. In the second phase, the key roles were identified. These included roles such as Country Managers, Country Directors, and Practice Leaders. The question then changed from '*How do I navigate my career at the World Bank*' to the question: '*What career experiences would lead to the successful performance in the specific job role*'.

To answer this question, a robust methodology was designed, and a range of job holders were interviewed alongside other stakeholders. The sample contained two groups drawn from the talent and performance metrics so that the research could compare the career experiences of successful job holders and those not so successful. The research uncovered key career experiences that significantly contributed to successful performance in the job role. The progression of holding certain job roles could predict the successful performance in the 'mission-critical' role. The results were set out as illustrative career paths (see Figure 8.4).

In the example career paths, the job roles identified the key career experiences. For example, prior to being promoted from the professional level of GG to the manager grade of GH, it was critical to gain team leader experience. Country Managers can be responsible for 10 to 50 members of staff, sometimes more. Team leadership experience was recognized as a determining criterion in predicting future successful performance.

The Career Management Unit published these career paths as part of a series of helpful guides on a dedicated page of the intranet. In addition, the Career Management Unit re-purposed the role of the career counsellors who had been heavily involved with the downsizing and redundancies to support staff on how

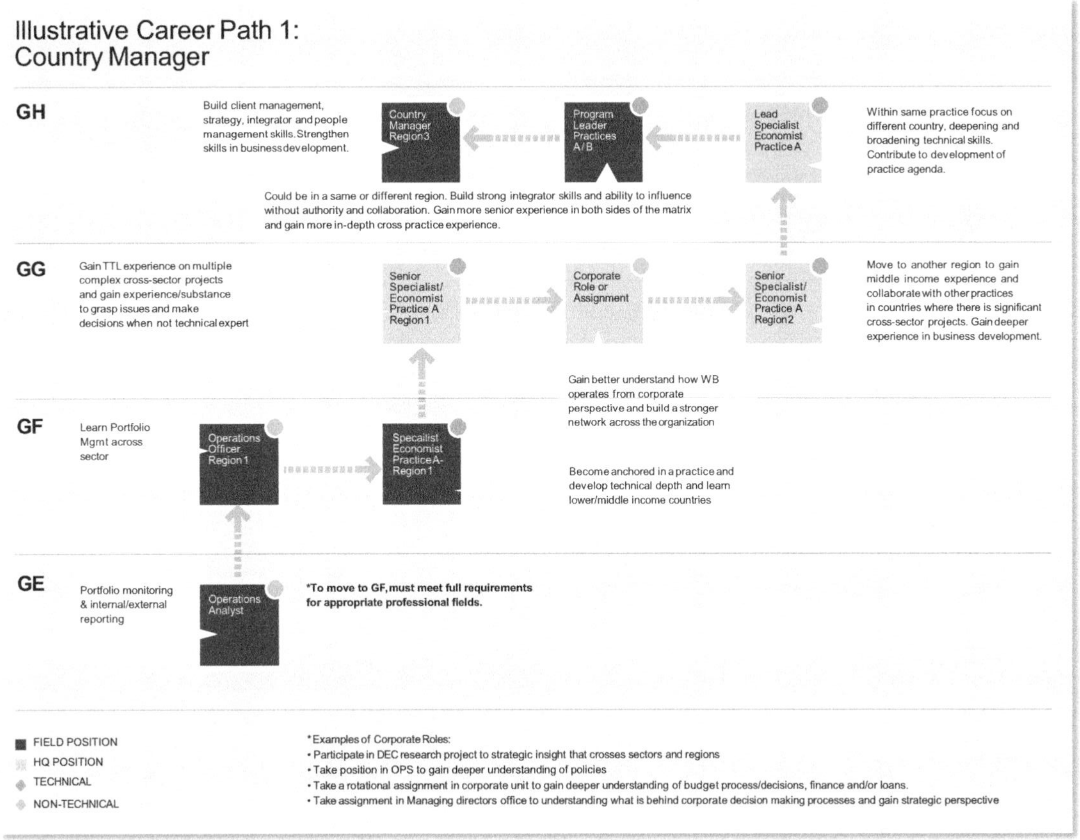

Figure 8.4 Illustrative Career Paths

to develop their careers. Workshops were delivered on topics such as 'Networking for Introverts' and 'Interview Skills'. Speakers such as Dorie Clark[61] and Daniel Pink[62] were invited as guest speakers. Senior leaders were invited to 'town hall' meetings to speak about their own careers and some of the challenges of balancing a career with family life.

There was a palpable buzz about career management in the Bank. Postcards were offered to individuals to be sent to their former boss, saying how they had helped develop the individual in the past. This reinforced the organization's view of what a successful leader should do and how they should manage their teams.

The next phase then focused on developing managers to be able to have a career conversation. All managers were trained on how to have a career conversation with a focus on the importance of the 'growth mindset'. Guides were written for individuals and for managers. Again, this reinforced the principle of having a more managed career.

Development programmes for senior leaders and junior staff were designed. The focus was on building the skills over a 12-month programme to advance the skillsets. Action learning projects were introduced, and delegates were able to present their work to senior leaders.

This work took around 12 months from the initial diagnostics to delivering career management for all. The next survey showed a ten per cent increase in employee engagement. The survey also measured whether managers and leaders were having the career conversations.

More importantly, there were significant business savings. The free-market approach had resulted in an average six-month selection process. The design and implementation of 'ready now' and 'ready with development' changed the time and resources required for selection from six months to six weeks.

In the final phase of the programme, the governance of the talent and career management process was implemented by introducing talent councils and boards. These supported the selection of talent pools and matched talent with critical business needs. They also ensured that every individual where applicable was mapped to their professional area of expertise, even when on assignments outside of their professional or job family. Talent brokers were introduced as a concept. This nominated middle and senior leaders to facilitate moves across the matrix and validate the readiness of staff in key talent pools. This work was then rolled out to other areas of the World Bank, including the administrative grades and other functional areas such as the Legal Department.

Underpinning all this work was the 'growth mindset' philosophy. Derived from the work of Stanford Professor Carol Dweck,[63] she posits that people hold one of two mindsets about intelligence: fixed or growth mindset. The growth mindset is a belief that basic abilities can be developed through dedication and hard work, informed through a love of learning and a degree of resilience. The fixed mindset is a belief that you believe intelligence and abilities are set and static. People with a growth mindset will see the same challenge as an opportunity to learn more.

When the annual survey was conducted a year later at the World Bank, the career management programme had led to a ten per cent positive increase in employee engagement.

More recently organizations such as Microsoft have embedded the 'growth mindset' to become part of the organizational culture and beliefs. In 2014 when Satya Nadella became CEO, the organization had plateaued and was siloed with divisions pulling in different directions. He is quoted as saying:

> Innovation was being replaced by internal politics. We were falling behind. With a focus on the growth mindset, the Microsoft's new mission statement is 'to empower every person and every organization on the planet to achieve more'.

Microsoft is now ranked fourteenth in the Fortune 500 in 2022, up from position 34 when Nadella took over in 2014.

8.8.2 Talent Marketplace

The concept of a talent marketplace was introduced at the International Finance Corporation (IFC). The Talent Marketplace was a simple yet impactful idea. Managers would post opportunities to work with their teams on specific projects of up to a day per week for a one- to three-month duration. So let us say that Manager A had a project and agreed to appoint an incoming member of staff (Employee A); in return, Manager B, who had agreed to release Employee A, would agree with Manager A that they would receive a member of their staff to work on a project in their area. This agreement would be sealed with a handshake. Talent Marketplace became an exciting place for development. Individuals would have the opportunity to work with a different set of colleagues and learn something new. Teams would have the opportunity for a different perspective on the work programme. Managers could benefit from the insights of their members of staff working in a new environment. Talent Marketplace became a practical tool to post opportunities and build relationships across the organization.

8.8.3 Questions to Test Career and Talent Engagement Using the 5-Point Likert Scale

- In the past seven days, I have received recognition and/or praise for doing good work
- My development is encouraged by my manager and/or colleagues

- In the past six months, I have talked to my manager or a colleague about my progress
- My manager holds regular career conversations to discuss my progress
- In the past year, I have had opportunities to learn and grow.
- At work, my opinions seem to count
- I feel valued and appreciated
- Colleagues are willing to put in effort beyond what is expected
- Colleagues are highly skilled in their field of work

In the next chapter, a framework for action is described with recommendations to build and sustain a healthy workplace culture.

Notes

1 Hartel, C.E.J. (2008) How to build a healthy emotional culture and avoid a toxic culture. In C.L. Cooper & N.M. AshKanasy (Eds.), *Research Companions to Emotion in Organizations*, pp. 1260–1291. Cheltenham: Edwin Elgar Publishing.
2 *Ibid.*
3 *Ibid.*
4 Wright, S. (2005) Organizational climate, social support and loneliness in the workplace. In N.M. Arkanasy, C.E.J. Hartel & W.J. Zerbe (Eds.), *The Effect of Affect in Organizations*, 1, pp. 123–142. Bingley: Emerald Publishing.
5 Hartel, C.E.J. (2008) How to build a healthy emotional culture and avoid a toxic culture. In C.L. Cooper & N.M. Ashkanasy (Eds.), *Research Companions to Emotion in Organization*. pp. 1260–1291. Cheltenham: Edwin Elgar Publishing.
6 *Ibid.*
7 Financial Reporting Council (2016) Corporate Culture and the Role of Boards. https://www.frc.org.uk/getattachment/3851b9c5–92d3–4695-aeb2–87c9052dc8c1/Corporate-Culture-and-the-Role-of-Boards-Report-of-Observations.pdf. Accessed on 22 June 2022.
8 Sull, D., Sull, C., & Zwieg, B. (2022) Toxic culture is driving the great resignation. *MIT Sloan Management Review*, January 11.
9 *Ibid.*
10 *Ibid.*
11 *Ibid.*
12 Sull, D., Sull, C., & Chamberlain, A. (2019) Measuring culture in leading companies: Introducing the *MIT SMR*/Glassdoor Culture 500. *MIT Sloan Management Review*, June 24.
13 *Ibid.*
14 Maitland (2015) The values most valued by UK plc cited in Financial Reporting Council (2016) Corporate Culture and the Role of Boards report.
15 https://www.mckinsey.com/business-functions/people-and-organizational-performance/our-insights/the-four-building-blocks--of-change. Accessed on 22 June 2022.
16 Robinson, D., Perryman, S., & Hayday, S. (2004) The drivers of employee engagement, IES Research Networks, report 408.

17 Suff, P., & Reilly, P. (2008) Going the extra mile: The relationship between reward and employee engagement. Institute for Employment Studies.
18 Suff, R. (2006a) Getting engaged: Employee satisfaction at the West Brom. IRS Employment Review 843, 24 March.
19 Tritch, T. (2003) B&Q boots employee engagement and profits. *Gallup Management Journal*, May.
20 CIPD (2006a) How engaged are British employees? www.cipd.co.uk/NR/rdonlyres/E6871F47-558A-466E-9A74-4DFB1E71304C/0/howengbritempssr.pdf.
21 Results tend to be controlled by senior management. Prior to the ABN Amro acquisition, when RBS was present in 30-plus countries, the RBS scores were typically broadcast to the UK population with little to no coverage of the results outside of the UK. Had RBS shared this information, the charts of red (low engagement) may have raised concerns about its capability to acquire an international bank (ABN Amro) in a further 20-plus countries.
22 Higgs, M. (2006) 'Demonstrating the value of total reward', presentation at Employee Benefits conference, 26–27 April 2006.
23 Corporate Executive Board 2007.
24 https://www.managementtoday.co.uk/engaged/article/645870 accessed 24 June 2022.
25 https://financialservicescultureboard.org.uk/assessment-results-2021/accountability2021/.
26 This figure includes the responses to the question 'I believe senior leaders in my organisation take responsibility, especially if things go wrong' with the following available responses 'neither agree nor disagree; disagree, strongly disagree'.
27 Edmondson, A. (1999) Psychological safety and learning behavior in work teams. *Administrative Science Quarterly*, 44 (1999): 350–383.
28 https://www.accaglobal.com/uk/en/technical-activities/technical-resources-search/2016/may/effective-speak-up-arrangements-for-whistle-blowers1.html.
29 Financial Reporting Council (2016) Corporate Culture and the Role of Boards. https://www.frc.org.uk/getattachment/3851b9c5-92d3-4695-aeb2-87c9052dc8c1/Corporate-Culture-and-the-Role-of-Boards-Report-of-Observations.pdf. Accessed 22 June 2022.
30 CIPD (2016). A duty to care? Evidence of the importance of organisational culture to effective governance and leadership https://www.cipd.co.uk/.
31 Financial Reporting Council (2016:13) Corporate Culture and the Role of Boards. https://www.frc.org.uk/getattachment/3851b9c5-92d3-4695-aeb2-87c9052dc8c1/Corporate-Culture-and-the-Role-of-Boards-Report-of-Observations.pdf. Accessed on 22 June 2022.
32 *Ibid*.
33 Interview with Senior Executive, October 2021 via Zoom.
34 https://www.gsb.stanford.edu/insights/how-narcissistic-leaders-destroy-within. Accessed on 23 June 2022.
35 Financial Reporting Council (2016:23) Corporate Culture and the Role of Boards. https://www.frc.org.uk/getattachment/3851b9c5-92d3-4695-aeb2-87c9052dc8c1/Corporate-Culture-and-the-Role-of-Boards-Report-of-Observations.pdf. Accessed on 22 June 2022.
36 Ulrich, D. (1996) *Human Resource Champions*. Boston, MA: Harvard Business Review Press.

37 Interview with Senior Executive, December 2021.
38 Interview with Senior Executive, December 2021.
39 Financial Reporting Council (2016:23) Corporate Culture and the Role of Boards. https://www.frc.org.uk/getattachment/3851b9c5-92d3-4695-aeb2-87c9052dc8c1/Corporate-Culture-and-the-Role-of-Boards-Report-of-Observations.pdf. Accessed 22 June 2022.
40 Buckingham, M., & Goodall, A. (2015) Reinventing Performance Management. *Harvard Business Review*.
41 Pfeffer, J. (2018) *Dying for a Paycheck*. New York: Harper Business.
42 *Ibid.*
43 *Ibid.*
44 *Ibid.*
45 https://www.theguardian.com/world/2017/jan/04/sweden-sees-benefits-six-hour-working-day-trial-care-workers.
46 Goh, J., Pfeffer, J., & Zenios, S.A. (2016) The relationship between workplace stressors. *Management Science*, 62(2): 608–628.
47 *Ibid.*
48 *Ibid.*
49 Pfeffer (2018).
50 Verhoek, Corinna (30 September 2014). Anti-stress legislation in Germany – how realistic is the prospect? – Ius Laboris Knowledge Base. *www.globalhrlaw.com*.
51 Vasagar, Jeevan (30 August 2013). Out of hours working banned by German labour ministry. *Telegraph.co.uk*.
52 Gibson, M. The most radical way to end vacation email overload ever. 15 August 2014. *Time*.
53 *Ibid.*
54 https://www.forbes.com/sites/jeannemeister/2021/08/04/the-future-of-work-is-worker-well-being/?sh=f7b4ba94aed0. Accessed on 25 June 2022.
55 Gratton, L. (2022) *Redesigning Work: How to Transform Your Organisation and Make Hybrid Work for Everyone*. Penguin Business.
56 https://www.cipd.co.uk/knowledge/fundamentals/emp-law/harassment/factsheet#gref. Accessed on 25 June 2022.
57 https://www.nationalbullyinghelpline.co.uk/gaslighting.html. Accessed on 25 June 2022.
58 https://www.cipd.co.uk/Images/line-manager-guide-bullying-workplace-conflict_tcm18-107061.pdf. Accessed on 25 June 2022.
59 https://www.gartner.com/en/newsroom/press-releases/09-30-21-gartner-survey-reveals-ninety-one-percent-of-hr-leaders-are-concerned-about-employee-turnover-in-the-immediate-future. Accessed on 28 May 2022.
60 https://dokumen.tips/documents/the-new-path-forward-new-path-forward-8–20102015-ceb-career-conversation.html?page=1. Accessed on 28 May 2022.
61 Clark, D. (2015) *Stand Out*. Portfolio.
62 Pink, D. (2013) *To Sell is Human: The Surprising Truth about Motivating Others*. New York: Riverhead Books.
63 Dweck, C. (2017) *Mindset – Updated Edition: Changing the Way You think to Fulfil Your Potential* (6th ed.). New York: Robinson.

9
A Framework for Action

9.1 Introduction

This chapter details a framework for action that can be adapted to support your organization in reducing or mitigating against toxicity.

There are seven key actions that need to be taken together.

1. Realign corporate values and measure engagement, inclusion, and respect
2. Enable psychological safety and support employees to speak up
3. Strengthen and enable leadership to act as role models
4. Promote and align HR policies and processes
5. Elevate well-being
6. Call out toxic behaviours
7. Transform career development and learning through the growth mindset

9.2 Framework for Action

See Table 9.1.

DOI: 10.4324/9781003330387-13

Table 9.1 Framework for Action

Realign corporate values and measure engagement, inclusion, and respect	Evaluate the Board's effectiveness in ensuring alignment with values and behaviours.	Board Workshop and Action Plan (See Figure 8.3 for questions for Boards)
	Measure the extent that the corporate values are embedded in the organization through an employee survey.	Engagement Survey Questions to Test Culture Values (see Table 8.3)
	Board and senior leadership oversight of the cultural reform agenda	The Board should provide a signed statement of intent and commit to a safe and inclusive workplace, that is free from sexual harassment, bullying, racism, and any other forms of discrimination
		Outline the case for change and the commitment to implement the framework for action
		Lead the discussion on their personal reactions to the findings by holding town-halls/all hands meetings/ team meetings and through other media channels
		Build the communication that connects the Board and Exco with the lived experiences of employees
Enable psychological safety and support employees to speak up	Embed and encourage a positive onus on employees to speak up and prevent disrespectful and harmful behaviours	Develop and deliver a 'code of conduct' for all employees in all locations (If global, then ensure that this is contextualized to the local environment)
		Ensure that the code of conduct is aligned with the organization's values and practices

Capture data and measure progress on psychological safety as part of the balanced scorecard and risk assessment	Set up a cross-functional working group/operational taskforce
	Establish the ability to capture data from many sources such as surveys, performance data, and 360-appraisals to provide insights on trends
	Establish a psychological safety dashboard
	Collect data via the people engagement survey on psychological safety and report by unit/division
Board and senior leadership oversight of the cultural reform agenda	The Board and Exco should oversee the implementation: • Set and monitor key metrics for progressing culture change • Conduct regular annual reviews and surveys using both qualitative and quantitative interventions
	Ensure regular communications (monthly/quarterly) to amplify the messages with diversity and inclusion initiatives such as Black History month, International Women's Day, etc.

(*Continued*)

Strengthen and enable leadership to act as role models	Train, promote, and develop leadership capability that ensures a consistent approach and understanding of a safe and inclusive workplace	Ensure all people leaders and managers at all levels: • Understand their responsibilities relating to the prevention of harm to any employee through inappropriate gestures, speech, etc. • Take the appropriate action on any incidents or reports of harmful behaviour • Effectively coach and engage with the individuals and the team on creating psychological safety in the workplace • Monitor progress through regular health checks such as pulse surveys and/or feedback sessions with independent consultants
	Promote and reward leaders who will act as role models that exemplify compassionate and collaborative leadership	Ensure all performance and talent management reviews are focused on:
		Effectively measuring and assessing individual behaviour in any management or leadership assessments
		Engaging in 360-appraisals to collect qualitative and quantitative data on leadership behaviours, including peer, follower, and leadership perspectives
		Promoting, rewarding, and recruiting individuals to leadership roles that exemplify and will act as role models of the desired behaviours

	Increase diversity in leadership roles to enable a more inclusive environment	Actively promote diversity through participation on leadership programmes at all levels
		Build talent pipelines for key leadership roles that provide for a rich source of diversity. These pipelines should include readiness within 12–24 months supported by regular leadership training intervention to boost capability
		Strengthen the talent pipelines by actively providing career experiences for key roles
Promote and align HR policies and processes	Provide guidance and support to leaders and HR Practitioners	Provide advice and guidance to leaders and HR practitioners to manage incidents of harmful behaviour in the workplace
	Build trust in the reporting system	Encourage stories of how reporting is safe and the consequences of action
		Encourage individuals to come forward and raise issues informally as well as formally and look on these as learning
	Provide guidance and support to leaders and HR practitioners	Provide advice and guidance to leaders and HR practitioners to manage incidents of harmful behaviour in the workplace
	Build and strengthen professionalism in HR and leadership	Ensure strong collaboration between HR and ethics and other leaders to improve preventative controls and strengthen professionalism

(*Continued*)

	Ensure regular consultation	Ensure regular employee consultation with employee representatives and ambassadors as well as groups representing women and diversity
Elevate well-being	Create a consistent and empathetic response for employees at all levels	Establish an Employee Assistance Programme (EAP) that offers counselling and support to all employees (and others) • Provide counselling and guidance for all employees • Support employees who may have experienced harassment and/or bullying • Offer early intervention strategies and guidance to support those impacted • Ensure reporting lines are sufficiently independent, i.e., ethics department rather than HR
Call out toxic behaviours	Measure toxicity	Measure levels of Toxicity (See Table 8.5 for Questions to Identify Toxicity)
	Publish the organization's Bullying and Harassment Policy and/or the Code of Conduct	Ensure there is a Bullying and Harassment Policy and/or a Code of Conduct that applies to all employees and contractors and measure ITS impact
		Ensure that there are clear examples of unacceptable behaviour and the consequences

Transform career development and learning through a growth mindset	Measure engagement on career and talent engagement using the 5-point Likert Scale	Suggested questions: • In the past seven days, I have received recognition and/or praise for doing good work • My development is encouraged by my manager and/or colleagues • In the past six months, I have talked to my manager or a colleague about my progress • My manager holds regular career conversations to discuss my progress • In the past year, I have had opportunities to learn and grow • At work, my opinions seem to count • I feel valued and appreciated • Colleagues are willing to put in effort beyond what is expected • Colleagues are highly skilled in their field of work
	Enable Career Management	Launch and embed career conversations that focus on development and learning Design career architecture to ensure transparency for career progression

Conclusion

In the research for this book, senior executives and others all spoke of their personal experiences of working within a toxic culture or for a toxic culture. This book has sought to expose the damage and destruction caused by toxic cultures.

In Part I, we set out to understand the key drivers of toxicity at a macro-level. Many books cover examples of toxicity and offer guidance on mediation at a micro- or individual level. Based on science and research, there are two key drivers that inform the framework for the Four Stages of Toxicity: 'Normalization of Deviance' and 'Cognitive Dissonance'. By taking a longitudinal perspective, the research, science, and history show us that organizational cultures do not become toxic overnight.

The four stages of toxicity reveal how deeply embedded toxicity can become. We become anaesthetized and unable to ask or challenge: Why else are we paying scant attention to the detrimental effects of toxicity? At the time of writing, more examples of toxic cultures have emerged, from the Post Office to the London Metropolitan Police, and more recently at No.10 Downing Street, the office of the UK Prime Minister.

The Post Office scandal exposed a flawed IT system where 738 sub-postmasters were prosecuted for criminal offences, including theft, false accounting, and fraud. Many of them lost their homes, reputations, and savings, and a few lost their lives. Over 20 years, a group of innocent, yet convicted, sub-postmasters fought to clear their names, and in 2021 the Court of Appeal ruled to quash all convictions. The rationale to implement the flawed IT system, Horizon, reveals one underlying assumption: that sub-postmasters could not be trusted. This assumption informed the decision to prosecute them in the criminal courts and to continue this approach despite evidence to the contrary. As Wallis notes,[1] "the Post Office had successfully fostered a cultural belief amongst its staff that Horizon was not capable of being the source of an accounting error. This meant that none of them were looking for errors".[2]

DOI: 10.4324/9781003330387-14

The toxic culture of the Metropolitan Police in London involved accusations of offensive behaviour, including accusations of two offices sharing pictures of murder victims, and the rape and murder of Sarah Everard by a serving Metropolitan Police officer. One former police commander writing in the *Financial Times* described how he had made a complaint about officers who had planted evidence on a young black man, "Supervisors turned a blind eye to my accusation, and I was bullied by colleagues who wanted me quiet".[3] The Independent Office of Police Conduct report highlighted a culture of highly sexualized, violent, and discriminatory 'banter' among Met officers, linked to "toxic masculinity, misogyny and sexual harassment, pervasive and persistent bullying, misogyny, homophobia and racism", as well as deeper structural weaknesses such as poor supervision, police teams being isolated from each other, and no safe ways to report malpractice.[4]

After allegations were reported in the media, an investigation was conducted relating to parties and social gatherings in No.10 Downing Street. From March 2020, the outbreak and spread of SARs Covid-19 represented a global public health crisis without parallel in living memory. In the United Kingdom, it had a seismic impact on every aspect of life in the country. In response, to help control the spread of the virus and to keep the most vulnerable safe, the UK Government put in place far-reaching restrictions on citizens that had a direct and material impact on their lives, livelihood, and liberties. The report found accounts of inappropriate behaviours in the workplace, including excessive alcohol consumption and a 'toxic work culture'. The report concludes that

> some staff wanted to raise concerns about behaviours they witnessed at work but at times felt unable to do so. No member of staff should feel unable to report or challenge poor conduct where they witness it. There should be easier ways for staff to raise such concerns informally, outside of the line management chain.[5]

These structural challenges, such as the immense power centred within the senior leadership and the short-term pressures for shareholder returns, or the reverence from the media and business schools that have devoted sycophantic articles to some 'leaders', have all contributed to toxic cultures.

In the second part, we explored the toxic triangle and the three dimensions or components of a toxic culture: toxic leadership, susceptible followers, and a conducive environment. It is purported that a toxic leader will not survive or have any impact without the other two components. Yet a conducive environment or susceptible followers seem to turn some leaders 'toxic'. This may help explain why, when an organization is judged to be toxic, the simplistic action of changing the leader fails.

Let us now turn to some outstanding questions. First, what can be done to prevent toxic cultures? Second, how far is a toxic workplace culture shaped by the national context? Third, can a toxic culture, or indeed a corporate culture, exist with the advent of remote working?

To respond to the first question, Part III identifies and proposes the tools and interventions to support and sustain a positive workplace culture. The RESPECT framework offers seven levers to inform and guide organizations on what to measure and what actions to take to maintain and embed a healthy workplace culture.

The examples in this book show that the elements of a toxic culture appear to be far more universal than not. We have discussed global organizations such as BP, Rio Tinto, RBS (now the NatWest Group), and VW, as well as national organizations, with examples from organizations that are headquartered in the Middle East, UK, Europe, USA, and Australia.

Some senior executives noted that certain types of leadership styles reflected national stereotypes. For example:

> Germans are very direct, and you go to Southeast Asia, and people are not that direct. Now if you put a German manager without training, managing diverse teams they will use their directness and that directness will be translated into very loud manager or a leader, and people will get scared because they are not used to that. So, while the intention of that individual is not to create a toxic culture or to be a bullying manager, the perception will be generated … and will bear the same results of a toxic culture.[6]

Finally, the role of the HR and the Board have been discussed throughout this book. The HR function is often blamed or criticized for a toxic culture. Many of the senior executives interviewed for this book raised concerns about the HR's desire and mantra to 'have a seat at the table', and in achieving this, had neglected their role as an employee champion. In the words of one Senior Executive:

> We are there because we are (the) people's expert, and that is the contribution the organization should look from us rather than seeing us as a business leader. You need to understand business, you need to understand where the money is coming from, you need to understand but it is all about people. And again, this will vary from organization to organization, but in my view most of the HR functions are subservient, we take orders and try to execute them without looking at what impact these orders will have. So HR needs to come out of that subservient mindset.

Some spoke of the need for the HR function to step up and take on the role of organizational justice, while others pointed to the impact of structural changes in the employment market with the demise of 'jobs for life' and a focus on hiring rather than developing internal staff. The demise of experiential training and the move to digital was called out as detrimental to a healthy workplace culture, as well as a *laissez-faire* approach to career management.

One senior executive recalled her early career at a UK Bank:

> "In the old days which is where I grew up for 16 years, there was training that you did internally and externally … So in order to be a corporate lender, you knew you had to do three jobs before that. And with those three jobs came six training courses, and you'd go and have to sit with some of it and do stuff and fill in the workbooks and things. I think it was very organized, very invested and accredited. It was like internal accreditation. You couldn't actually move on to the next course or the next job until you were silently competent of something. But that was back in the day when we had money for the learning and training, and even regional training managers who would keep an eye on your training plan and help you tick it off.
>
> And if you remember, all of the big companies after the early 90s crash, they all lost their training centres. They all had these beautiful training centres, and then they all got rid of those in the 90s. And then they digitized a lot of the learning, and people didn't appreciate the type of jobs that meant that you had the right experiences to move on to a different level job, or a promotion. In that, we lost the security of jobs for life, and we lost the security of very clear career pathways, and we lost the security of having the money to invest in training. That's when it all went. And I think it started in the early 90s.[7]

Yet the role of the HR function is often and justly criticized for always taking the side of the 'manager'. In 2022, the HR function at Apple, one of the world's largest organizations at the time of writing, has been subject to a *Financial Times*[8] investigation that revealed the HR function or "People team" acted as a risk mitigation unit to protect bad managers. One former Apple employee described a 'toxic work environment' and 'gaslighting'. In seeking to refute allegations from her manager, she prepared a paper for HR and was told, 'If a manager wants to get rid of you, they'll get rid of you. HR will do whatever the manager wants'. Has the HR function in becoming a 'business partner' lost one of its primary roles as the 'guardian' for organizational justice?

The world of work can be brutal. According to an eminent Professor, J. Pfeffer,[9] many modern management expectations such as long hours, economic insecurity, and work-family conflict are impacting engagement, increasing turnover, and damaging health. More concerning is that around two-thirds of employees fall into the 'not engaged' or 'actively disengaged' engagement categories – meaning that these workers experience no positive emotional engagement in the work they do: they simply disliked their jobs, or are dissatisfied, bored, or unhappy at work. A study in 2018 revealed that more than half of UK workers feel under excessive pressure and exhausted, and that nearly 40 per cent feel their jobs make no meaningful contribution to the world. In *Sedated*, Dr James Davies[10] argues that the impact of modern capitalism has and continues to have a devastating impact on mental well-being. With £18bn being spent annually every year on the NHS and with 25 per cent of the entire UK adult population prescribed a psychiatric drug every year, the problem continues to grow.

In 2021, a new Health and Safety Regulation came into force. Building on previous regulations concerning the organization's responsibility to protect its employees' physical and psychological health, and to 'prevent work related injury and ill-health', the new regulation known as ISO 45003 focuses on well-being in the workplace. Described as a psychosocial risk-based approach, organizations are now required to identify hazards such as the working environment and how work is organized. This valuable regulation places more emphasis on measurement, such as pulse surveys to monitor the workplace environment.

There is an opportunity to build healthy and sustainable workplaces. Toxic organizational cultures and leadership are devastating for individuals, teams, organizations, and other stakeholders. Organizations can no longer assume that publishing values and statements are good enough. The time demands action to build and continually sustain positive workplace cultures. It is time for work organizations to make a choice: to create workplaces and implement management practices that have positive impacts on physical and mental well-being, and not the reverse.

Notes

1 Wallis, N. (2021) *The Great Post Office Scandal: The Fight to Expose a Multi-Million Pound IT Disaster Which Put Innocent People in Jail.* Bath: Bath Publishing Limited.
2 Ibid (2021:120).
3 Otter, S. The toxic culture of the Met threatens policing by consent. (10 February 2022) https://www.ft.com/content/b7e5840d-1b38–46d5-b2c1-1a0d7205916c. Accessed 30 June 2022.
4 https://www.ft.com/content/5d639b30–5bf8-4c50–8783-b5f7a2388b68. Accessed 30 June 2022.
5 Cabinet Office. Findings Of Second Permanent Secretary's Investigation into Alleged Gatherings on Government Premises During Covid Restrictions. 25 May 2022. https://s3.documentcloud.org/documents/22036979/2022-05-25_final_findings_of_second_permanent_secretary_into_alleged_gatherings.pdf. Accessed on 30 June 2022.
6 Interview with Senior Executive, November 2021.
7 Interview with Senior Executive, October 2021.

8 Financial Times, 4 August 2022. The women calling out Apple's handling of misconduct claims.https://www.ft.com/content/96160847-af3f-44b6-8129-1e39a73a28d3?accessToken=zwAAAYLFiYE6kdOWFghHrz9EttOBKR45pzoo0w.MEQCIBmJ3d-Vk4XzlNChcoh39mInL_OY9_qkwTKejEslDEmxYAiBGcC39hxzkyLuuug1gluK-S5yCpGFH4O9WqbAXXUcmaog&sharetype=gift&token=85647a97-af24-4bd1-ac2f-95b97aaca4de.

9 Pfeffer, J. (2018) *Dying for a Paycheck*. New York: Harper Business.

10 Davies, J. (2022) *Sedated: How Modern Capitalism Created Our Mental Health Crisis*. London: Atlantic Books.

Index

Note: **Bold** page numbers refer to tables; *italic* page numbers refer to figures and page numbers followed by "n" denote endnotes.

ABN Amro: acquisition by RBS 45–6, 50, 65, 96–7, 122
action framework: toxicity reduction 241, **242–7**
Aegon Asset Management: capability framework 30
agility **206**; organizational values **202**; and psychological safety 214; World Bank 233
American International Group (AIG): toxic culture 18–19
American Psychological Association 9n2, 13
Anglo American: safety record 34–5
Apple corporation 33; criticism of HR role 251

Balfour Beatty 68
Boards: Corporate Governance Code (UK) 175; diversity, need for 175–6; and organizational culture 176; and organizational values **204**
Boeing: 737 MAX 8 crashes 78, 81; acquisition of McDonnell Douglas 79; bottom line focus 78; broken promises to employees 80; case study, vignette 79–82; Dreamliners, grounding of 80; employee ranking system 80; fines 81–2; fraud 79; 'more for less' ideology 80–1; performance pressures 78–82; safety concerns ignored 79, 80, 81; whistleblowers ignored 81
BreatheHR (UK) 12
BrewDog: vignette 177–8
British Petroleum (BP): accountability, lack of 102–3; Board collusion 106; budget cuts 77, 85, 90, 92, 95, 99, 100; business units 94–5; Deepwater Horizon spill 78, 99, 103; fines and clean-up costs 12, 107; management structure 94; safety issues 34, 91, 92–4, 107; singularity cult 101, 102; sustainability rhetoric 93; Texas City refinery disaster 99, 100, 101, 102
Browne, John 77, 90, 92, 95
bullying: characteristics 185–6; costs 135; and cultural values 176; cyber 230; definition 126; examples 229–30; excuses for 126; leadership style 86–7, 124, 126; pervasiveness 187; Rio Tinto 186–7, 190–1; tactics **127–8**, **188–9**; toleration of 189–90; Wells Fargo 124; *see also* corporate bullies; gaslighting

capability framework: Aegon Asset Management 30
capital: reputational 33–4
career management: lax approach to 251; World Bank 232–6
Carillion: acquisitions 68; and cognitive dissonance 69–70, 74; collapse 67; high dividends 70, 71; House of Commons report on 71–2; KPMG, collusion with 71, 72–3; *Making Tomorrow A Better Place* 69; misleading accounts 69; Normalization of Deviance 70, 71; organizational weakness 68; payments policy 69; public-sector projects 67; regulators' failure 73–4; spending spree 68; supply chain 69; toxic culture 71, 72; vignette 72–3

Challenger disaster 41–2, 44; analysis 42; Groupthink 98; and Normalization of Deviance 42
change: and corporate culture 26, 27
change management: developing talent and skills *28*, 29–30; dimensions 28–31, *28*, 205; fostering understanding and conviction *28*, 29; reinforcing with formal mechanisms *28*, 31; role modelling 28–9, *28*, 205
Chartered Institute of Personnel and Development (CIPD) 2, 208, 217, 229, 231
Chief Executive Officers (CEOs): misbehaviour 191–2; narcissism study 132–3; and organizational culture 217; vignette 121–3; writings on 121
Clark, Tim 214
coaching: performance appraisal 215
cognitive dissonance 6, 11; avoidance 60; and Carillion 69–70, 74; definition 54–5; and organizational identity 62; triggers 82
Collins, Jim: writings on CEOs 121
Columbia Accident: culture failure 44
competency framework: examples 29–30
control techniques 141
corporate bullies: psychopaths 123–4; types **126–7**; *see also* bullying
corporate communication: and culture 29
corporate culture *see* organizational culture
corporate manipulators: psychopaths 123
corporate misbehaviour: and corporate reputation 191–2
corporate psychopaths 133–40; character traits 133–6, 137; criminal psychopaths, comparison 133–4; damage inflicted 138; disruptive tendencies 137; economic costs 135; liars 139; manipulative abilities 135; negative associations 135–6; organizational destroyers 134; personal traits 138; positive associations 135
corporate reputations: and corporate misbehaviour 191–2; definition 60; negative factors 33; and organizational character 60; and toxic cultures 3
corporateness: and culture 31–5; definitions **60**; intangible assets 33; meaning 31–2
Coutts Bank: acquisition by RBS 47, 122
cultural values: and bullying 176; manipulation of 176; RBS 176
culture/s: attributes 15; collectivist 198–9; and corporate communication 29; and corporateness 31–5; definitions 14–15; failure, NASA 43–4; individualist 199; of intimidation 142; of invincibility, NASA 44–5; and leadership 14–17; levers 28–31; *see also* healthy emotional cultures; organizational culture; toxic culture/s

The Dark Triad: personality disorders 129–40, 145–146
Davies, James: *Sedated* 252
Deepwater Horizon spill: BP 78, 99, 103
Deloitte: performance appraisals 223–4; performance management system 222–3
demands: unrealistic 140
Diagnostic and Statistical Manual of Mental Disorders 124
discrimination: zero-tolerance approach 218–19
divide and rule management 142
Downing Street: social events during COVID-19 lockdown 249
Dweck, Carol 236

employee champion: HR as 220, 250
employee disengagement 251–2; measurement 209–10, **210–12**, 212
employee engagement: drivers 205, **206–7**, 208; Likert Scale 209, 237–238; surveys 205, **206–7**, 208; World Bank 236
employee resignations 231; reasons for 201; and toxic cultures 200
employee retentions: key factors 202
employees: community work 226
ethical behaviour: and slippery-slope effect 51; *see also* unethical behaviour
extrinsic motivation: compensation 26, **27**; conditions 26, **27**; in positive/toxic work cultures **27**; security 26, **27**; *see also* intrinsic motivation

Festinger, Leon: *A Theory of Cognitive Dissonance* 54; *When Prophecy Fails* 54
Financial Conduct Authority (FCA) 1, 12, 96
Financial Reporting Council (FRC) 73, 175; on good governance 199–200; on leadership 217; on organizational values **204**

Financial Services Culture Board (FSCB) 209–10; assessment framework questionnaire **210–12**, 212
flexibility: work hours 225–6
followers: active 154; colluders 157, **159**; conformers 157, **158**; coping strategies **155**; with Dark Triad traits 161, **163–4**; definitions 152–3; follower-centric approach 152; leader-centric view 152; Machiavellian 161, 162–3, **163–4**; narcissistic 161, 162, **163–4**; passive 154; positive and negative 160–2, **160**, 167; proactive 154; psychopathic 161, **163–4**; relational view 152; resistance strategy 165–6; survivors 166–7; susceptible 157–60; toxic, and toxic leaders 164–5; types 154, 165; *see also* leaders
followership: definitions **158–9**; examples **158–9**; expectations of 153–4; and leadership 151–3; in toxic cultures 156; and toxic leadership 154–5

gaslighting: examples 230–1
Global Financial Crisis (GFC, 2008) 1; and corporate culture 12; and leadership 115–16; and RBS 122
Goodwin, Fred (CEO, RBS) 29, 30; disgraced 48; focus on quantitative data 65; leadership style 65–6, 86–7, 90, 95, 121–2; leaves RBS 47; personal expenditure 107; reputation 63–4; strategy execution 65; *see also* Royal Bank of Scotland (RBS)
Groupthink: Challenger disaster 98; RBS 98
growth mindset philosophy: Microsoft 236; promotion **247**; World Bank 236

halo error: leaders 121
harassment: sexual 230; toxic behaviour 229
Harvard Business Review: on leadership 123
Harvard Business School: and RBS 65
Hassan, Steven: *The Cult of Trump* 144
Hayward, Tony (CEO, BP) 102–3, 107
health effects: long work hours 224; and toxic culture 225; *see also* mental health
Health and Safety Regulation (2021) 252
healthy emotional cultures: conceptualization *198*
healthy workplace culture: building 8–9
heart disease: and leadership behaviour 13
High Potential Motivator Indicator (HPMI): intrinsic motivation 24
Hubris Syndrome 189–90
Human Resources (HR): ambivalent role 220–1; criticism of role at Apple 251; as employee champion 220, 250; identifying toxic leaders 222; and organizational culture 220; policies and processes 221–2, **245**

Independent Office of Police Conduct 249
ING Bank: "gangster culture" 116
instability: toxic workplace 171–2
International Finance Corporation (IFC): talent marketplace 237
intimidation: culture of 142
intrinsic motivation: accomplishments 24, **24–5**; affiliation 24, **25–6**; autonomy 24, **24**; factors 24; in positive/toxic work cultures **24–6**; *see also* extrinsic motivation

Kelley, Robert: "In Praise of Followers" 153
Kotter, John: *Leading Change: Why Transformation Efforts Fail* 28
KPMG: collusion with Carillion 71, 72–3

language: degrading 141
leaders: deference to **89**; halo error 121; as heroes 116; as role models 115, 216–20, **244**; transformational 121, 123; *see also* followers
leadership: agile leadership theory 116; approaches to 116–23; cult of 64; and culture 14–17; and followership 151–3; FRC on 217; and GFC (2008) 115–16; *Harvard Business Review* on 123; and Machiavellianism 131; and narcissism 132–3, 219; and organizational identity 63–4; transformational 172; *see also* toxic leaders/leadership
leadership behaviour: and heart disease 13; and organizational culture *16*, 115, 118
leadership style: bullying 86–7, 124, 126; and corporate culture 66; Goodwin, Fred 65–6, 86–7, 90, 95, 121–2; national stereotypes 250
Lehman Brothers: collapse 47
Lewin, Kurt 10n8

Likert Scale: employee engagement 209, 237–238; and well-being questions 228

McDonnell Douglas: acquisition by Boeing 79
Machiavellianism 130; and leadership 131
McKillop, Tom 48–9
managers: as role models 29
mental health: costs 13; impact of modern capitalism on 252
Metropolitan Police: toxic culture 249
Microsoft: growth mindset philosophy 237; toxic culture 184
motivation: components 23; hygiene factors 23; Pink on 23; *see also* extrinsic motivation; intrinsic motivation

narcissism 130; CEO level 132–3; characteristics 133; and leadership 132–3, 219
NASA: Columbia Accident 14, 44; contractors, relationship 43–4; culture failure 43–4; culture of invincibility 44–5; layers of bureaucracy 45; Marshall centre 42–3; Normalization of Deviance 41–2; Space Shuttle Challenger disaster 41–2, 44
NatWest: acquisition by RBS 47, 64–5, 85, 96
naysayers: toxic culture **89**
Normalization of Deviance 11; acceptance of the unacceptable *84*; Carillion 70, 71; and Challenger disaster 42; definition 40; factors 70; NASA 41–2; RBS 47–8, 49–50; triggers *82*; VW 87
norms: organizational culture 16; toxic 34–5

organizational character: and corporate reputations 60; dimensions 60
Organizational Citizenship Behaviours (OCBs) 161
organizational culture: analysis *16*; artefacts 15; awareness **17**; and Boards 176; and CEOs 217; and change 26, 27; definition 41; errors, treatment of 90; espoused beliefs 15–16; espoused values *16*; and GFC (2008) 12; and HR 220; and identity 62, *63*; and leadership behaviour *16*, 115, 118; and leadership style 66; levels 15, *16*; norms 16; structure *16*; and toxic culture attributes 201; underlying assumptions 16; value realignment **242**

organizational identity: and cognitive dissonance 62; and culture 62, *63*; elements 62–6, *63*; external view of 63; image-culture gap 62; image-vision gap 62; and leadership 63–4; and stakeholders 62, *63*; vision-culture gap 62
organizational values: agility **202**; Board's responsibilities **204**; collaboration **202**; consensus on 202; customers **202**; diversity **203**; embeddedness in company 203–4; execution **203**; FRC on **204**; innovation **203**; integrity **203**; measurement *28*, 205; performance **203**; respect **203**

perfection: demand for 141
performance appraisal: alternatives to 214–16; coaching 215; continual feedback 214–16
performance management systems: characteristics 181; Deloitte 222–3; key steps **182**; negative outcomes 184–5, 222; persistence 183–4; and toxic culture 183; unintended outcomes 183
performance pressures: Boeing 78–82; toxic culture 77–82, 83, 85–6, **88**, 180–1
personality disorders 124; prevalence among executives 137; taxonomy **125**; The Dark Triad 129–40, 146; types 137
personality types: and roles 145
Pfeffer, Jeffrey: *Dying for a Paycheck* 224
Pink, Daniel: *Drive-The surprising truth about what motivates us* 23
positive cultures 23–31
Post Office: IT scandal 248
power: abuse of 140
productivity: and work hours 224–5
psychological contracts: aspects 61
psychological safety: and agility 214; enablement **242–3**; and team learning 213
psychopaths: characteristics 130; corporate bullies 123–4, 156; corporate manipulators 123; corporate puppet masters 124; in organizations 117; types 123; *see also* corporate psychopaths

RESPECT remedy: toxic workplace 197, 250
Rio Tinto: bullying 186–7, 190–1
role modelling: and change management 28–9, *28*

role models: leaders as 115, 216–20; managers as 29
roles: influences on 145; and personality types 145
Royal Bank of Scotland (RBS): ABN Amro acquisition 45–6, **47–8**, 50, 65, 96–7, 122; Achilles heel 122; branches, downgrading of 64; centralization 64; complexity of operations 49; core values 29; Coutts Bank, acquisition 47, 122; cultural values, changes 176; Edinburgh headquarters 122; efficiency drive 64, 66; external view of 63, 95; failure, reasons for 46; and GFC (2008) 122; global domination, obsession with 85; Groupthink 98; and Harvard Business School 65; losses 47; NatWest, acquisition of 47, 64–5, 85, 96; non-acceptance of failure 40–1; Normalization of Deviance 47–8, 49–50; paranoia 95; performance management 92; personal insights 61; resilience norm 49, 50; Scottish directors 97; singularity cult 97–8; toxic culture 66–7; UK Government bailout 47; *see also* Goodwin, Fred (CEO, RBS)

safety issues: BP 34, 91, 92–4, 107
safety record: Anglo American 34–5
Schein, Edgar H. 5; *Organizational Culture and Leadership* 14
singularity cult **88**; BP 101, 102; RBS 97–8
Society for Human Resource Management (SHRM) 12
Space Shuttle Challenger disaster: NASA 41–2
staff turnover: Wells Fargo 98
stakeholders: and organizational identity 62, 63; reverence from **88**, 95–7
Stumpf, John 95, 99–100
succession planning 219–20

talent councils and boards: World Bank 236
talent marketplace: IFC 237
team learning: and psychological safety 213
teams: behaviours and beliefs **218**
Texas City refinery disaster: BP 99, 100, 101, 102
Tourish, Dennis: *The Dark Side of Transformational Leadership* 123
toxic: etymology 3, 19
toxic behaviours: calling out 229, **246**; CIPD guidance 229; examples 229–30; harassment 229
toxic culture/s 17–22; AIG 18–19; consequences 1, 12, 13–14; and corporate reputations 3; costs 12, 151; creation 19, 107; definitions 3, 19, 20–2, 107; drivers 4, 5–6, 40; and employee resignations 200; examples 1; followership in 156; and health effects 225; leader, deference to **89**; loyalty, demand for 84, 87, **88**, 90–5, 143; measurement **213**; Metropolitan Police 249; Microsoft 184; naysayers, treatment of **89**; in NHS 12; norms 34–5; and organizational culture 201; origins 3–4; and performance management systems 183; performance pressures 77–82, 83, 85–6, **88**, 180–1; prevention 250; in public sector 12; questions about 2; RBS 66–7; reduction, action framework 241, **242–7**; reverence from external stakeholders **88**, 95–7; singularity, cult of **88**, 97–107; stages 4, 5–6, 84–107, *84*, **88–9**, 108, 248; triggers 82–4, *82*; Uber 32, 176; World Bank 18; *see also* positive cultures; Toxic Triangle
toxic leaders/leadership 6–7, 113; behaviour, examples **154**; characteristics 117–18; definitions **118–20**; and followership 154–5; identification by HR 222; impact 120–3; meaning 117; personal narratives 143–5; resistance to 165–6; survivors of 166–7; terms for **117**; toleration of 86–107; and toxic followers 164–5; at VW 86; in the workplace 140–45
Toxic Triangle 5, 6–8, 113, *114*, 156
toxic workplace: checks and balances, absence of 174–6, **180**; favouritism 173–4, **180**; instability 171–2, **179**; measurement **179–80**; perceived threats 173, **179**; RESPECT remedy 197, 250
toxicity *see* toxic culture/s
Trump, Donald: toxic personality 144–145

Uber: toxic culture 32, 176
unethical behaviour: acceptance over time 51; and conformity effect 52; and whistleblowing 51; *see also* ethical behaviour; Normalization of Deviance

Unethical Pro-organizational Behaviour (UPB) 180
USA: 'Great Resignation' (2021) 200

values *see* cultural values; organizational values
Vaughan, Diane 11, 40; on culture failure at NASA 43
vignettes: AIG 18–19; Boeing case study 79–82; BrewDog 177–8; Carillion 72–3; on CEOs 121–3; NASA, Columbia Accident 14; Uber, toxic culture 32; VW, toxic culture 57–9; VW CEO fined for false testimony 105–6; World Bank, toxic culture 18
Volkswagen (VW): centralized hierarchy 94; CEO fined for false testimony, vignette 105–6; cheat devices, use of 34, 55, 56, 56–7, 57, 58, 59, 87, 100; 'clean diesel' campaign 55; corporate values 55; 'dieselgate' timeline *104*; fines 2, 87; global ambitions 85–6; humiliation of managers 56; job losses 101; lawbreaking, denial of 103; and Normalization of Deviance 87; rhetoric and reality 56; toxic culture 57–9; toxic leadership 86; and US car market 56

Warren, Elizabeth 100
Watt, James 177–8
well-being: corporate business 227; individual vs organizational 228; priority rating 227, **246**; questions, and Likert Scale 228; *see also* mental health
Wells Fargo: bullying 124; fake accounts 91–2, 95, 99–100; fines 12, 95; global ambitions 86; illegal activity 1, 9n1; sales pressures 98–9, 101; staff turnover 98
whistleblowing 52, 216; and unethical behaviour 51
work hours: flexibility 225–6; health effects 224; and productivity 224–5
working from home (WFH): positive and negative outcomes 227–8
workplace stress: costs 13; health problems 13; *see also* toxic workplace
World Bank: agility 233; Career Advisory Panel 233; career management 232–7; career management principles 233–4, *233*; Career Management Unit 233, 233–4; career paths 234, 236; Country Manager appointments 233; employee engagement 236; growth mindset philosophy 236; management development 236; talent councils and boards 236; toxic culture 18

zero-tolerance approach: discrimination 218–19